the gift of
an ordinary day

Also by Katrina Kenison

Mitten Strings for God

the gift of
an ordinary day

A MOTHER'S MEMOIR

KATRINA KENISON

SPRINGBOARD PRESS

NEW YORK   BOSTON

Springboard Press
Hachette Book Group
237 Park Avenue, New York, NY 10017
Visit our website at www.HachetteBookGroup.com

Printed in the United States of America

First Edition: September 2009

Springboard Press is an imprint of Grand Central Publishing.
The Springboard name and logo are trademarks of Hachette Book Group, Inc.

Grateful acknowledgment is made to the following for permission to reprint previously published material:
Clarissa Pinkola Estés: Excerpt from *La Curandera: Healing in Two Worlds*, by Clarissa Pinkola Estés. Copyright © 2009, reprinted with kind permission of the author, Dr. Clarissa Pinkola Estés, and Texas A&M University Press.

HarperCollins: Excerpt from *Grasshopper on the Road*, by Arnold Lobel. Copyright © 1978 by Arnold Lobel. Reprinted by permission of HarperCollins, New York.

Houghton Mifflin Harcourt Publishing Company: Excerpt from "St. Francis and the Sow" from *Mortal Acts, Mortal Words* by Galway Kinnell. Copyright © 1980, renewed 2008 by Galway Kinnell. Reprinted by permission of Houghton Mifflin Harcourt Publishing Company, Boston and New York. All rights reserved.

Paulist Press: Excerpt from *Hope for the Flowers*, by Trina Paulus. Copyright © 1972 by Trina Paulus. Paulist Press, Inc. New York/Mahwah: NJ. Reprinted by permission of Paulist Press, Inc. www.paulistpress.com.

Library of Congress Cataloging-in-Publication Data
Kenison, Katrina.
    The gift of an ordinary day: a mother's memoir / Katrina Kenison.—1st ed.
    p. cm.
    ISBN 978-0-446-40948-3
    1. Motherhood. I. Title.
    HQ759.K46 2009
    306.874'3092—dc22
    [B]
                                        2009003135

10 9 8 7 6 5 4 3 2 1

Book design by Giorgetta Bell McRee

For Steve, unsung hero

*Every step in the dark turns out,
in the end, to have been on course
after all.*

—JOHN TARRANT

contents

introduction

$\mathscr{T}$he book you hold in your hands is not the book I intended to write. What I envisioned was something shorter, simpler, and less personal.

Ten years ago, when my sons were six and nine, I wrote a small collection of essays about my efforts to slow life down in a world that seemed to be moving too fast. As a young mother, I wanted so much for my children, and I expected quite a bit of myself, too. And yet, somewhat to my surprise, motherhood was forcing me to reexamine all of my preconceptions about what it meant to live well and to do well by my family. Trying to do it all, have it all, and give it all to my children, I realized that in fact I was setting a pace that left us scattered and exhausted.

It dawned on me that what I really wanted was to enjoy those fleeting years with my husband and our sons rather than race through them. Writing was a way to remind myself to savor the quiet pleasures of everyday life, to pay more attention to people than to things, and to allow my young sons the time and space to play, daydream, and begin to figure out for themselves who they were and what they cared about.

The book grew directly out of my own experiences with my two little boys—baking bread, sleeping in a tent in the backyard, telling stories at bedtime, coloring Easter eggs. I felt so certain then that a good life was right at hand, if I could only remember to keep it simple and unhurried.

My book, *Mitten Strings for God: Reflections for Mothers in a Hurry*, didn't really say anything about slowing down that hadn't been said before. I simply offered a few more thoughts on the matter as it pertained to children. My husband and I had a joke that year that while he was downstairs after dinner taking care of the kids, I was upstairs writing about them. The good news was, it didn't take long. The book almost wrote itself.

It also struck a chord with other mothers who felt as I did and who shared my desire to run around less and stay at home more. In a culture that emphasizes activity, enrichment, and early competence as the tickets to adult success, we tend to equate full engagement calendars with full lives. In a few brief essays, I tried to offer a glimpse of another way. A decade later, I still receive letters from mothers eager to share their stories of how my book inspired them to find more realistic, livable, enjoyable rhythms for their own families.

Meanwhile, my own little boys grew up. The five-year-old who once nestled himself under my arm while finger knitting a long blue mitten string for God is sixteen now, shaving and driving. His older brother, who used to climb into my bed with his beloved copy of *James and the Giant Peach,* is reading Plato at a college halfway across the country.

I always thought that someday, when my sons were older, I would write a second book, a kind of sequel to the first. But as my sons grew into adolescence and our family life became more complicated, I felt less and less sure of my ground. It was one thing for my husband and me to decide that we would opt out of T-ball and elaborate birthday parties in favor of pickup baseball games in the backyard and unscheduled weekends. But it is quite another to try to shape family life with two teenage boys who have their own agendas, social plans, and strong opinions.

My original intent was to write about the unprecedented expectations and pressures experienced by today's teenagers and parents and how important it is to offer an antidote to that pressure at home. I wanted to remind myself as much as anyone that there are alternatives to our culture's narrow definition of success, and to suggest that we'd be doing all our sons and daughters a service if we'd relinquish some of our collective anxiety over their unknown futures and simply trust them more to find their own way.

But as my two sons became teenagers themselves, our stable, orderly life flew apart. Instead of growing in wisdom, I was searching for answers. The idea of trying to offer anybody advice about anything seemed ludicrous. When I tried to write, what came out seemed messy and complicated, as messy and complicated as our own everyday lives. So I realized that I had a choice: I could give up on my idea altogether, or I could take a longer, more circuitous route. I could try to tell my own midlife story of living, loving, and letting go, knowing that doing so would also mean owning up to all that I don't know, all that I'm still trying to figure out.

Unlike the first book, this one hasn't come easy. For one thing, writing about teenagers, I soon realized, is even harder than living with them. They are extremely private creatures, after all, demanding of respect. There were many lines I could not cross. As for myself, I am not a parenting expert or a therapist or a teacher. I'm just a mother confronting the vicissitudes of middle age—change, loss, a twenty-one-year-old marriage, children leaving home. And none of it is smooth sledding. All I really have to guide me these days is my own response—joy, gratitude, sadness, fear—in the presence of all that seems most precious now, as my two nearly grown sons strain inexorably against the ties that bind us.

It is, of course, a universal drama—children grow up, they leave home, clocks tick in empty bedrooms, and untouched gallons of milk turn sour in the fridge because no one's there to drink them. Parents mourn the loss and, at the same time, discover the will to reinvent themselves. I know I'm not the first mother who's found it hard to let go, who's yearned for change only to resist it when it comes, who's found it painful at times to accept the fact that my sons are pulling away, moving out into lives of their own. Nor will I be the last.

And so I offer the story of my midlife searching and mothering over the course of five unsettled years, in the hope that other mothers will recognize aspects of themselves in these pages and remember that, unique though our own experiences may be, none of us really travels this path alone. Parenthood is what binds us. Our own doubts and questions awaken empathy for parents everywhere, and our fierce love for our own children deepens our compassion for all children. Walking in the woods with a friend, or gathered around a dinner table when the candles have burned low, or sitting in a circle in a church basement, we share our struggles, open our hearts, tell about our lives and our children's lives, in an effort to make sense of things, to learn the hidden truths of ourselves, but also, of course, to share the small discoveries that may somehow ease the way for someone else. This is how it's been for me.

K.K.

~ 1 ~

change

> *To exist is to change, to change is to*
> *mature, to mature is to go on creating*
> *oneself endlessly.*
> —HENRI BERGSON

*W*hen my children were small, I would sometimes lie in bed in the early morning and try to envision the day ahead. Not the schedule we would keep or the activities in store, but rather the attitude I wanted to bring to these things. Imagining myself being patient, calm, accepting, I would create a picture in my mind of the mother I wanted to be for my two young boys. Of course, at some point the day's challenges would always get the better of me. Jack would stick a bead up his nose and tell me it had magically disappeared. Henry would spill his third glass of orange juice in a row. And I'd catch myself being impatient, critical, brusque—not the kind of mother I'd envisioned at all.

Back then, I took comfort in knowing that when things got tough, we could always regroup and start over. I could take a deep, slow breath, pop my cranky children into a tub full of bubbles, toast bagels, let the storm clouds blow over. (Well, the bead up the nose did require a trip to the ER.) Still, I felt so certain that tomorrow would be just another day, another chance to try to get it right—followed by another, and another after that, and hundreds more, all more or less like the very day I was struggling to get through at that moment.

It seemed to me during those early years of child raising that my sons' childhoods would go on forever. I couldn't imagine any life other than the one that consumed me right then, a life shaped by the joys and demands of raising young children.

From the time my older son was three months old, I had a job I could do from home, editing an annual anthology of short stories. For a former literary editor not quite willing to forgo her publishing career, the setup was ideal—I was getting paid to read. With a little self-discipline, I could easily slip back and forth between work and children. If the boys were occupied, I'd grab a pile of literary magazines and retreat to the couch. When they were small, paid child care bought luxurious stretches of uninterrupted time at my desk. Later, I arranged my schedule around theirs, glad for a workday that ended at three, for our sacred weekday afternoons.

For years, I felt fulfilled in both realms, fortunate to have work I loved and continually challenged by the requirements of motherhood. My life's purpose seemed clear—I could keep a toe in my professional shoes and be a stay-at-home mother at the same time, certain that I could best sustain and nurture our family life simply by being there. My morning meditations among the pillows might set a tone or an intention, but the real practice, I came to see, was in the ritual of starting over, day after day, caring for my husband and children, striving for balance, trying to meet my deadlines and, at the same time, meet our basic needs for rest and laughter and togetherness.

I learned a lot about myself, and many lessons in mindfulness, during those long days. Intense and demanding as they are, the years we spend with our young children can also be deeply, viscerally gratifying. We know exactly where we are needed and what we need to be doing. Immersed in the physical and emotional realm of parenthood, we develop reserves of patience, imagination, and fortitude we never dreamed possible. At times, the hard work of being a mother seems in itself a spiritual practice, an opportunity for growth and self-exploration in an extraordinarily intimate world, a world in which hands are for holding, bodies for snuggling, laps for sitting.

As our sons grew up, my husband and I marked their heights on the side of a pantry cupboard, savored every milestone, and marveled at how well settled we were, completely absorbed in lives that revolved around our children, work and school, and friends with whom to share it all. For a long time, life unfurled predictably, steadily, like fat ribbon from a spool.

The changes, when they began, were subtle at first. Somehow our treasured family ritual of reading together at bedtime slipped away. No one asked for stories anymore. Baths were replaced by showers, long ones, at the oddest times of day. The three-year gap between our sons, insignificant at six and nine, seemed to stretch into a chasm, unbridgeable at eleven and fourteen. Baseballs stopped flying in the backyard. A bedroom door that had always been open, quietly closed. Board games gathered dust on the shelves. And then one day, toward the end of my older son's eighth-grade year, I looked at him over breakfast and realized I had absolutely no idea what he was thinking about. And when, for heaven's sake, had he grown that hair across his upper lip?

Sensing the ground shifting beneath my feet, I resisted this new, unknown territory, already nostalgic for what I'd so recently taken for granted. I missed my old world and its funny little inhabitants, those great big personalities still housed in small, sweet bodies. I missed my sons' kissable cheeks and round bellies, their unanswerable questions, their innocent faith, their sudden tears and wild, infectious giggles, even the smell of their morning breath, when they would leap, upon waking, from their own warm beds directly into ours. I missed the person I had been for them, too—the younger, more capable mother who read aloud for hours, stuck raisin eyes into bear-shaped pancakes, created knight's armor from cardboard and duct tape. Certainly my talents didn't seem quite so impressive anymore, my company not as desirable as it once had been.

If I thought the journey from childhood into teenagehood would be orderly and predictable, the transformations steady and almost imperceptible, I was wrong. Our family did not glide easily from one phase of life into the next, but then, perhaps no family ever does. The confluence of my own midlife and my sons' adolescence hit us like a blast of wind, blowing the front door wide open, hurtling through the house, and rearranging the furniture of our lives. Some of the chaos undoubtedly came with the territory, and some we surely brought upon ourselves; by the time our older son stepped across the stage to receive his eighth-grade diploma, we were rolling up the rugs in the living room.

I am a person who thrives in the familiar comforts of home, a nester, a sanctifier. Since earliest childhood, I have marked and claimed spaces—from the fairy cave beneath a weeping willow tree in my grandmother's backyard, furnished the summer I was four with soft striped blankets, china teacups, and stacks of picture books, to the rambling, green-shingled house on a short cul-de-sac that my husband, sons, and I inhabited so fully and for so long that none of us thought we would ever, could ever, live anywhere else.

In the midst of an upscale, well-groomed suburban neighborhood, ours was the funky house, having been built originally as a barn two hundred years ago. Its history as a home for livestock was still evident in the ancient, oddly stained beams and low ceilings, the vision of the 1920s architect revealed in the leaded glass casement windows, the handmade fireplace tiles, the tiny bedrooms, old-fashioned kitchen, and unlikely floor plan. Idly house hunting and then enchanted by this particular house's eccentricities, my husband and I wondered how we would fill those little upstairs bedrooms. We made an offer anyway—only to learn, the following week, that I was already pregnant with our second child. It seemed like fate. By the time we brought Jack home eight months later, we felt as if we'd always been there.

As our children grew, we created gardens and traditions, laid stone paths through the flowers and installed a swing set under the towering pine, planted trees each Mother's Day, tended to vegetables growing in the backyard and to close, abiding friendships with the neighbors on all sides. Standing outdoors sometimes at night, looking in through the lighted windows at the familiar, cherished rooms, I imagined our house as a living, breathing organism, animated by us and filled to the brim with the stuff of our lives, every moment, memory, word, and gesture of our family's history contained within its embracing walls.

For thirteen years we were held, loving that house so much that it seemed almost to love us back. Until the day when, to my surprise, being held began to feel more like being restrained. Slowly, almost without my knowing it, I had begun to hunger for something, or someplace, else. Someplace wilder and a little rougher around the edges, with a wider sky, perhaps, a longer view from the kitchen window, and a deeper kind of quiet than could be found in any suburban neighborhood.

In my mid-forties, with our children on the brink of

adolescence, I longed for something I could scarcely name but that our orderly, well-defined life seemed no longer to provide. Watching my sons growing and changing so visibly, almost from one day to the next, I sensed something inside me breaking loose and changing as well, something no less powerful for being invisible. It was almost as if, having strived for years for predictable comforts, urban conveniences, and the security of our well-established routines, I was suddenly haunted by all the things I hadn't done, the dreams that might never be realized, the sense that the tidy, civilized life we'd worked so hard to create didn't quite fit the person I really was, or, rather, still thought I might be.

I didn't want to leave my marriage or quit my job. I had no interest in a makeover or a sports car, and we couldn't afford a second home. Yet I was beginning to understand the reckless impulses that drive so many of us at midlife headlong into mysteries and mistakes, new identities and unlikely adventures. If some essential part of me was already disappearing as my children moved into increasingly wider orbits, well then, I wanted to reach out and claim something else to take its place. Freedom was one word for it; I nursed a new, uncharacteristic itch for more space, empty roads, dark night skies.

Who knows, really, where dreams begin? Perhaps they first take shape in the unknown realms of sleep or in the far corners of our consciousness, gaining size and substance off in the distant wings of awareness, until one day, just out of the corner of your eye, you see it—the hazy shape of a new idea that is suddenly too big and insistent to ignore.

Perhaps my own first impulse to pull up stakes and move away had its earliest stirrings in such a dream. Off at the edges of perception, as my husband and I considered high schools for one son and imagined possible futures for the other, arose a disconcerting sense that perhaps the comfortable old shoe of a life that had fit so well for so long wasn't quite the right size anymore.

What began as a fantasy of light and space and room to stretch evolved, without my even realizing it, into yearning— for the opportunity to write a whole new family chapter, in a place where we might expand our understanding of what it means to live well. A place where, despite the challenges of adolescence, our sons might find some kind of counterbalance to the social and academic pressures they had already begun to experience in the well-stratified world beyond our own front door.

Much as I wanted both my children to benefit from whatever material advantages we could offer them, it began to seem even more important that they also come to appreciate the value and the beauty of ordinary things, gifts that come with no price tags attached but that can nevertheless seem increasingly out of reach in our noisy, fast-paced, overcrowded world—the snap of an apple picked from a roadside tree, the silence of deep woods after snow, the majesty of a clear night sky, the solitary bliss of a swim across a lake on a summer afternoon.

Neither my husband nor I was bound to a location for our livelihoods. I could read short stories at a kitchen table. When we first moved to the suburbs, Steve had been a publishing executive, commuting by train each day to the city, earning a salary that could easily support us all. But he had left that career to try his luck with a start-up; when that and then a second venture failed, he'd launched a small business of his own from a corner of our guest bedroom. For a couple of years, life went on as usual—vacations, music lessons, private school. And then, one tax time, we simply added up the money that was coming in, compared it with the money going out, and realized that something would have to change.

Thus began a year of soul-searching deliberation and many, many late night conversations. What holds anyone in place? How do we know where we belong? Could we be just as happy in a smaller house somewhere else, where the cost of living might be lower? Somehow, we needed to learn to live on less, so we asked ourselves if life in a slower, quieter, less populated place might actually suit us better. We could go anywhere. Or not. There was much to be said, as my husband kept insisting, in favor of tightening our belts and staying put, in the only home our two sons had ever known. More than once I wondered if the longings that plagued me were legitimate or whether my midlife crisis was just taking the form of boredom with all that was familiar.

After nearly a year of indecision and uncertainty, of endless house hunting in every corner of the New England countryside, and of countless house showings of our own (flowers on every table! clean towels at every sink! spotless toilets!), we were exhausted and more confused than ever about what we really wanted. In the end, we got ourselves into the regrettable position of having sold our old house without managing to find a new one.

By the time we finally had to confront the painful task of dismantling the home we now regretted selling, our romantic vision of a simpler new life in the country seemed like a pipe dream. We'd lost our zeal and confidence for going forward. After having tried and failed to make a desperate, last-ditch deal to keep our old house, we had to accept that there was no going back.

Shaken, we went on autopilot, filled boxes, and labeled them "Deep Storage" or "Accessible Storage." In fact, almost everything we owned was going into storage of one kind or another—including, or so it seemed at the time, our capacity for rational thinking. Hard-pressed for some kind of plan, and for a roof over our heads, my husband and I arranged to move in with my parents until we sorted things out.

A month before our older son was to start high school, we left our beloved house, gave away many of our possessions, packed the rest, and embarked on what turned out to be a three-year quest for home, roots, and a new life elsewhere.

On the day we locked our back door behind us for the last time, bade our best friends and neighbors good-bye through one last wash of tears, and followed the moving vans north, we were also, without quite realizing it, closing the door for good on our sons' childhoods and bidding farewell to the life we'd so carefully constructed and then so swiftly dismantled. Three and a half years later, when we finally sliced into the boxes of Beanie Babies and baseball cards, these once precious talismens had lost their magic. Both of our sons were full-blown teenagers. We were in new territory altogether.

Over these last difficult, unsettled years, change has seemed to define us, and at times I've wondered if it would, in the end, undo us. Our children have braved new schools, new towns, new lives entirely. After thirteen years in one place, we suddenly found ourselves with claim to no place, unsure about where we would live or even exactly what we were looking for. We were completely in flux. But I've come to see that even though the particular details of this midlife journey may be unique to us, our story of upheaval is not all that unusual. As I look around at the families we know, I realize that almost every one of them has endured transformations of one sort or another as their children moved through adolescence.

The changes are various, some exhilarating, others heart-breaking, some deliberately set in motion, others completely unexpected. It almost seems as if the strict requirements of life with young children tether us for a time, creating limits and enclosures that hold fast through elementary school. We know our children need security, rhythm, and routine in order to thrive, so we sacrifice, perhaps at great cost to ourselves, to provide those things. It's what parents do, if we possibly can. But as high school looms, even the steadiest families begin to rock.

As writer Phyllis Theroux observes, "We set off like captains of clipper ships outfitted with the latest gear and tackle to race across the ocean. Then, somewhere midcrossing, we realize that the expedition is essentially beyond our control. That time coincides with children becoming adolescents. Adolescence is a mutinous, confusing time when everybody is trying to get off the boat."

Not many of us actually jump ship. But the fact is, midlife—which hits most parents just about the time our children are hitting their teens—finds a fair number of restless, graying seekers out charting new courses, often through unexpectedly rough waters. Whether we choose change or it chooses us, the only thing we can know for sure is that security of any kind is an illusion. The life we know is always in the process of becoming something else.

I have friends who, having put careers on the back burner while raising children, are suddenly realizing that it's now or never and are heading back into the workforce as their children spend fewer waking hours at home. Couples we know who have struggled to keep unworkable marriages together for the sake of their children decide, as those children become teenagers, that they have held on long enough. Families that appeared tightly knit seem to unravel overnight. Others find themselves caring for elderly parents who, though vibrant just months ago, suddenly seem astonishingly frail and all too mortal.

A few weeks ago, good neighbors on our street were stunned to lose their house to foreclosure; they aren't sure where they'll go next. On all sides now, people I care about are having heart attacks, losing jobs, starting businesses, moving to follow new dreams or revive old ones, remaking their lives in all kinds of ways and for all kinds of reasons. Most of the changes fall into the realm of challenges, not easy, perhaps, but inevitable bumps on the road of life. Others, however, are simply devastating.

As I look back over the last few years, my mind fills with memories of indelible moments when I've been abruptly, painfully reminded that we can take nothing and no one for granted.

It is early on a March Sunday, my husband and I just waking up to a gray dawn when the phone rings. My husband answers, grabs the back of a chair, and asks in disbelief, "Who's dead?" My best friend's son has been stabbed, killed while trying to stop a fight near his college campus.

It is October, my birthday, and I'm having lunch outside with two dear friends from my old neighborhood, basking in the sunshine of a perfect autumn afternoon. Happy to be reunited, we're eating deli sandwiches and complaining about our crow's-feet and sagging eyelids, wondering if we'd ever have the nerve for face lifts, joking about finding ourselves a group rate somewhere. A week later, one of these friends, just my age and in the bloom of health, is diagnosed with advanced stage four ovarian cancer, enters treatment, and begins fighting for her life. No one is complaining about wrinkles anymore.

My book group has gathered on a February evening to drink

wine, catch up with one another, and discuss a recent Oprah selection. We go around the circle, each of us offering a few sentences about what's going on in our lives, what's happened since we last met. There is a pause as a good friend takes a deep breath, looks up, and announces in a voice shaking with pain and determination, "I'm getting a divorce."

At the age of forty-six, my brother has become a dad at last. But his son is born seven weeks early and is fighting for survival in the ICU, a three-pound scrap of humanity not quite ready for life on this earth. I look at my kid brother in his hospital scrubs, his eyes full of tears, his heart bursting with pride and hope, and realize that he's not the same person he was just yesterday; that no matter what happens to that tiny little boy in the incubator, my brother has been forever transformed by fatherhood.

These are just my stories, the ones that happen at this particular moment to be very close to home. But every woman I know has her own ready list of tragedies, trials, wake-up calls, and, yes, opportunities for transformation.

I remember the book my own mother, then on the brink of forty, was reading when I headed off to college in the fall of 1976. In that bicentennial year, Gail Sheehy topped the bestseller list with *Passages*, suggesting that midlife is no safe harbor after the turmoil of young adulthood, but rather a critical turning point in the life cycle, a time when our heightened vulnerability also offers us unprecedented opportunity for growth. Sheehy struck a huge chord with her reinterpretation of the midlife crisis, or "passage," as a necessary element of the spiritual journey into self-knowledge and renewal. "If you want to grow," she proclaimed, "you must be willing to change." Thirty-plus years and thousands of self-help books later, this is no longer news. Yet, truth be told, I still feel broadsided by the changes that have hit me over the last few years and am deeply sobered by the enormous losses so many close friends have suffered.

Many nights I lie awake, worrying about what's next. Difficult times are inevitable, and I have no doubt that my own losses and disappointments will continue. Somehow, I need to learn to weather them, to strengthen my belief in the rightness of things as they are, even as I transform this deepening awareness of mortality and suffering into a more accepting kind of faith.

Before long, I will turn fifty. Soon, one son, and then the other, will leave home. And I am overcome these days with a new sense of urgency about all of it. For years I have been caught up in the work of raising children, earning a living, turning pages on the calendar, checking items off a list. But time that once seemed to move so slowly has all of a sudden begun to go way too fast. Childhood doesn't last forever after all, nor does any season.

Change, it is said, always goes hand in hand with opportunity. Growing older, I begin to see that finding fulfillment in this next stage of life will demand a kind of surrender that seems beyond me now, a new way of being and caring that I can barely begin to imagine. I suspect I have a lot to learn about letting go.

I recall my younger, intensely ambitious self with a wince—how avidly I set my sights on the future and how hard I worked at becoming the person I thought I ought to be, in pursuit of the life by which I thought I could define myself. So many aspirations—for a rewarding career, security for my family, success for my children, a marriage that worked, and a life that mattered. I wanted it all. And I believed that if I nurtured those dreams, tried hard enough, and planned well enough, they would one day come true. The funny thing is, now, as my children begin to pull away, it is the present moment that concerns me most. Yet try as I might to pay attention, I find myself confronted with all sorts of unexpected and conflicting emotions—pride in my sons, of course, and gratitude for what we've had, but also an almost heartbreaking sense of just how short life really is, and how incomprehensible. How in fact life is not all about planning and shaping, but about not knowing, and being okay with that. It's about learning to take the moment that comes and make the best of it, without any idea of what's going to happen next.

It's been quite a few years since I began my days by imagining them first from bed. But now I think it's time for me to visualize again, if only to remind myself to begin each day with gratitude for what is rather than worrying so much about what still might be. I now know that although each day does indeed afford us an opportunity to start again, the days are numbered after all. Instead of regretting what's over and done with, I want to be glad for life as it is right now, accepting that we are, each one of us, struggling along as best we can to become the people we are meant to be. Instead of mourning the passage of time, I want to live with a sense of abundance in the here and now, knowing that what we have is exactly enough. Instead of wishing that my sons could be somehow other than they are, I want to remind myself to see, every day, what is already good in each of them and to love that.

We are entering a kind of homestretch here, the end of family life as we've always known it, the end of the day-in-day-out, zip-your-jacket-here's-your-sandwich kind of mothering by which I've defined myself for so long.

My sons will be graduating from high school and leaving home before I know it. Although we've spent the last three years in transition, in borrowed rooms and temporary arrangements, the real changes have only just begun. In the months ahead, our family will move at long last into a house of our own. One son will begin his freshman year at a large public high school where, on the first day, he will know almost no one. The other will be a senior at the small alternative high school where he has grown, in the last three years, from a shy, diffident boy into a quietly confident young man. My husband and I will drive, supervise, proofread, cheerlead, negotiate curfews and car privileges, and write lots of checks.

And then, just a year from now, our older son will pack his bags and head off to college, and our family will begin the inevitable shrinking and shifting that will conclude with my husband and me looking at each other over dinner, in a childless house, wondering how it all ended so quickly.

~ 2 ~

best

To freely bloom—that is my definition of success.
—GERRY SPENCE

*H*e stands sometimes, lost in thought, with wrists crossed, palms twisted toward each other, dreaming melodies. He sleeps deeply, as if hurled onto the bed from a high place, head thrown back, mouth open, arms and legs bent at odd angles, feet in the air. But in the morning he's the first one up, taking the pulse of the day. After his shower, the hair on his head sweeps forward, as if he's just blown in on the wind. His eyes are green, then gray, changeable as the sky. He hunches over the sports page at breakfast, devouring every scrap of baseball news along with his Rice Chex, laughing out loud at the funny parts, which may of course be funny only to him.

Before a single word is spoken, he can sense the mood in a room. He embodies a silence that is quieter, deeper, than not talking. He needs fewer words than most, but more music. His fingers carry memories of sonatas, jazz riffs, Broadway melodies. He wears his shirt unbuttoned over a faded tee, his pants baggy, his shoes often half-tied. When he walks out the door, he always calls good-bye, and coming home, he asks, first, "How was your day?" If the dishwasher is full of clean dishes, he empties it.

Evenings, he sits at the piano and, from some unknowable place within, brings forth his own heartbreaking improvisation on the old Nat King Cole tune "Blame It on My Youth." In the hallway, I pause, a basket of laundry in my hands, surprised by a sudden lump in my throat as the house fills with sound.

As an eighth grader, this boy who never asked for much asked for just one thing—to go to high school in a place where he wouldn't get lost in the crowd. It seemed to my husband and me a fair request. He was looking not for escape, but for a place to grow, a place where a shy, unusual kid, small for his age and all too easy to miss in a world of larger, louder personalities, might be seen and valued.

The public school in our suburban town was good, but exactly where he didn't want to be. So we began to look around. It seemed there was a wealth of possibilities nearby, all manner of private schools promising individual attention, small classes, care. We added up costs, calculated commuting distances, and signed up for the SSAT, surprised to learn that an achievement test taken at thirteen could set a trajectory for life.

One windy autumn night, my husband and I drove from Massachusetts to New Hampshire to visit a small alternative boarding and day school on a country road just a few miles from the house where I'd grown up. Back then, I'd known the school only by reputation, as a place for artsy kids who wanted to sit at potter's wheels, study Shakespeare, learn the constellations. Although the campus was practically in my own backyard, I had never once set foot there; to a public school girl like me, it was the counterculture. So it was with some sense of irony that I found myself visiting for the first time thirty years later, wondering if this small, idealistic high school might be the right place for our son.

It was dark when we arrived, and there were no lights to

guide us. We parked the car and wandered for a while, having no idea what any of the strange, shadowy buildings might be or where we were meant to go. There were no signs to point the way. Standing alone on this gusty, wide-open hilltop, far from town and lights and civilization, the two of us felt as if we'd come not to visit a school, but to receive instead a direct audience with the sky. A full moon lurked behind fast-moving, translucent clouds. When they parted, we could get our bearings for just a moment, make out a dirt path, and take a few steps toward campus. Then, plunged in darkness again, we'd stop, disoriented and wondering what on earth had brought us here.

Eventually that night, we did find our way to the library and the informal session we'd come to attend. We were impressed by the dedication of the teachers, the love they expressed for their work, the engaged, articulate students, the cozy room. But what I remember most is an odd feeling I had while standing outside in the dark. As the moon by turns illuminated and obscured the cluster of old farm buildings that constituted High Mowing School, I assured myself that this brief exploration would end soon enough, that my husband and I would get in our car and drive home, back where we belonged—after all, we had a good life already and all sorts of schools to choose from that would not require moving from one state to another. At the same time, some wiser part of me knew quite well that, like it or not, our journey had already begun.

I have another memory from just a bit later in that unsettled year that seems, in retrospect, equally pivotal. The more my husband and I talked about the possibility of moving, the more we tried to convince ourselves to stay put. Life was rich and good, we told ourselves, our children were thriving and would surely be fine, our dearest friends lived next door, our dark green shingled house was the vessel into which we'd poured every memory we had of parenting, of our children's child-hoods. The best part of our lives had been played out right here—Christmases, birthdays, sing-alongs, untold numbers of baseball games, campouts, and dinners on the back porch. Surely we could figure out high school, work out a budget, settle back into the life that was already ours, and find a way to satisfy my restless middle-aged soul without pulling up roots and overturning our entire existence.

Our blueberry bushes were amazing that year, abundantly fruitful all summer, blazing red come fall. On an unseasonably warm late autumn afternoon, I climbed out of the car, a pile of mail in hand, and paused on the path between our overgrown flower garden and the little stand of blueberries. The leaves had not all fallen, frost had yet to claim the last of the chrysanthe-mums and cosmos; we were suspended in that fleeting, pre-cious moment just before true cold. On this loveliest of days, it was easy to believe that we were already in exactly the right place, that we would be here always. The yard was bathed in deepening shades of gold and red, and the air carried the sweet scent of damp leaves, earth, fallen apples, wood smoke. Standing there in the light of early dusk, I ripped open the envelope containing my son's SSAT scores.

In that instant, I knew two things for sure: Our son was not the number on that piece of paper. And somehow, no matter what it took, we would see to it that he came of age knowing that who he is as a person is more important than how well he performs on a test. By the time I walked through the back door, something inside me had shifted for good.

Most parents do not up and move as their children enter high school. Yet we all aspire to find for them the environments in which we think they will best thrive and grow. No matter where we fall on the financial spectrum, no matter what our circumstances, as parents we feel compelled to put our children's needs first, doing whatever we can to ensure that they are the recipients of the best educations and experiences we can provide. For thirteen years, my husband and I had shared a common sense of purpose, a commitment to spend whatever time it took and whatever money we had in order to give our two sons the best lives possible. If there was another agenda there, an unconscious one, it went without saying: Of course we also dreamed of happy, productive futures for our sons, and we would give them every advantage we could, in the hope that they would go on to live the good, satisfying lives we envisioned for them. It is human nature, after all, to want the best for our young.

The question we now had to ask ourselves was, What exactly did we mean by "the best"? Was it the life our children had always known, in a house we had never planned to leave, in an affluent suburban town where "the best" is generally assumed to mean a full load of honors classes in the high school, a varsity sport or two, and a part in the school play? For some, even for many, that might very well be the ideal. But when it came to our older son, we had long since realized that "the best" was not always the obvious; it was usually something we had to figure out for ourselves.

As the parents of two very different boys, we'd also learned early on that a good choice for one might be exactly the wrong choice for the other. A vision of what's "best" isn't the best at all if it doesn't support a particular child's growth or fit his temperament. One of the greatest challenges I've faced as a mother—especially in these anxious, winner-takes-all times—is the need to resist the urge to accept someone else's definition of success and to try to figure out, instead, what really is best for my own children, what unique combination of structure and freedom, nurturing and challenge, education and exploration, each of them needs in order to grow and bloom.

It's not easy. I've watched my sons come of age in a world in which they often feel that their worth is measured by what they have and by what they do, who they hang out with, how they dress, talk, and perform in classrooms and on athletic fields—external yardsticks that don't even begin to reflect the inner life of the soul, imagination, curiosity, character, and desire.

As the mother of boys with temperaments that often seem in direct opposition to each other, I sometimes feel as if I'm trying to grow a fern and a cactus in the same small pot, so different are their ways and needs and gifts. Yet with each of my sons I find myself walking a fine and precarious line between encouraging them to strive for excellence, to work hard and do their best, and also allowing them the space and time to grow up at their own pace and in their own way.

Watching my own two boys respond to the world, I'm continually reminded that a real education is not just a simple transfer of information, not a competition, but a gradual and at times unfathomable process of awakening compassion, deepening understanding, and fostering the development of imagination, curiosity, and will. Learning well doesn't always mean scoring high. It also means acquiring the tools necessary to take on the most challenging work of all—becoming the person you are meant to be.

I know, of course, that there are young people coming of age today who are destined to lead, to write the great stories of their generation, to break old records, to chart the courses of companies and countries, to leave bold marks upon the culture and big changes in the world. And they will find their way and answer their callings, as the great leaders and innovators always do. But I also suspect that in all likelihood, my own two children will walk less visible paths. My greatest hope, for both of them, is that they will also lead deeply meaningful lives of no less importance or artistry. But in either case, it will surely not be money or talent, prestige or power, that brings them true contentment.

What my husband and I began to realize, as our son neared the end of his eighth-grade year, was that no matter where we ended up living, or where our children went to school, we owed both of them this: the willingness, on our part, to refine and redefine our own idea of what "the best" might really mean.

Rather than try to project who our older son might or might not one day turn out to be, we needed to try to appreciate and understand who he was right now. And then we needed to meet him there, loving and accepting him just as he was, supporting his journey of self-discovery, crooked and long though his path might turn out to be. When we began to see it this way, our own path suddenly seemed clearer.

"Before you tell your life what you intend to do with it, listen for what it intends to do with you," writes Quaker minister Parker Palmer. There was no single compelling reason for us to move at all, but the more attentively we listened, and the more we opened ourselves to the possibility of change, the more we sensed that it really was time to go. Perhaps life did intend something different for us from what we knew, and perhaps we could figure out what that was by heading in the direction of what seemed best for our son.

As one of my friends, whose daughter chose to homeschool herself after ninth grade, points out, "The definition of the 'best' is pretty limiting in our culture, and it doesn't seem to take into account the fact that <u>every kid is different.</u>" Her older daughter had homeschooled and then gone on to graduate with honors from Stanford; her younger wanted to sing, study advanced math, and track wolves in the wilderness.

"I've had to make decisions with my daughter that made her feel happy and fulfilled now," my friend explained one afternoon on the phone, "instead of pushing her to do things just because they'd look good someday on a college application."

My husband and I, both products of conventional middle-class upbringings and public schools, have followed predictable paths; both of us are, by nature, quick to speak and learn and do. Parenthood has changed us, though, gradually, irrevocably opening our eyes to other ways. I remember a lecture by the spiritual teacher Jon Kabat-Zinn that we attended years ago, when our first son was just a toddler.

"Our children drop into our neat, tightly governed lives like small, rowdy Buddhist masters," he suggested, "each of them sent to teach us the hard lessons we most need to learn." Certainly our son had been doing his job since birth, blessed as he was with a constitution and a temperament that continually challenged us to slow down and to reconsider our own assumptions about what the best might really mean.

At thirteen, he was just waking up intellectually, yet he was also possessed of a deep emotional intelligence and a wisdom that belied his age. A musician, a dreamer, a loner, he knew he wasn't ready for the social and academic pressures of the fast lane. He would not thrive in the crowded classes in our town's public school. His test scores, astonishingly low, would no doubt exclude him from the local private schools that might have been viable alternatives. But he had never taken such a test before; his mind didn't work that way. So those numbers, I knew, reflected neither his intellect nor his potential. They did not begin to define his spirit or to describe his character. But they did remind us that, as always, our son needed to be allowed to forge his own way. The fact that we were already poised to move seemed, then, to be a sign.

For over a year, my husband and I had tried to summon the courage to give up the life we had in favor of a life we could only imagine, trying to picture ourselves elsewhere as we looked at towns and schools and houses, always wondering how we'd know, in the end, if we were really meant to go and where we were really meant to be. The fact that we couldn't fully explain our impulse to move made it hard to justify. But in the end, it came down to this: We outgrow phases of life as inevitably as children outgrow favorite toys and last year's winter jacket.

Painful as it was to acknowledge, the good suburban life that had suited us so well for so long didn't quite fit anymore, for all sorts of reasons. The social and academic pressures to compete and to excel, to live and act and dress a certain way, would surely intensify in the years ahead, and we found ourselves wanting an alternative to that for both our sons. Perhaps, we reasoned, a little more space, a little more freedom, and a little less scrutiny would be good for all of us. We began to realize that choosing a place to live, choosing a high school, and choosing a way of life that felt right and true and financially manageable were, in fact, all part of the same choice. It really was time to go.

We did not put most of our furniture into storage and take up residence in my parents' house without grief for what we were giving up. But a few things came into clearer focus as we began the work of bringing one long life chapter to a close and embarking on a new one. We could love the home we'd had and leave it anyway, leave it without knowing what would replace it. Really, we had no choice. But we also came to see that a gift can only be received with an open hand, and in order to find out what life was about to offer us, we would first have to release our hold on what was already over. That in itself proved to be quite a challenge and certainly a good lesson for our sons to learn.

"All journeys have a secret destination," writes philosopher and theologian Martin Buber, "of which the traveler is unaware." My husband and I couldn't claim to understand all of the forces that combined to loosen our hold on one life and propel us headlong into another, but we shared a sense that we wanted both our sons to grow up knowing there are alternatives to our culture's prevailing definitions of success and to the unspoken assumptions that had been an undeniable part of all our lives in our comfortable suburban town. Fortunate as we'd been to have that life, we were ready to relinquish some of its advantages in favor of new possibilities.

Perhaps, away from some of the expectations they had absorbed since childhood, our sons would in time discover their own best selves. Perhaps we two middle-aged parents would discover ours as well.

~ 3 ~

solstice

When all's said and done, all roads lead to
the same end. So it's not so much which
road you take, as how you take it.
— CHARLES DE LINT

I am driving home from a much needed summer vacation, my sons sound asleep in the backseat. Alone with my thoughts, I allow my mind to drift back to a moment just a month ago, when I stood stock-still, weeping, outside the coffee shop in our old hometown, a moment when the reality, the enormity, of what we were about to do hit me so hard that I wasn't sure I could take even one more step in the direction we'd already decided to go.

I knew every store on the street; the people walking by were people I'd seen before. All over town, in houses I knew as well as my own, my friends were waking up, making breakfast, starting the day with husbands and children, children my own two sons had grown up with. It was all so familiar, so dear, so much a part of me.

Home wasn't just our dark green house on a dead-end street, it wasn't just our hammock in the backyard, my tomato plants sprawling through their metal cages, the kitchen sink where I'd done the dishes for thousands of meals. Home was this whole perfectly contained universe—town, friends, acquaintances, the streets we traveled every day, the restaurant where our two-year-old had once pitched backward in a high chair and knocked himself out cold, the baseball diamonds where our sons had learned to throw curves, the library where we'd borrowed and returned hundreds of books, the church where Henry let himself in with his own key to practice the organ after school.

And we were about to leave it all. Panic stopped me in my tracks, heart hammering in my chest and eyes filling with tears, as if I'd just walked head-on into a wall. Our sons were enrolled in their new schools, my parents were busy clearing out bedrooms for us, but beyond that, whatever it was that we were going to was still an unanswerable question. I could touch and taste and smell every nook and cranny of what we were about to give up, but none of us had a very clear vision of what would ultimately take its place, and the fear of not knowing had me in its grip.

I had grown accustomed to these black moments, sort of, for as the day of our move approached, I was having to talk myself off the ledge every couple of hours: Check the to-do list again, empty another closet, donate more books to the rummage sale, keep packing. Breathe.

Once the job was finally done, once we'd said our last good-byes, unloaded all our earthly possessions into a rented storage space, put sheets on the beds at my parents' house and clothes into dresser drawers, release and exhaustion set in. School would start in a couple of weeks. Meanwhile, we'd given ourselves a week in neutral territory, a small rented cabin in Maine, where we could rest and recover.

Now, coming back, my husband and I are in separate cars, each of us, surely, lost in our separate reveries as well, wondering just how we'll start composing this new life chapter, what words we'll inscribe on the bright, empty pages of next week, next month, next year. Driving home—home, amazingly enough, for now being the all too familiar red Cape where I grew up—I can only marvel at the big, looping circle of life that has somehow brought me, at age forty-five, right back to where I started from.

If someone had told me on the day I graduated from college, full of big plans and intent on a career in book publishing, that the road to New York City, Cambridge, and suburban Boston would ultimately lead me all the way back to my own parents' dinner table—balding husband, two sons, and family dog in tow—I'd have thought it a bad joke, not at all funny. As it is, I'm utterly torn in this moment between laughter and despair, so strange does it feel to be driving our old Toyota minivan along the very stretch of interstate I traveled countless times in high school.

Back then, I'd have been cruising in my best friend's blue Chevy Nova, riding shotgun home from the beach, salt-crusted and sunburned. Windows down, lemon-streaked hair blowing in the wind, sharing Newports and comparing tan lines with Barbara and Joanne, singing along to Neil Diamond's "Sweet Caroline" on the radio as Barb's bare brown foot nudged the gas pedal to the brink of eighty. That scene is so close and real in my mind's eye that it might have been yesterday.

It is almost unfathomable that more than a quarter of a century separates me now from that teenage girl and her half-formed dreams. Harder still to believe that she's grown up to be me, a middle-aged mother of two, trying to fit back into the rooms and unspoken rules and family dynamics I thought I'd left for good the day I headed off to New Haven, a first husband (both of us way too young to be married to anyone), a first job as an editorial assistant (my dream come true), and a first apartment, furnished with flea market treasures that seemed to me the cutting edge of thrift.

Since that long-ago day when I launched myself so whole-heartedly into my adult life, I've never really come home again, except for the occasional overnight visit, holiday gatherings, family dinners. No wonder my husband and I have found it so difficult, over these last months, to explain to our friends and families our decision to give up everything we'd worked so hard to establish, to move away from "the good life" to, well, a stopgap life in which everything is temporary and unformed. Moving in with my parents, because we sold our own house without knowing where we were going? At times, we can barely explain it to ourselves.

Fear, excitement, sadness, loss—it is as if all the emotions I've stuffed away for months, in order to get the job of packing and moving accomplished, are rising up in me now at once. I pop in the Grateful Dead CD my brother gave me as a tongue-firmly-in-cheek "housewarming" gift. ("So," he'd said, laughing, "I hear you guys are moving back in with the parents—guess that means you'll be cranking up Neil Young and the Dead and reliving your lost youth.") And all of a sudden, there are a whole lot of people in the car with me—self-conscious, hair-flipping teenage self; current middle-aged, wrinkle-fighting self; seventeen-year-old best friends; two nearly grown boys of my own flesh and blood; forgotten high school crushes; be-loved, long-suffering husband.

I glance back at my two sons—completely conked, heads lolling, mouths open, just the way they slept as toddlers—and it is as if all the years and chapters of my life, past and present, are colliding, surging up and blending into one another right here on the highway, to the strains of Jerry Garcia and the band.

The song is "Sugar Magnolia," and it is in my blood. I know every note, every lyric, so well, so completely, that thirty years evaporate in an instant. I shut off the air-conditioning, put down all the windows, and begin to sing along.

Releasing my grip on everything—our dear house, our old life, my old image of the way life should be—has brought me face-to-face with my own greatest fear: the loss of control. But for better or for worse, I remind myself now, we have already let go. Our sons' childhood bedrooms—seemingly sacrosanct, unchanged for years—are no more. The spaces we created, furnished, and tended for so long are dismantled and in an instant have vanished from the face of the earth. Overnight, a new family has moved in and laid claim to the house that once seemed like a living, breathing extension of us. I *am* terrified— what if we've made a huge mistake and there's no going back?

But at last, hurtling down the highway with my old high school music turned up loud, I'm feeling just the smallest stir of excitement as well. Uprooted as our family is, we are also suddenly and completely unfettered, and there is an undeniable freedom in that. Looking back, I see that the choices I've made over the years actually do make some sense now. Marriage, divorce, New York City apartments, career, second husband, moves, homes, children, friends, activities—all of these decisions, big and small, add up to something, a life that appears in retrospect not random at all but, rather, pretty coherent. Even the mistakes, from this vantage point, appear to have been part of some larger plan.

Looking ahead, however, I can discern no such pattern, no trail with an arrow on it pointing the way. All I can really do is give in to the moment at hand—then pause, consider, and take one more step forward into the unknown. In the meantime, though, this is it: life in all its weird messiness, three generations about to try living together under one roof, sharing a refrigerator, divvying up the newspaper, figuring out bathroom protocol, quiet time, and computer rules.

Can we rise to this task we've set ourselves—start fresh, find a home, and create a life with some balance and meaning—even while parenting two sons through the demanding years of adolescence and high school? I'm still not sure. But the reality, or so I tell myself, is that I've never really been in control anyway. I glimpse the perfection of my own life only in retrospect, rarely in the moment, when I can barely see beyond the end of my nose. And try as I might to hold on or to avoid change, the best I can hope to do is make my way through all these ups and downs one day at a time, viewing the inevitable seasons of transition and transformation as opportunities to relinquish the old beliefs and possessions that no longer serve me all that well anyway.

Our sons are as different in their needs and desires as two boys could possibly be. Right now, one is eager to get on with the challenges of high school, while the other cries himself to sleep most nights, furious at us and desolate for all he's lost. My husband, who made the best case for staying put, is making a valiant effort now, for my sake, to put a good spin on changes he never sought. And I, who set all this upheaval in motion in the first place, feel the weight of that responsibility. Yet all of us yearn to reweave and strengthen the fabric of our life as a family. In our own ways, we must each begin to shift attention away from the life that was, so that we may allow ourselves to open to the life that is.

As this long, hard summer of moving and upheaval turns at last to fall, I realize that, with a little care and attention, the mundane details of life do have a way of falling into place. Our sons start school and take relief in the order prescribed by schedules and homework. My husband settles into our newly rented office space and begins to expand his business beyond its old guest bedroom limitations. My mother and I figure out how to share not only housework but a house. I learn—though not without some strain—how to be a mother and a wife in this house where I am still, first and foremost, a daughter. Day by day, we begin to piece together new routines as the old ones fade just slightly into memory.

Jack enters sixth grade and has to learn French, secure himself a place on the basketball court at recess and in the rigid pecking order of middle school boys. Henry assimilates quietly into high school, taking his time, as usual, to make friends. He plays keyboard in a jazz ensemble, grows his hair long and nurtures the new beard sprouting on his chin, withholds judgment on everything—the move, the school, his new classmates. My parents dust off the Ping-Pong table in the basement, stack extra drinking glasses in the kitchen cupboards, and adjust to a household that's suddenly noisier, messier, and more crowded than most seventy-year-olds would willingly put up with.

Even so, we are under no illusions. Our makeshift living situation works because we all understand that it is not meant to last. A month after we move into my parents' guest bedroom, and in defiance of my own promise to put a moratorium on all big decisions for a while—especially those involving down payments—I slip away one afternoon and go house hunting.

When Jack once asked me to describe my dream house, I conjured, to his horror, a cottage with sloping wooden floors, a screen door that would bang shut and fasten with a hook, daisies in a mason jar on a big screened porch table, walls that could be whispered through, beds covered with faded quilts, afternoon light filtered through pines.

To a boy who favors wall-to-wall carpeting, overstuffed sectional couches, and digital everything, my rustic vision was cause for grave concern. My husband, on the other hand, is dubious but not altogether surprised when I phone him out of the blue from a New Hampshire hilltop and tell him I think I've found our new home—a two-hundred-year-old summer cottage that satisfies all my romantic longings. Here, on a narrow country road, is a solitary place that seems to embody the kind of space and timeless peace I've been dreaming of.

The small red-shingled saltbox is empty on the afternoon I see it first, silent, as if waiting in the hushed stillness for human life to return. Outside, in the slanting light of a late September afternoon, the touch of a long-ago gardener is everywhere in evidence. Peonies sprawl along the stone wall, ancient lilac bushes frame the driveway, mint and thyme multiply at the kitchen door beneath a rampant vine of lacy clematis climbing to the rooftop in full ivory bloom.

Tall ferns sway gently in the breeze, softening every edge, filling each neglected garden bed alongside scraggly, toppled roses and spikes of goldenrod. A black, three-foot-long snake dozes, still as stone, on a wedge of granite by the barn. On the narrow screened porch there is a jumble of wicker chairs, an old metal glider, its cushions faded from decades of afternoon sun, and a small square table set, as if for all time, with binoculars, notebook and pen, a reading lamp, and a well-thumbed copy of Peterson's *A Field Guide to the Birds*.

Beyond the windows there, a grassy lawn gives way to a steep decline, fields, stone walls, and a wide-open view of mountains, two gentle peaks looking like nothing so much as a pair of softly rounded breasts. There is not another house in sight, just a dilapidated gray cottage far across the field and an old shed on the other side of the road. There is something eternal here, ancient and quiet and still.

Two days later, my husband walks through the tiny, crooked rooms, peers into the dank, hand-dug cellar hole, and shakes his head. He wants me to be happy. He thinks I've lost my mind. His response sobers me, but my own attraction to the place only intensifies.

Again and again in the days that follow, I find myself returning to the house, to see how the mountains look at different times of day, to find my way along the trails in the woods across the road, to linger at the pond, or to steal glimpses of the empty porch, so inviting on these luminous autumn afternoons. It is far from practical, this dilapidated old cottage. And given the work to be done, it will be no bargain at any price. Yet try as I might, I can't make myself stay away, can't stop shaking my reluctant, sleepy husband awake in the middle of the night to point out yet another attribute I'm sure he, in his pragmatism, has overlooked.

Although the house shows the wear and tear of its recent history as temporary housing for actors from the summer stock theater up the road, it has clearly been much loved in the past, the treasured summer retreat of an unmarried schoolteacher and her bachelor brother. Almost more of a toy house than a real house, frozen as it is in another time, adrift in a sea of tall field grass edged by woods, the small red cottage seems to promise a way back to the kind of life I yearn for—simple, slow, in closer touch with earth and sky and natural rhythms.

No one else, it seems, is beating a path to the old red door wreathed in clematis vines. Certainly there's no reasonable explanation for my sudden sense of urgency about this house, this land. After all, we had agreed to leave all our options open, burn no more bridges, live with my parents for a year, and then figure out what to do next. Yet it's as if I've been overtaken by some obsession or need that will not be satisfied until our futures are securely allied—our family, this place.

Finally, after weeks of vacillation, we make an offer to buy the cottage and the surrounding acres of rocky field "as is," with no inspection. After all, we reason, the house will need a complete gut job and renovation anyway, so why pay good money just to shine a spotlight on its many shortcomings? In return for our laissez-faire approach to house buying, we save a few thousand dollars on the price and get ourselves a quick closing.

On the glorious late October morning that we sign the papers, my husband and I stop in town afterward for coffee and muffins to go and drive up to the cottage, keys in hand. At my insistence, we carry two beat-up wicker chairs from the porch and set them outside at the top of the hill. There is not a sound, nor another soul in sight. No car drives by. A few bright leaves still cling to the maple trees, flares of red against a pure blue sky. Our new home is less than a hundred miles from our old. And yet we are so far from that familiar, close-knit suburban cul-de-sac, from the well-worn grooves of our old sensible, predictable, densely populated lives, that we might as well be on another planet. I take Steve's hand, turn my face to the sun, breathe in the sharp autumn air.

But try as I might to summon joy, this is not the celebratory moment I've been hoping for. A pall of buyer's remorse settles over us both. There is no getting around the fact that we are here today because I have been seduced, drawn beyond all reason to the serenity of open land, a view of fields and mountains, the layers of history in a crumbling cottage, the possibility of a future that is nothing more, at the moment, than a vague picture in my mind's eye. And we're here because my more sensible husband, in his desire to please me, is willing to go along with—if not embrace—a vision he most definitely doesn't share. We may be sitting side by side in these two mismatched chairs, but we're definitely not in the same place. I look out across the dry, faded grasses, watch a lone hawk ride a current across the empty valley, and venture a private prayer: Please, please, let this be all right.

The house has an oil tank in the garage and minimal baseboard heat, but it isn't insulated or winterized. There's no possibility of doing anything here until spring. Living at my parents' house through the dark dormancy of winter, we think about how to proceed. We consult with an architect to sketch out possible renovations, but his idea of transforming our humble cottage into a kind of Colonial hybrid seems ridiculous to us.

Finally, I have the notion that before ripping out a single wall, we should simply move in and live in the house exactly as it is for a while. This way, we can have a place of our own for the following summer—and give my parents a much deserved break from daily life with teenagers. More important, we will learn something, I'm sure, by taking our time. We'll have a chance to discover what dawn looks like here and where the sun sets at night. We'll slow down the pace of change, test our commitment to this place and our new way of life. But most of all, we'll come to know the house—and to know ourselves in this quiet landscape—before plunging ahead with the next big step.

As the last of the snow melts away in April, I make it my project to get the house ready for us, determined to uncover its secret charms—and to convince my skeptical family that we belong here, here as much as anywhere. For what I'm realizing, as we prepare to move for the second time in less than a year, is that this life path we're following now isn't exactly well marked. It's more like one of the faint, overgrown trails in the woods across the road than a paved roadway—barely visible at times, not found on any map, discerned more by feeling and intuition than by knowing. It seems that in buying this derelict cottage, we've already forsaken the route of efficiency anyway. Much as I might wish for a GPS for life, it seems that we're destined, for now, anyway, to bushwhack.

Only when we return to open up the house in the spring do we begin to discover just what we have—a thriving maternal bat colony that inhabits not only the attached shed and garage, but the spaces behind each loose shingle and every other dark cranny as well; a leaky roof; crumbling foundation stones; rot; and carpenter ants. (Some of the discoveries come later, when, for instance, a few days of hard rain are followed by humid sunshine and I watch, transfixed, as a black, rank mold begins to grow across the slick floors and up the freshly painted walls.)

All winter long, I've doubted the powerful feelings that first drew me to this spot. I've questioned my own infatuated persistence and regretted dragging my husband into an impractical purchase he'd resisted from the start.

"You had to have it," he's pointed out more than once.

"I'm so sorry," I've said many times in return, really meaning it. Now, though, there's nothing to do but make the best of what we have and try to summon some faith that we're on the right track after all, or that, at the very least, we'll eventually end up there.

Mornings, I arrive with a large take-out coffee and sit for a while on a rock in the yard. I throw a ball way down into the field for Gracie to fetch and then laugh as she flies down the hill, in her element. The only thing missing now is sheep.

Five years ago, as I made a delayed and reluctant final peace with the fact that there would be no more babies in our lives, the urge for a puppy came on strong. It seemed that turning forty, and facing the end of my childbearing years, had unleashed some powerful, latent maternal urge that could be satisfied only by the acquisition of some small dependent creature requiring constant care. For months I tried to resist, and then, on a whim, I answered an ad in the paper and made an appointment "just to look" at an eight-week-old border collie puppy. Thirty minutes after I first touched my nose to Gracie's tiny black one, she was throwing up in my lap as we headed for home. She came of age catching fly balls in the backyard, an eager participant in any game involving little boys and moving objects. But we always believed she deserved a larger playing field. Now, watching her torpedo through the tall grass, crouch in anticipation, and then leap up high to catch ball after ball in midair, I realize that for Gracie, anyway, who could care less about bats and mold, these wide-open acres truly are a bit of heaven on earth.

Our morning routine is meant to tire her out before I get to work, but it serves another purpose as well. Gracie is my role model for joy, my living, breathing, bullet-fast reminder that the good life is always the life of now, that the only moment is the present moment. I need only pause long enough to drink it in, throw the ball one more time and then another, gaze at the mountains, and awaken to the beauty of the day.

And then, fortified and acclimated once again to solitude, I head inside, put an Alison Krauss CD on my portable stereo, and clean furiously. The previous owners, like the owners before them, took away only what they wanted from the house, leaving the rest behind. So we now possess not only a cottage, but a century's worth of random cast-off furnishings as well. I make countless trips to the dump, methodically ridding our new home of its assorted ashtrays, stained dish towels, questionable pillows, and moldering throw rugs.

Much of what we inherit, however, we keep. The furniture will do. And it seems as if we're being offered a peek at the history of the house in the artifacts that have accumulated here for generations—the pliant decks of yellowed playing cards, the satiny wooden chessmen in their brittle cigar box, the commemorative plate depicting the coronation of Queen Elizabeth, the collection of 1940s license plates nailed up in the garage, the childlike oil sketch of Mount Monadnock that hangs on the porch.

For some reason, I am particularly pleased by the discovery of a stack of faded beach towels in the closet, worn soft and thin from years of use. And I can't even consider tossing out the movie listing tacked to the kitchen wall some long-ago August week, when the theater downtown was showing *Misty, The Naked Edge, The Last Sunset,* and *Gone with the Wind.* The books in the upstairs hall, with titles like *A Sense of Hummus, Country Moods and Tenses,* and *The Flowering of New England,* evoke a simpler, more innocent era of longer attention spans, fewer distractions, and less technology. A time when people, perhaps, really did do less and read more. I sniff the musty pages, dust the books, and put them back on their shelves.

I attack the bathroom with Clorox and hot water; enlist Steve to play hooky from work one day to help me strip wallpaper in the bedrooms. But when the wallboard itself disintegrates along with the paper, we give up. Two coats of paint over the whole mess will get us through for now. I assess the porch—it needs a screen repaired, a thorough scrub-down, and half as much furniture. Day after day, alone in the house, I empty mousetraps of wizened corpses, wash floors and windows, sweep up bat guano.

The kitchen, however, has me flummoxed. With its forty-year-old brick linoleum, worn straight through in places, blackened, bubbled, and pocked everywhere else, the room will never again look or feel quite clean. The single work surface is the top of the washer and dryer, conveniently lined up alongside the old gas stove. There are three small open shelves, already stacked with glasses and dishes, a circa 1950 metal sink unit, an old refrigerator propped up on blocks to keep it from tipping over on the slanted floor, a drawer full of tinny silverware in a red plastic tray, and a cupboard's worth of aluminum pots and pans, just like the ones I played with in my grandparents' basement four decades ago. Every windowsill and corner is furnished with an ant cup. Perhaps the same zealous tenant also left behind the economy-size pack of D-Con under the sink.

I've assured my skeptical family that we will make this fun, that living here will be its own adventure. Lying awake on the first deathly still, sweltering June night that we spend in the house, I can only wonder if and when that fun will begin. There is no disputing that I've been the driving force behind this venture, not only the purchase of the house, but also the brilliant idea that we should spend the summer here, making do and getting by, exchanging familiar twenty-first-century comforts for the cottage's old-fashioned, pastoral charm. This scenario, a kind of grown-up version of playing house, is my dream, no one else's. Now, wide awake, sweating in the oppressive heat of an airless, unseasonably muggy June night, under a roof with nary a shred of insulation, I am losing my nerve.

My husband is right. In our, or rather my, eagerness to put down new roots, we've been terribly naive. Can we really take on the daunting project of turning this poor old cottage into a solid, fully functioning house? Do we even want to try? Already, Steve has warned me that he is less than enthusiastic about the prospect of camping out here for the next few months. For the moment, he's humoring me. He'll give it a try for a few nights; beyond that, no promises. My parents, he points out helpfully, will be glad to take him back.

Having spent the last few weeks scrubbing and painting, I have to admit that the bloom is off the rose for me, too. I'm still not at all sure I can even cook a decent dinner in the grimy little kitchen, let alone manage to actually live alongside the bats and the ants and the mice. By the time we had lugged our suitcases up the steep, narrow stairs this afternoon and plugged in a few fans, the boys were already plotting sleepovers elsewhere and extended visits to our old hometown. In the hot, oppressive dark, June bugs bang against the window screens and a mosquito whines at my ear, as if to assure me that I'll spend this night awake.

Then I hear another sound, muffled sobs. I get up, step across the hall to Jack's room, and slip in beside him, a sweaty, miserable boy who is sure his mother has gone off the deep end and is dragging him along for the ride. It takes a few minutes, but finally he turns his cheek on the wet pillow, stares at the wall, and says angrily, "Other people move, and they manage to at least find a normal house to live in. We already had a perfect house and a perfect life, and good neighbors and everything we needed. But we gave it all up for nothing."

He is crying hard, gasping, and giving voice to every terrible thought I've spent the night trying to push away. "*You* needed to move to the country. And then," he continues in a furious whisper, "you couldn't even buy us a real house, you bought this stupid old shack that's not nice at all. I hate it. I hate everything about it and I don't want to live here. If we had to move, I don't know why you and Dad couldn't at least have found us a decent house instead of this stupid shack full of bats. I would never even invite a friend here. This place is so embarrassing that I wouldn't want any of my friends to see it. Ever."

The words cut deep, mostly, of course, because I'm afraid Jack is right. He finally wears himself out and falls asleep, but now I'm too upset to rest. Back in bed, I shed some tears of my own. If I could undo it all, I finally admit to myself, roll back time and make the choice to stay right where we were, in our old green house in our busy, friendly neighborhood, instead of moving at all, I would. Instead, in my idealistic search for simplicity, I've managed to make our lives far more complicated than they were before, certainly more complicated than they need to be. I am hot, exhausted, and utterly discouraged. And my family is ready to mutiny.

Sometime toward dawn, it occurs to me that what we really need is to have a party.

The summer solstice is three days away, on a Friday, and I ask everyone I can think of to come for dinner. We don't know many people in town, but we do have two close, longtime friends who live here, and we've met a few others who seem to have good friend potential. I am hoping, hoping desperately, that celebrating the year's longest day by filling the house with people and good things to eat might lift our spirits. At the very least, Jack will see that I'm not too embarrassed to invite friends over. But just maybe, in the course of decorating, cooking, and sharing food, we will actually manage to enjoy ourselves, make peace with our shoddy little house, and begin to lay claim to this small corner of earth that has, for better or worse, exerted such a pull on my soul. With determined good cheer, I borrow all my mother's candlesticks, make a shopping list, and wait to hear from the twenty or so people I've invited.

One new friend says she wouldn't miss it. No one else calls back. Thinking it's always better to be prepared than caught short, I go ahead and bake a twelve-pound ham anyway, make salads, Chinese sesame noodles, and a yellow solstice cake, shaped like a sun and adorned with daisies and carrot-colored day lilies from the yard. I fill a big cooler with ice and drinks and stack every plate we have on the dining room table. I assign jobs—Jack to make a bright cardboard sun to hang on a tree by the driveway, Henry to fill all the old pitchers and canning jars in the house with wildflowers, ferns, and grasses. Steve, glad to escape to the air-conditioned comforts of his office, promises to be home by six.

The afternoon of the party, I have another flash of inspiration— we should build a fire pit out on the hilltop, a kind of shrine to the view, where we can come to watch the sun slip away. It is a hot day, but I coerce the boys into helping me lug rocks, gather sticks, pile firewood. We arrange chairs and an old wooden bench in a semicircle, looking out to the mountains, and lay a fire.

The evening could be a disaster, and it nearly is. One couple I've invited arrives in party attire, sips at glasses of water, looks around, and then leaves five minutes later with hardly a word. Not a good start. But three other people show up and, mercifully, they stay. And as it turns out, three are enough, on this night, to make a celebration. As we gather around the feast laid out on the table, our friend Kerby surveys the candlelit room, the pitchers full of field flowers, the sloping painted floors and crooked doors, and exclaims, "This place is absolutely perfect. Don't change a thing."

I will be forever grateful to him for those words, just the right words at just the right time. Of course the house itself is so far from perfect that we've begun to feel like idiots for buying it. But what is perfect is the moment, a moment of pure grace at the end of a long, hot, awful week during which we've doubted every decision we've ever made.

Thanks to three friends, and candles, and the somewhat grudging efforts of my sons and husband, we really do manage to create something remarkable on this June night—a sense, once again, of home. As dusk falls, we carry our plates out onto the screened porch and enjoy a wonderful dinner. Candles flicker, Paul Desmond is on the stereo, plates are filled and filled again, and the mountains turn pink, then purple, and then fade to black as the bats begin to emerge, flicking into the darkening sky first by ones and twos and then five and ten at a time.

As the moon rises, huge and heavy and almost close enough to touch, we rub bug spray into arms, necks, and ankles and troop outside to gather around our extravagant fire. We push marshmallows onto the ends of sticks, then watch them turn brown and oozy in the flames. Voices hush to whispers. For the first time, and in good company, we open ourselves to the sights and sounds and smells of night on this broad hilltop—the wide bowl of sky, blanketed with stars, the mesmerizing fire, the cool, damp grass and summer air.

After a while, Kerby begins to speak: "Let us go then, you and I, / When the evening is spread out against the sky . . ." An English teacher, he recites T. S. Eliot's entire poem "The Love Song of J. Alfred Prufrock" from memory, with the kind of passion and deep, urgent connection that is perhaps possible only among friends, in the dark, by a fire. No one moves. We are suspended here, held captive under the spell of poetry. It is a moment to remember. And I realize that whatever it was I'd hoped to accomplish this night has indeed occurred. Surely each one of us, sitting close by one another on the crest of this hill, feels blessed to be here, grateful that fate, or circumstance, has led us tonight to this particular spot in the world and no other.

It is well after midnight, the fire dying down to embers, when we all finally stand and stretch, reluctant even now to bring this long, lovely night to an end. Here in the darkness we have discovered, to our amazement, that in June these wild, untended fields are alight with fireflies, that they spark and tumble like falling stars through the tall grasses.

~ 4 ~

ordinariness

*The ordinary acts we practice every day
at home are of more importance to the soul
than their simplicity might suggest.*
—THOMAS MOORE

*Y*ears ago, long before my husband and I ever thought of moving, a psychic predicted not only that our family would end up elsewhere, but that we would one day find ourselves with a life so much easier and more satisfying than the one we knew that it would feel almost like a vacation by comparison. It struck me as a nice, unlikely, pie-in-the-sky sort of idea, and at the time I barely gave her words a second thought. But as we begin to grow used to living in our new-old house, grow accustomed to the owl's lonely call beyond our bedroom window and the urgent yips of coyotes rising from the field below, to walks before breakfast and late afternoon swims in the pond, I find myself remembering her premonition.

As the long, uneventful summer unfolds, we relax. For the first time in quite a while, life does feel almost effortless. There is no place for the boys to go and not much for any of us to do. Although my husband heads to work every day, and although I have short stories to read and deadlines to meet, it occurs to us that much of the time we actually do feel as if we're on vacation. The screened porch is the nicest office I've ever had; working there, I can easily pretend that I'm not.

There is something about this hilltop, with its view of meadow and mountain, that invites daily contemplation and repose. There is something, too, about the ordinary, everyday rhythm of life here that is surprisingly satisfying, as if in forgoing for a time some of the technology and twenty-first-century material comforts we usually take for granted, we are more able to open ourselves to each day's small tasks and simple pleasures.

The solstice dinner was a turning point, laying the stage for many more festive evenings. In a way, that unlikely little party set us free, for we were reminded of something important that night—the whole point of entertaining is not to impress people, but to welcome them. Spreading the blue-and-white-checked tablecloths that came with the house, setting the mismatched dishes on card tables on the porch, I'd realized how easy it is to get so caught up in making the right impression that we forget the simple satisfaction of just being together with people we like, of making time and space for family and friends.

My twelve-pound ham taught me a valuable lesson, too: A funky, ill-equipped kitchen bestows its own blessing. No one expects anything much to emerge from it, there are no standards to meet, no tests to pass, no fancy appliances to live up to. At first, I thought any cooking I managed in that counterless room would be akin to Samuel Johnson's oft quoted view of women preaching: like "a dog's walking on his hind legs. It is not done well; but you are surprised to find it done at all." In fact, though, I discover that I can prepare very satisfying meals by putting the chopping board in the sink and spreading out my ingredients on top of the clothes dryer.

I buy some cloth napkins and six brightly colored mugs,

leave a wooden box of silverware on the dining room table, the cooler in the hall, and candles everywhere. With that, we are ready for guests on a moment's notice. There is not even a chance of impressing anyone, so all pressure is off. No need to be showy or try to get gourmet with the menu, and our visitors are more than happy to rough it with us, to step into the time warp of our summer, squeeze in around our small porch table, and share produce from the farm stand, cooked with love and just a little effort. Making dinner, whether for four or ten, has never been so much fun.

The paradox of this is not lost on any of us. In our old well-appointed house, having company was always a bit of a production, calling for much planning and schedule juggling, housecleaning and table setting. Here, in our make-do quarters, it's no big deal. Often, after dinner we read aloud, something it certainly never occurred to us to do with friends before but that seems like ideal entertainment in our current circumstances.

For overnight callers, we've hung a flowered plastic shower curtain across the back of the upstairs hall and nestled a bed under the eaves—instant guest quarters, as long as the guests aren't too particular. Overflow crowds are accommodated by our old tent in the yard and the weathered picnic table that came with the house. If Jack began the summer feeling sorry for himself, it is not long at all before even he finds himself under the spell cast by easy days, impromptu parties, and starstrewn nights.

We eat nearly every dinner this summer on the porch, watching the bats issue forth as the sun slips away. Mornings, we carry breakfast out on trays and linger in the sunshine, enjoying the light and each sighting of hummingbirds among the phlox blossoms. I can clean the whole house in an hour or so, dragging a shop vac behind me to suck up dead flies and grime from the windowsills. Beyond that, there isn't a lot to do to keep up the place. Sweep the bat dung, change the flowers in their vases, dust pollen from the porch furniture.

It seems almost as if we are living outside, so connected are we to the long arc of the sun, the nocturnal travels of the moon, the ever changing panorama of mountains and sky, the background music of birds. We feel the opposite of deprived. For the first time in years, there is time for idleness. On weekends, we eat homemade doughnuts at the farmers market, ride our bikes to the next town for pond swims and ice-cream cones, go to concerts on the village green.

This sense of ease, I realize, is something I have been craving and that our two sons have never really experienced. Having grown up with all the advantages and activities of suburbia, they aren't quite sure, at first, what to do with themselves now that the distractions and activities have been stripped away. We are no longer surrounded by neighbors and ready playmates, there is no swimming pool down the street, no array of day camps and summer sports programs from which to choose.

Our boys have never in their lives lacked for something to do; on the contrary, my challenge has always been to keep them from having and doing too much, to keep them from overindulging in the vast banquet of choices we've all taken for granted. Now, I face a different challenge altogether—filling the days. Certainly, if one of our reasons for moving had been to explore an alternative version of "the good life," here is our chance—an opportunity to do less and to appreciate more.

At first, my sons do get bored. They complain about the lack of neighbors and the absence of a plan. And then they find things to do—shoot baskets, play cards, listen to baseball games on the radio, play badminton in the yard. Afternoons, there might be an argument over who will get the chaise longue in the porch corner, the best place of all for reading or napping, but the hammock is not a bad consolation prize. Many books are read in both places.

Settling in, we learn that we really don't need as much space to live in as we thought we did. Jack is now convinced that the red cottage is just the right size, six small rooms and a porch. Henry loves that nobody ever has to shout; we are always within earshot of one another. But several house inspections confirm our growing suspicion that the structure has been so compromised, and is so rife with problems, that it would make more sense to take the whole thing down and build from scratch than to try to restore it. The fact that half of the house's original two-hundred-year-old timber frame was sliced away decades ago to create two flimsy upstairs bedrooms makes the decision somewhat easier; there really isn't all that much to save anyway.

And yet age itself lends the original rooms a timeless, humble beauty, visible in the wavy panes of glass in the windows, the wide pine floorboards, the hand-planed doors, painted and re-painted countless times. Most of what is here has lasted for two centuries, was made slowly, painstakingly, by human hands— moldings, mantels, wrought-iron latches, rough-hewn beams, the stair rail, one long sapling mounted on the wall with horse-shoes and worn smooth as silk by the trailing fingers of all our predecessors. These details, too, seem to remind me of our pur-pose in being here: Slow down, notice, and appreciate.

The day will come soon enough when we'll have to move yet again, have to deal with demolishing the house, dispensing with all its contents, and beginning to build anew. But for these few months, at least, we are granted a glimpse both of the past and of what our future life here might look and feel like. We have a chance to reorder some of our priorities and to figure out what kind of home we might eventually create on this spot, how some of the things we love about this old house might somehow find their way into a new one.

In the meantime, living here, in a cottage that we all grow inordinately fond of despite knowing that we will one day knock it down, I realize something else, too—that a house is but one step in the journey toward belonging, that the land we choose to settle on becomes a kind of haven as well, although this home, too, must be consecrated, slowly and over time. Watching, listening, learning, I begin to feel at ease where I am, come to know the language of the wind, the daily path of the summer sun, the proximity of stars. And so it is that the contours of this landscape slowly inscribe themselves on my heart, on all our hearts, as sense memories accrue by layers, one day blending seamlessly into the next.

"I don't think anyone 'finds' joy," writer Dawna Markova observes. "Rather, we cultivate it by searching for the preciousness of small things, the ordinary miracles that strengthen our hearts so we can keep them open to what is most difficult." Living together in the old cottage, improvising and making do, we do find ourselves paying attention to the small things, learning to appreciate not just the house and all its quirks, but also the pace that being here seems to impose on us, the easygoing mood that comes with paring down, living with less, doing less, expecting less.

I am sitting on the glider one afternoon, surrounded by piles of work but taking my time to savor a long story in *The New Yorker*. A glass of iced tea, made with mint snipped just outside the door, sweats rivulets on the table at my side. I look up after a while, to see Henry completely absorbed in his own book over in the corner. Jack is off someplace on his bike. Neither

Henry nor I have said a word for over an hour. In this silence, time seems to have slowed to a leisurely crawl. It is high summer, hot and still, with just enough breeze to keep us comfortable on this lazy, uneventful day. The sky is clear. The long view across the tall grasses to the stone walls and distant, blue green mountains fills me with serenity.

My restlessness of the last few years has quieted here. And it seems that my own newfound sense of well-being has even spread outward, lightening all our spirits. On a steamy night in June, my family had threatened to decamp from our new home because it failed to meet their standards of comfort and convenience. Three months later, we are not only used to our small red cottage that smells of bats, but have actually begun to cherish our time here, already aware that we will all remember this particular summer as a special, even magical, interlude.

It is worth thinking about. If happiness really could be bought, surely most of us would feel much more satisfied than we do, blessed as we are with such an abundance of good food, beautiful places to live, accessible education, entertainment, and opportunity. Yet our impulse, our human nature, seems always to be to strive for more. More wealth, more recognition, more stuff.

As essayist Anna Quindlen has suggested, perhaps our whole concept of success needs to be redefined, by "satisfaction of the spirit, rather than by power of the résumé." It may well be that success lies as much in our ability to behold the world before us in gratitude and wonder as it does in owning things and doing things. And it may be, too, that happiness really is a state of mind we choose for ourselves, a way of being that we cultivate from one moment to the next, rather than the result of realizing our ambitions or acquiring whatever it is we think we most desire.

In some ways, I've always felt inadequate to the task of preparing my sons to meet the challenges and pressures of twenty-first-century adolescence. I want so much for them to know the rigors of hard work and the pride of succeeding in their efforts, to have the experience of doing their best and being recognized for that. But the message that we must have more, accomplish more, and be more is pervasive, and I find myself by turns succumbing to that pressure and then feeling more determined than ever to resist it.

I think the word *ordinary* has a bad rap. We encourage our children to strive to lead extraordinary lives, in the belief that such striving is not only admirable but necessary if they are to realize their goals and grow into fulfilled, successful adults. Many of us live in fear that our children may not live up to their potential, may fall behind their peers, may fail to embody our—or the culture's—notions of success.

But as I've watched my sons and their friends meet the demands of their lives, as I listen to other parents share their worries about college rankings and admissions percentages, their children's future careers and life choices, I can't help but wonder, What is the cost of all this striving? And what gets lost in our relentless push to achieve, have, and do more?

It's easy, given the times we live in and the implicit messages we absorb each day, to equate a good life with having a lot and doing a lot. So it's also easy to fall into believing that our children, if they are to succeed in life, need to be terrific at everything, and that it's up to us to make sure that they are—to keep them on track through tougher course loads, more activities, more competitive sports, more summer programs. But in all our well-intentioned efforts to do the right thing for our teenage children, we may be failing to provide them with something that is truly essential—the time and space they need to wake up to themselves, to grow acquainted with their own innate gifts, to dream their dreams and discover their true natures.

Without quite intending to, what we are really doing this summer in the red cottage is giving ourselves, and our sons, a break. Although we are all at loose ends for a while, although our sons miss the solid structure of their old lives, before long they are adapting. And then, somewhat to my surprise, contentment sneaks up on us. It turns out that life is rich and full enough right here.

Knowing hardly anyone in town, we are freed by our anonymity to relax. If there is a place to be, or a thing to do, well, we're clueless. The need to improvise—whether it's making dinner or coming up with a plan for the evening—makes us playful again, more spontaneous, and easier to please. And that is good for all of us.

My husband and I have agreed to a time-out of our own for the summer—no more talking about whether we've done the right thing or not. In fact, we are taking a complete recess from the relentless planning and thinking and questioning that seem to have consumed us now for years. And what a relief it is, to give up worrying for a while and to open our minds instead to the possibility that things will simply work out for the best.

Years ago, I copied into a notebook some well-known lines by the fourteenth-century mystic Julian of Norwich: "All will be well, and all will be well, and all manner of things will be well." I've always loved the reassuring cadence of her optimistic theology. Finally, I begin to allow myself to believe it. By winter, perhaps, we'll have a sense of what to do next. In the meantime, the answer to every question really does seem to lie in letting go, settling into the long, spacious days and restful nights—all the windows open, all the doors unlocked—and trusting that, for the moment, anyway, we are exactly where we need to be. Whenever I manage to do that, when I can give myself over to the moment at hand, I am suffused with peace.

What began for all of us as a trial—starting afresh in a new town, in a shabby little house, where everything was different from what we were accustomed to—turns out to be, instead, a kind of reeducation, as we find ourselves surprised by delight in the ordinary moments and the modest pleasures of everyday life. Surprised, too, to find that happiness hasn't much to do with perfect surroundings, with having a lot or doing a lot. It comes with living simply, taking care of one another, allowing time in the day for ease and pleasure and play. In our own ways, we all forge strong connections to our new home, or rather home-to-be, as the weeks pass.

When school starts in September, it is Jack who campaigns to stay on. We should enjoy our life here, he insists, until the cold drives us back to the better-insulated comfort of my parents' house for the winter. By now, no one cares much about the splintery upstairs floor, the bright green indoor-outdoor carpet on the porch, or the meager, ill-equipped kitchen. We are used to them. Soon the bats fly south, and then the carpenter ants are gone, too, holed up and dormant for the winter. Other than the unseen animal that scrabbles its way each night to a burrow beneath the living room floorboards, we have the place to ourselves and a little oil heat to take the edge off the autumn chill. We find storm windows in the garage, stuff some paper towels for insulation around the back door, and pile more blankets on the beds.

Days shorten, frost comes, Concord grapes ripen and sweeten on vines in the backyard, wild turkeys parade across the field, and no one wants to leave. The maple and oak trees turn, imperceptibly at first and then completely, a dazzling show of golden yellows and coppery shades of orange and brown. At sunset, bathed in light, the mountains blaze with color. The empty fields of November, with their crumpled grasses and frozen spikes of goldenrod, are as beautiful, in their own way, as the abundant, rippling green seas of June. I make hot cocoa for breakfast, soup for dinner. We give ourselves another night, and another after that.

We know that when we do move out, it will be a long time before we'll spend a night in our own home again or watch the sun come up over "our" mountains. Finally, though, even our extra sweaters are not enough. Fall is over. No one has been really warm for days. On the Saturday after Thanksgiving, we borrow my dad's pickup truck and load it up with the things we'll need for the winter. We decide to leave everything else right here till spring, when we hope it will feel a little easier to clean out the old house for good. Then we shut off the heat and the water, prop open the refrigerator, drain all the pipes, lock the door for the first and last time, and hang the rusty key on its nail.

After a year of rootlessness and uncertainty, we have found our footing, surprisingly enough, in a rotting, two-hundred-year-old summer house destined for the wrecker's ball. Living here for just six months, making do in the house just as it is, we have figured out what we needed to know—that it is okay not to have everything; that it is possible to have a meaningful and satisfying life without moving too fast; that sometimes "making do" actually means making room for more, more than we can possibly imagine.

Although the old red saltbox isn't meant to be our house, we will call this hilltop home. And somehow, we will find a way to make sure that the new house pays homage to the one that stood here first, and to this land all four of us have finally come to love. One thing we've learned this summer is that a house is not an end in itself, any more than "home" is just one geographic location where things feel safe and familiar. Home can be anyplace in which we create our own sense of rest and peace as we tend to the spaces in which we eat and sleep and play. It is a place that we create and re-create in every moment, at every stage of our lives, a place where the plain and common becomes cherished and the ordinary becomes sacred.

~ **5** ~

doors

The big question is whether you are going
to be able to say a hearty yes to your adventure.
—JOSEPH CAMPBELL

$\mathcal{J}$oseph Campbell suggested that there is a unique track, a particular life adventure, waiting for each one of us, and when we step forward to embrace our adventure, doors begin to open that we never saw before, doors that could not open for anyone else.

It was Campbell's belief that our real work in this world is to achieve integrity between what we believe and how we live. "The privilege of a lifetime," he wrote, "is being who you are." But Campbell also warns that the journey is difficult, that a thousand distractions, and countless obstacles, stand between us and our own truth.

I would add that the journey is ongoing. Not a day goes by that I don't still need to remind myself that my life is not just what's handed to me, nor is it my list of obligations, my accomplishments or failures, or what my family is up to, but rather it is what I choose, day in and day out, to make of it all. When I am able simply to be with things as they are, able to accept the day's challenges without judging, reaching, or wishing for something else, I feel as if I am receiving the privilege, coming a step closer to being myself.

It's when I get lost in the day's details, or so caught up in worries about what might be, that I miss the beauty of what is. The process of uprooting our family and then trying to map out a new life plan elsewhere has led me, over and over again, down the worry path. There have been days—there are days still—when my husband and I simply look at each other and ask, "What on earth were we thinking?"

Yet even though we did not set out to sell a house, buy a house, tear down a house, and build a house, it's impossible to imagine now that it could have been otherwise. What happens, I suppose, is that we decide to step up to our life adventure and then invariably find ourselves surprised by the journey.

Twenty-five years ago, I thought the self-confident, dark-haired man in a pink button-down shirt sitting across from me at a publishing conference table was the handsomest guy in the room. By the time he finally asked me to marry him, I'd had "a hearty yes" on the tip of my tongue for four years—but I never could have foreseen the husband he would be, or the father, or that one day we would find ourselves together on a New Hampshire hilltop, splitting wood with our two sons and stacking it in the back corner of a grassy field.

Gazing into the eyes of my firstborn son, I could not begin to see the young man he would become, the music that would define his life, or even that, all too soon, the time would come when he would be ready to leave home. Three years later, meeting his brother for the first time, I couldn't imagine that one day he would sit at the kitchen table doing math problems that I couldn't even read, let alone begin to solve. When I kissed his soft newborn neck, I could not conjure the aftershave or acne in his future, the fights to come over yard work and messy bedrooms, or the pleasure of listening to my two sons play jazz duets in the living room after dinner.

Moment by moment, we have the opportunity to say yes, to move into our lives and open ourselves to the adventure—but that doesn't mean that we ever really know where we're going or that we can predict what we'll find when we get there. If we're lucky, though, the life we end up leading is one that makes us feel alive.

Once our extended summer idyll is over and we have to move forward again, there is no avoiding our anxiety about putting all our resources into one patch of rocky countryside that we are still just getting to know. This is not just about schools and kids and midlife restlessness anymore, it is about me and my husband and all the years to come, years beyond high school and college and boys who still live at home. Both of us have nurtured all sorts of dreams for our future, ideas about where we might live "someday," how we might travel, new career paths we might pursue, what retirement would feel like, and what kinds of freedom await us once our sons are grown. Now, reality sinks in.

Embracing one adventure inevitably means closing the door on countless others. We will not have that cabin on a lake I've always dreamed of, or a retirement in Maine, or new jobs in the city, or our pick of ethnic restaurants on a Friday night. In exchange for space, privacy, and a playground of stars at night, we are giving up for good the energy and intellectual stimulation of urban life, the proximity of old friends, the cultural amenities we've always taken for granted, whether we availed ourselves of them or not. We are committing ourselves now not only to a house or a piece of land, but to one small New England town, a new, unknown community, and all the myriad details, seen and as yet unseen, that constitute a way of life. Building a house, at least in our minds, is about putting down roots for the long haul. In the meantime, though, Henry is already halfway through high school. If we don't get on with it, he will never really get to live here at all.

We are hoping that if we're ready to break ground by spring, we'll have a finished house a year later and move our family just one more time. Jack will begin his freshman year of high school in his new hometown. Henry, if all goes well, will have a year in which to sink his roots in with ours before heading off to college. Time is of the essence. But the prospect of finally forging ahead—of committing our time and our energy, not to mention the rest of our lives and all of our money and then some—is daunting.

So I worry. We will be consumed with construction while our sons are consumed with being teenagers. Just as I'm wishing that we could all be settled again, wishing simply to savor our last years of living together as a family, we are squeezed back in with my parents for yet another year, juggling the relentless demands of two jobs, two teenagers' schedules, and all the daily, high-stress details of house building.

We don't know the first thing about managing such a project. All we really have are some specific ideas about what we want and a limited amount of money, left from the sale of our old house, to spend to get it. By the time we part ways with the first architect, who, after considerable time and expense, still can't understand why we want the new house on the same site as the old, we're wondering if we really have the will or the energy to build a new house, not to mention a new life, from scratch.

As a teenager, I dated a boy whose family lived in a capped cellar hole. His parents had gotten the foundation poured for their new house, he told me, and then found themselves without the incentive or funds to continue, so they had simply finished off the basement and moved in. I spent a night or two in that underground burrow, watching TV in a windowless living room with scatter rugs layered upon a cement floor, wondering how anyone could live in a home where you had to step outside to see what kind of day it was.

Now, as my husband and I begin to draw up house plans of our own, memories of that cellar hole home haunt me. It could happen to anybody. I imagine every terrible scenario—one of us will get seriously ill and die, leaving the other with a half-done house; we'll have a terrible fight and split up, the unfinished house symbolizing our failed marriage; we'll run out of money partway through; a natural disaster will strike, and we'll find ourselves left with neither a place to live nor a savings account.

And yet, as the saying goes, the train has already left the station, and we are on it. The old house has to come down, a new one has to go up, the sooner the better. For months, we try to articulate our vision and pore over plans with architect number two, who understands intuitively that the only way to make up for the loss of one old farmhouse is to create a new and better one in its place. Having fallen in love with the hand-cut beams in the old house, we ask him to design an exposed timber frame for the new. When we say "not too big," he takes us at our word and makes the rooms smaller. When we say "informal, rustic, and full of light," he pays attention and adds more windows. We begin by re-creating our favorite part of the cottage, the screened porch, sketching out the new one, long and narrow like the old, in the very same place, just a few feet farther back from the road.

And then, week after week, in meeting after meeting, we talk and watch as the house takes shape on paper from there, simple spaces designed to bring the outdoors into every room and to nestle new forms into an old landscape without disturbing it too much.

A week before Christmas, just as we approve the final design, I lose my job. Rarely do the big, life-changing moments announce themselves; rather, the phone rings, you pick it up, thinking of something else, and suddenly the voice on the other end of the line is telling you that the world is no longer what you thought it was. I had worked for one publishing company, in various capacities, for my entire adult life, twenty-six years in all, and my career there ends, one snowy afternoon, with a phone call.

I sit at my desk in our rented office space, trying to absorb this news, too shaken even to walk down the hall to tell my husband. The timing couldn't be worse. We need my salary, are counting on every penny of it to help pay for the house we are now committed to building. And the work, the connection to books and writers and literature, has defined and shaped the person I am. I can't imagine what else I might do. For sixteen years, from the time Henry was three months old, I've read short stories and put together a book a year, ordering my days around the demands of deadlines and children, managing all of them, I thought, pretty well.

Getting fired hurts. It makes you question every positive thing you've always assumed about your professional self. It turns confidence into insecurity, makes you understand that you are both dispensable and replaceable, that the job you've been doing matters far more to you than to the company you are doing it for. I'd had one employer since I graduated from college—longer than I'd been married, longer than I'd been a mother. I'd begun work as a temp in a pre-digital age, pasting book reviews into scrapbooks, and then moved up through the ranks to proofreader, copy editor, editorial assistant, New York editor. For years before children, my colleagues had been my family; books and authors, my life. I married the sales director.

Our beloved, erudite boss made the toast at our wedding, and a few years later, when I wanted to have babies and work at home, he made me the editor of an annual volume of short stories, a job I expected to do for a few years but that soon came to feel like a calling. Now, several mergers and acquisitions later, someone slashing a budget has decided that my job can be done just as well, and for a lot less money, by a younger, in-house editor.

A day or two later, trying the words on for size, I confess to a new friend that I've lost my job and am scared to death. "That's wonderful!" she exclaims, throwing her arms around me. "Now you can finally do all the other things you're meant to do with your life!" There is a tiny part of me that wonders what those things might be. But the bigger part—the part that takes refuge in a long-held professional identity, the part that loves getting paid to do something that comes as naturally as breathing, the part that thrives on the structure imposed by deadlines and steady work with a beginning, middle, and end— that part of me feels as exposed and raw and vulnerable as a naked person who's been shoved out of a warm bed onto a cold, hard floor.

Of course, the beauty and the curse of any steady gig is that it has a way of holding you in one place, keeps you doing that one familiar thing, perhaps even for longer than you should. My career as an editor had allowed me extraordinary freedom through all the years of child raising. I didn't intend to read short stories forever, but I hadn't thought of quitting, either. It had never even occurred to me that I wouldn't have a choice.

If you share a house with teenagers, you know exactly what it's like to live under surveillance, to be monitored for the slightest inconsistency in thought, word, or deed. Observed by the merciless eye of youth, we are judged without pity and, as often as not, found wanting. Where once they gazed upon me lovingly, my adolescent sons are now more than happy to point out my every fault and shortcoming. If I somehow fail to notice the furrowed lines in my forehead, Jack makes sure to alert me to their arrival. When I sing out of tune, Henry gently points out that people can hear me. My failures—to remember to buy orange juice, to correctly identify the Tropic of Capricorn, to refrain from embarrassing my teenage son in front of a friend—are pointed out to me on a daily basis. And so, having long since toppled from my maternal pedestal, I particularly dread telling my children that I, their reasonably successful, multitasking, wage-earning mother, have been sacked. It is humiliating and hard to explain. I still don't quite get it myself.

To my surprise, their reactions are not unlike my friend's.

"Now you can write a book!" says Jack.

"You can work on the house," says his brother. "And have time to read novels."

Instead of seeing my sudden unemployment as a cause for shame, they seize right away on the idea of unexpected opportunity. Never once does it seem to occur to either of them that I have failed or even that I should take the blow too personally. Wiser than I knew, they are already envisioning new occupations for me. The idea that we will now have to budget even more carefully, adjust to having less, and make some sacrifices doesn't seem to scare them, either.

My husband studies our lengthy building control estimate, tallies up the bills, and casts an eye upon our dwindling savings account. But even he takes this latest setback in stride. "We'll figure it out," he assures me. "We'll be okay." Maybe the upheavals of the last two years have taught all four of us a few things after all.

Our family began shifting toward a new shape on the day we

left our old home without knowing where our next one would be. Any sense we might have had that we could anticipate what would happen along the way has already proved an illusion. Dependent as I was on the comfort and security of my job, and regular advances and royalty checks, what I'm getting now, instead, is just one more reminder that nothing is permanent and that loss—even the loss of a seemingly steady job and the identity that goes with it—is an unavoidable part of the much larger, natural cycle of death and rebirth within our lives.

I could choose to worry, to turn my clammy fear about "what next" into anger at being dismissed so summarily. Or I could try to follow my sons' lead and accept this unexpected ending not as a disaster, but as yet another chance to move in a new direction. And isn't this, after all, the lesson I would most want the two of them to learn? That we can't always choose what happens to us, can't always pick the hand we're dealt—but we can choose our response and decide how to play the hand we have.

My sons watch me closely this Christmas, to see if I am going to be okay but also, perhaps, to learn how, or how not, to handle grown-up hurt. Looking for some small blessing in the midst of this misfortune, I find it, of all places, in their eyes. If there is indeed a gift in losing my job, it is here, in the opportunity to help my own two children begin to understand that we give short shrift to the mysterious twists and turns of our lives if we measure them only in terms of our careers, our annual incomes, and the prestige and security conferred by those things.

Life knocks us all off course at one time or another, I tell them, and right now it's my turn. I let them see me cry a little, I accept every hug that comes my way, and then I remind myself, over and over—just as I would tell a son who got cut from the baseball team—that when a door closes, another one always opens. I am simply going to need to keep an eye out for it, so that when I see it, I'll be ready to walk through.

It takes a few months for the door to close for good on my publishing career. I still have the year's reading to complete and all the details of a final book to wrap up. Just as I had felt compelled to say good-bye to our old house by cleaning every last corner, now I want to do right by the annual volume that has borne my name for sixteen years. If I am not going to die there with my boots on, then at the very least I can step with some grace out of the editorial shoes I've worn for so long.

So each day's work offers up its own challenge—can I be grateful for what I've had and at the same moment embrace the practice of letting it go? Can I accept that with every letter, every phone call, every task, I am disconnecting the wires and severing my connections to the only profession I've ever known? At the same time, can I manage to keep a clear eye on the road beyond, the road that may lead to some new endeavor I can't even conceive of yet?

Hard as it was at the time, pulling up stakes and moving had also freed us to embrace a new place and a new life. Now, in much the same way, being stripped of my identity as an editor is releasing me into yet another new space. I haven't been without a regular job since my sophomore year of high school, and I've never been let go from one of them. All through college, I worked; afterward, I went straight into my first editorial job; and ever since then, publishing, and then publishing and children, determined the shape and rhythm of my existence. What kind of rhythm, I wonder, will I come up with on my own?

If our family needs a symbolic act to dramatize all the dismantling and undoing going on in our lives, we certainly have one in the demolition of our beloved, problematic red cottage. For months, as spring approaches, Steve and I wrestle with the question of how to claim the bits and pieces that seem to us worth saving—the venerable, rough-hewn beams, over two hundred years old, the wide, painted floorboards, sections of trim and hardware, the plain doors, so simple in design yet irreplaceable.

We meet first with a pair of restoration professionals, who arrive in a tidy white truck and cheerfully propose two days of salvage work to the tune of a hundred dollars an hour—and who offer to make rustic cupboards and tables with our reclaimed wood and then sell them back to us.

We walk our builder through the house, only to hear, not for the first time, that saving anything is more trouble than it's worth. A carpenter friend advises, Take the floorboards, leave the rest. Another says, Save the beams, if anything. The one thing everyone seems to agree on is that it will cost us more in time and money to save and reuse parts of the old house than it will to build every bit of it new. Salvaging antique house parts, we are told again and again, is an indulgence for hobbyists or for rich folk who aren't in any hurry and don't mind spending extra.

I have always imagined us as the sort of people who would rescue a house, not tear one down. I love the literature of reclamation, the stories of fearless do-it-yourselfers who, against all odds and sound advice, buy a derelict house that no one else wants and painstakingly bring it back to life, uncovering scraps of history and irreplaceable features each step of the way. For years, I've paged through home magazines, studying the alchemy by which forlorn, neglected buildings are transformed into quirky, character-laden homes that transcend time, whispering secrets from the past even as they shelter their owners in the present.

I watched with admiration as my friend Edie, a single woman eking out a living as a freelance writer, poured heart, soul, and every cent she could earn or borrow into restoring a listing old farmhouse over the course of ten long years, her patience in the end rewarded by a cozy home layered with history, character, and charm. That was the kind of story I wanted for myself, the narrative I'd foreseen when we first considered buying the red cottage. We would take the house back to its bones, then lovingly rebuild it, preserving its humble, bohemian appeal even as we lifted it gently into the twenty-first century.

I envisioned myself as a sort of house heroine, not a house wrecker. So coming to terms with the idea of knocking down the house had been hard enough. To me, it seemed almost akin to adopting a child, only to give up and send the child back—the kind of thing you would feel guilty about for the rest of your life. I'd taken some small comfort, however, in the belief that we would salvage all the good parts and figure out a way to use them in the new house that we'd build on the old footprint.

Now it seems that no one is willing or able to help us make that happen—unless we want to pay dearly for our folly. There is no way to structurally incorporate the old beams into the new timber frame, our framer assures us. Our builder has no interest in retrofitting old parts to new spaces, and we have no extra money to pay him to do it. And we are running out of time. A wrecker is scheduled for six a.m. on a Tuesday in early June. We have a week to get the house emptied and ready. I feel as if, once again, I am letting the house, and myself, down, failing even to come up with a reasonable way to save the best parts, let alone the whole thing.

One of the first people I met in New Hampshire was a transplanted former dancer from New York City with the unforgettable, entirely appropriate—and appropriated—name eQuanimiti Joy. eQuanimiti had lived here for some time, in various incarnations. Some people remember knowing her by another, more pedestrian name, back when she worked as a cashier at the health food store, acted in local theater productions, and shaved her head. By the time we arrived, however, she had fully blossomed, a rare, exotic orchid in a small-town garden full of familiar native plants.

Tall and slender, with spiky hennaed hair, unerring good taste, and a contagious, ever ready laugh, eQuanimiti stood out, the only person in town who could regularly be found dashing into the post office in a lime green miniskirt, high heels, a cropped, bright orange jeweled sweater, and a rakish 1960s hat to set it all off.

To exchange a greeting with eQua at the PO was to brighten your morning. But to set foot inside her domain—an eccentric shop in a converted mill building at river's edge, down behind Main Street—was to brighten your whole outlook on life. eQuanimiti could as easily have chosen to call herself Creativity Joy, so effortlessly did she turn ugliness into beauty, trash into art, cast-off clothes into high fashion, junk into treasure, bad days into good ones.

In her Unique Boutique, eQua sold her paintings, vintage clothing, appealing odds and ends, and various age-defying lotions and potions. But what she really trafficked in was laughter and soul wisdom, by both happenstance and appointment.

You could pay eQuanimiti to sit with you in her private back room, tucked in at her grandmother's old kitchen table, where she would listen to your woes and give you such provocative homework assignments that by the time you walked back out into the world, you were already seeing it with new eyes. Or you could wander in, fondle a Buddha's smooth belly, try on a hand-painted scarf for size, purchase a two-dollar box of Indian incense, and strike up a conversation. Either way, you'd come away with more than your money's worth. For what eQuanimiti offered all who passed through her decorated doorway was not just advice or adornment, but a whole package, a way of seeing the world that invited you to put your trust in it, to have faith that the powers that be would come through for you no matter what.

"You're responsible for the wanting and the clarity," she said to me once, her eyes sparkling behind her bright blue glasses. "And guess what? The universe is responsible for the rest!"

It was eQuanimiti who first led me to the empty building across the parking lot from her shop that would become both the storage space for all our possessions and our rented office space. eQuanimiti who decided, within about thirty seconds of laying eyes on me, that she would be my friend, cheerleader, and spiritual adviser. eQuanimiti who, just when I need them most, says a few words that seem to change my life, or at least the way I look at my life.

I am lingering in her shop one afternoon, a little lonely and overwhelmed, yearning for what I see in retrospect as the respectable straightforwardness of my former life, a life that included a regular paycheck, a nice, solid house, a nine a.m. yoga class, and an afternoon car pool. I confess that I can't imagine how we will ever manage to tear down a house, build a house, move in, pay our bills, and actually get ourselves pulled together again.

"You know," she says, uncommonly serious for a moment, her short coppery hair sprouting like a bright halo around her face, "you are not alone in this. There are partners everywhere, partners who are waiting and willing to help you, if you would only let them. They are right in front of you, you just haven't noticed them yet." I'm not sure she's right, but I certainly like the idea of getting some help. At the very least, I decide to start looking.

And so, when I spot a cupboard made of about six different kinds and colors of old wood for sale downtown at the Sunday morning flea market, two days before demolition, I stop.

"Do you like working with old wood?" I inquire of the stocky, liberally tattooed, and prematurely gray-haired man in a black Ramones T-shirt sitting nearby. "Because if you do, I have a whole houseful that could be yours for the taking." The man tosses his cigarette to the ground and rubs it out carefully. I can tell by the smile that spreads now across his round, boyish face that here, sitting on a stool in a parking lot as if he's just been waiting for me to pass by, is the partner I've needed all along.

Later that afternoon, my demolition angel shows up with his teenage son in tow, a pile of ropes and bungee cords, and a trunk full of saws, hammers, and crowbars. Steve Graves, I suspect, has never met a piece of scrap lumber he didn't love. Where others have seen old junk, extra work, and no payoff, Steve sees treasure.

We have found each other in the nick of time. There is nothing in the old house that seems useless to him. Even the square, hand-forged iron nails are well worth the effort required to pull them, one by one. Cupboard doors will surely find new life elsewhere, and who knows what might be done with the two-hole seat from the outhouse? Certainly it is worth saving it to find out.

As far as I'm concerned, the less of the house that ends up in the dump, the better, and given that, it is easy to come up with a deal that feels like a win for both of us. Steve can take anything he wants here, and in return, he'll build us a table someday and perhaps figure out a way to bring some of this old wood back into the new house. The doors he promises to set aside for me, in the hope that when the time comes, I'll have figured out a way to use them.

Still, even our carefully orchestrated salvage operation doesn't fully prepare me for the experience of watching a house die. As the hours pass the next day, to the sounds of hammers dislodging floors and crowbars prying shelves from the walls, all I can think is, Here we go again, erasing and destroying, rubbing out a past that we could never fully appreciate, heading toward an unknown future, and being called upon, once more, to let go, to accept that nothing lasts forever—not childhoods, or careers, or idyllic summers, or even two-hundred-year-old houses.

As the remains of stairs and mantels and cupboards are carried out and piled on the lawn or loaded into the back of Steve's borrowed truck, it seems as if life itself drains from the house. All afternoon I keep vigil in the yard, unwilling to leave yet not quite able to set foot inside and watch.

Finally, the poor red cottage seems to release a last exhausted breath, an old, cold, earthen smell, like an exhalation of trapped air from another century. Like a piece of rotting fruit, then, the house slumps into itself, the dark, empty windows staring sadly out across the field. Or so it seems to me, as I mourn the passing of a home that had been ours only briefly but that had so readily offered up its secrets—live simply, be in the moment, build memories, stay close.

"I won't forget," I whisper to the empty shell, to myself, and to the quiet land, land that always has and always will bear the weight of us all, past, present, and future inhabitants of this place, each of us striving in our time to hallow the earth here, to invest in it, to mark it and claim it for a while as our own.

By dawn the next morning, we are ready. No one is going

to work or school today. Instead, we buy a few dozen dough-nuts and boxes of coffee and prepare to bear witness to the house's dramatic final moments. As the sun rises over the mountain, a small self-selected audience arrives, quiet, reverent at first in the early light—my mom, the architect, our builder, a quiet girl from Henry's class with a camera around her neck, Steve Graves, freshly showered after his all-nighter with the crowbar.

We have said our good-byes to the house and made our peace with this day's work. Now, on this magnificent summer morning, the mood is almost festive. At long last, we say to one another, we are on our way. The backhoe guy is a little late, though, so the boys get a head start on the job, tossing a few rocks at the kitchen window, thrilled by the sound of glass breaking without blame or consequence. What is left now is just an empty, lifeless husk, not a home at all, so we let the teen-agers go at it, testing their arms and their aim as they methodi-cally, joyfully smash every remaining window, whooping with laughter as each pane shatters and falls.

In the midst of moving from one Manhattan apartment to another, E. B. White once wrote that being between addresses is akin to being a lobster without a shell, so tender and na-kedly vulnerable are we when home is neither here nor there and the comforts of roof and wall and best-loved chair are temporarily nonexistent. We, of course, have a roof over our heads at my parents' house, the security of food and shelter. And yet, as the humble little house we bought with high hopes such a short time ago vanishes now from the face of the earth, it feels as if a part of me, some solid, protective cov-ering, is disappearing, too.

It is warm in the sun, but I am shivering anyway, shaken by the inescapable violence of house razing, the finality of it all.

Once again, we find ourselves on a threshold, and there is no turning back. Our two sons, thoroughly in the moment, revel in the spectacle of destruction. As the great claw finally swings through the garage roof, bats shoot up through the gaping hole and spin away into the morning sunshine, disappearing into nearby trees.

So fragile, this house that has managed to withstand the elements for two centuries. It crumples now without protest, as easily as a dollhouse made of balsa wood. Another swing of the claw, and there, revealed for all to see, is half of the upstairs bathroom, sliced in two and suspended in space—the porcelain sink where we brushed our teeth two times a day, still clinging to the wall; the mirror, remarkably intact; the bright pink bath towel I left behind last summer, still hanging, folded neatly in thirds on the towel bar, the red-and-green wallpaper with its scenes of tiny black villagers riding to market in horse-drawn carts. One last glimpse of all of this, and then with a crash and a great cloud of dust, it, too, is gone.

Soon there is nothing here at all but a pile of rubble and a startling, wide-open space where just moments ago a house still stood. It happened so fast that we are all momentarily stunned into silence. I try to picture what might come next, but instead what I see is the stark, inevitable truth of time; what I hear is the silence of all the moments that have ended. I can hardly bear the weight and texture of this moment as it, too, slides with all the others into memory.

I don't wish for the red house back, not really, yet in a way, I wish for everything back that ever was, everything that once seemed like forever and yet has vanished. I wish for my own girlhood bedroom with its dark brown desk, the monkey with real fur from the 1964 World's Fair, the pile of coloring books under my bed. I wish for my grandparents, both long gone, and Saturday night suppers at their kitchen table, in a house whose smell of bath powder and pipe smoke I will remember always. I wish for a chance to relive an afternoon with my brother, when I was mean and made him cry by grinding a cookie into the dirt beneath the swing set at our very first house. I wish for my horse, sold thirty-odd years ago, and the dim corner of her stall in a barn long since demolished, her sweet breath on my neck as I brushed her flanks and day-dreamed about a boy named Joel who might want to kiss me. I wish for my college apartment, the hot plate and electric skillet that made up my first kitchen, the fall morning I lay in bed there reading *To the Lighthouse*, shaping the words in my mouth, reluctant to let them go. I wish for my husband as he was twenty-five years ago, the first time he ran his fingers through my hair and asked if I would see him again; and for my own younger self, in love with the idea of marriage and so certain of our togetherness. I wish for the first bedroom we ever shared, in the back corner of his Cambridge apartment, wind whistling through the old window sashes as we pressed close, sleeping naked together no matter how cold it was. I wish for my two sons at every age they've ever been, for each of them as newborns at my breast in warm, darkened bed-rooms; as stout toddlers, shy kindergartners, exuberant little boys filling every space, every moment of my existence with their own. I wish for Easter mornings and Christmas morn-ings and birthday mornings and all the hundreds of ordinary weekday mornings—cereal poured into bowls, fingernails clipped, quick kisses, and good-byes for now.

Standing here on an empty hilltop in New Hampshire, as a bulldozer slowly pushes the debris of a small red house into a neat pile, I allow, just for a moment, the past to push hard against the walls of my heart. Being alive, it seems, means learning to bear the weight of the passing of all things. It means finding a way to lightly hold all the places we've loved and left anyway, all the moments and days and years that have already been lived and lost to memory, even as we live on in the here and now, knowing full well that this moment, too, is already gone. It means, always, allowing for the hard truth of endings. It means, too, keeping faith in beginnings.

Fall. There is a rush on, a sense of urgency at last, to secure a roof before snow flies, to get the new house closed in and tight to the weather. All summer, we've absorbed the hard lessons of building and waiting, learning patience. Once the old house was gone, it took us a week to determine the precise locations of the four corners of the new one, to get the angle toward the mountains exactly right. And then the excavators were late. It rained, and concrete had to be postponed. The framers, scheduled for the end of June, had to be moved to the first of August; meanwhile, the cost of lumber, tile, paint—and everything else—goes up.

Our simple design harbors hidden complexities. Schedules and budgets, we begin to see, are imaginary constructs, best-case scenarios as flimsy as the paper we print them out on. The house will cost what it will cost and be ready when it's ready, a thousand details, hundreds of small crises, and countless mistakes and decisions from now.

We choose windows, shingles, and clapboards and watch the trucks arrive, delivering the raw materials of house building. I stare at the plans for hours, marking electrical outlets, trying to imagine where we will plug in the vacuum cleaner, the toaster; anticipating bookcases, traffic flow, and morning light; conjuring the spot where, after dinner, we will want to sit with the newspaper, sip mugs of tea, and read; figuring out where the frying pans and cookie sheets will go, how wide the kitchen sink should be.

All day, the job site is a cacophony of music, whining saws, electric drills and hammers, shouted instructions, jokes, and laughter. The carpenters' dogs rove through the fields and rush my car, jumping and barking furiously, when I pull into the drive. The men shoot bows and arrows down the hillside after lunch, nap in the sun, hover around a fire in a metal ash can on cool days. They are unfailingly polite to me, yet I know they'd rather I not hang around here. It's not my house yet, it's their workplace, and I am an intruder on the day's business.

Evenings, in gathering darkness, Steve and I walk through the silent, newly framed spaces, by turns eager and anxious, trying to envision beyond the mess of sawdust, tools, discarded coffee cups, and the sharp, piney smell of raw wood to real life as it might one day unfold here, banana muffins baking in the oven and baseball games on TV and piles of socks being sorted into dresser drawers. Progress is slow. It will be a while.

There are eleven doors from the red cottage, wrapped up in a tarp at the edge of the yard. We are looking for economies, ways to save our money, and for the first time in sixteen years, I am not spending the month of September trying to catch up on a summer's backlog of short stories. I figure it will take me a week or two to strip the paint off the doors; then, when the time comes to frame doorways, they'll be ready. Our painter offers to deliver the doors to an empty barn he uses for indoor projects, eight miles up the road in the next town over. I can work there, he says, even on rainy days, and no one will disturb me.

After the stresses of being out of a job, mediating through months of personality conflicts between our builder and the architect, worrying about rising costs and innumerable delays, and trying to maintain peace among the three generations spending a long hot summer at my parents' house, it is a relief to be alone, to pick up a paint scraper and tackle a mindless, physical job. School has returned my sons to routine and me to freedom, and I am grateful for the wide-open stretches of solitude.

Day after day, I put on paint clothes, pack a few things into the car—rubber gloves, lunch, water, a snack for Gracie—and drive to the barn, tucked away on a quiet country road across from a broad hayfield. I carry four sawhorses outside and lay out two doors at a time. It is messy manual labor, slathering on the remover, waiting for the skin of paint to blister and bubble, then slowly, methodically scraping, layer after layer, beginning with our own cottage white on down through farm greens, timeworn yellows, and stubborn brown varnishes, until at last the original milk paint is revealed, two hundred years old, translucent and tough as glue.

Working outside in this secluded spot, I fall into a rhythm, a kind of industrious contentment. Time slows, for there is just this one thing to do—scrape and sand. My thoughts fly freely at first, but always, after a while, something happens. My mind quiets, and I feel the day open to me, or perhaps it is my own heart that opens, in gratitude for these long, peaceful hours. Alone and in silence, I rejoice in the world's splendor.

Crows wheel through the field across the road, their indignant cries shredding the stillness. A blue jay settles onto a branch above my head and adds his raspy voice to the morning. Gracie dozes in the grass, chin between her front paws, content to be close. The maple leaves, just touched with color when I first arrive in September, turn as the weeks go by to vivid oranges, yellows, and reds, their brilliant fire only intensifying the blue vacancy of sky. The chirr of crickets and field insects starts slowly in the morning, building with the heat of the day, and I listen, seeking to learn the rhythms of this place, and to make the most of these days, by noticing everything.

I have not found myself with this kind of open-ended solitary time since childhood, when I used to disappear for hours into the woods behind our house, drifting aimlessly along the trails, just to see what I could see, just to find what I could find. Now, it is as if I need to reawaken perception, learn all over again how to quiet the clamor of voices in my own head in order to tune in to nature's subtle music, to fully inhabit these hours by paying attention to everything going on around me. And so, working away with my tools, brushing, scraping, sanding, I allow myself to imagine that I'm also taking part in a kind of private communion here, receiving with reverence the sights and sounds and smells of the day.

As the sun climbs its way up through trees and turns my patch of shade to light, the air warms. By twelve, I'm stripped down to my T-shirt, pant legs rolled, sweating in the thin, dry heat of an autumn afternoon. Each side of a door takes more than a day to finish. This is slow work, after all, stripping one layer after another, more paint and history than I ever could have imagined.

Yet the doors themselves reward my efforts, each one slightly different in detail, utterly simple in design. Hand-planed, solid, not perfect, yet perfect in their homely imperfections, they have opened and closed upon two centuries' worth of stories and secrets. I've opened and closed each one of them countless times myself, never once noticing whether the panels were raised or flat, whether the tops and bottoms were square, how the pieces dovetail so neatly together at the corners. Now I study them. And, as with everything else these days, the longer I look, the more I see. Perhaps the wood they are made of came from towering pines that once stood on our land, trees that were felled by the callused hands of a long-ago farmer to clear a space for his house to go and then were used in the building of that house, hard by the dirt road between one seventeenth-century New England village and the next. To reclaim them, to bring them back to the place where they belong, feels right, as if in some small way I am finally honoring not only the carpenter who crafted them, but the red cottage itself, simply by offering up the gift of my time, by caring enough about the past to ensure these old doors a place in our future.

One day, I walk with Gracie up the hill to an orchard, one of the few remaining here in a region that was once widely known for apples, and chat with the old man in the roadside stand, presiding over his heaping bushel baskets of gold-flecked Macouns and sweet McIntoshes. As far as the eye can see, the trees sprawl, heavy with fruit; the grassy paths beckon, and I promise to return later, to sample each variety and fill one of his paper sacks. He refuses my money, insists instead on giving me apples. "Pick yourself one for now," he says, "and take another two for later," and then he thanks me for visiting.

Another day, famished, I hike the mile into the village and treat myself to lunch on the shady porch of the little café there, the only customer on this weekday noon. Across the road is the pond we biked to with our boys two summers ago, deserted on this fall day, the diving dock pulled up on shore for winter. I wander over, down the wooded path to the water's edge, where I throw sticks for Gracie to swim after, trail my fingers through the dark, cool water, and then sit for a while, alone on the empty beach.

Sunlight shafts through the trees and bounces off the water, still as a reflecting pool. In the silence, in this wide emptiness of clear sky and shimmering lake, it occurs to me that something in my life has shifted, almost without my realizing it. There is no one, anywhere, at this moment wondering where I am or what I'm up to. There are no manuscripts awaiting my attention, no deadlines to meet, no phone calls to make or letters to write. There is no paycheck coming my way. No one is asking for my opinion. No child is waiting for a ride somewhere or missing me.

After years of finding a sense of purpose and fulfillment in my role as an always productive, always available mother, editor, school volunteer, neighbor, and friend, I sense life calling me now to a new place, a way of being in which I can no longer define myself by what I do, who needs me, or how much I accomplish in the course of a day.

Certainly no one needs these old doors; no one else even cares about them. Yet the satisfaction I feel, scraping and sanding for hours until my hands are sore, is profound. It is work that I'm doing just for me, in homage to a past I only briefly brushed against and in respect for a future that we'll inhabit for just a while. But right now, for one golden stretch of autumn, I feel blessed to have this time. Time bent toward no ambition beyond revealing the hidden beauty in a few old doors that will outlast us all.

It occurs to me that perhaps I don't have to push at life quite so hard after all, that sometimes the best thing we can do is allow our lives simply to take us where we need to go. The truth is, I don't have any idea what goals I should be focusing on or how I ought to compose my life at this juncture—life in a new house, without regular work, without two children at home, without my old, tightly knit web of neighbors and friends.

But as all the identities I worked so hard to construct over the years begin to slough away, I feel myself reconnecting with my own quiet center. It is as if I am, at last, catching a glimpse of myself not as I might wish to be, but as I am. I see a woman who is less ambitious than she once was. Someone less self-conscious, less invested in appearances, but also less "special" than the person I always thought I was meant to be. I see my own ordinariness. And I see that to be ordinary is okay after all.

Inside, the child I used to be is still alive, as ardent and eager as ever. The little girl who loved swimming in lakes, eating three kinds of ice cream at once, and buying new shoes is still, amazingly, me. Yet the lines in my face, my softening belly, the new, spidery red veins in my legs, give no hint of her existence. What is visible instead, I suppose, is the humility bestowed by marriage, pregnancies and parenthood, time and experience, sadness and joy, unrealized dreams and hard-won understanding. I'm still shocked, sometimes, when I catch sight of this person, this new-old me, in a mirror. Looking at recent photographs, I have wondered lately, Where did I go? Yet just beneath the surface of the middle-aged woman, rarely glimpsed now, the girl within still dances, an inner, secret self whose existence sometimes surprises me. She is as real as the outer me, still patiently awaiting my acceptance and recognition.

Here, alone with a stack of old doors and a bucket of Ready-Strip, it seems that I am peeling away not only paint, but the layers of my own carefully constructed persona. Until at last I myself am stripped, taken all the way back to a being I barely remember, a person who seems surprisingly young and hopeful and tender. I make room for her. And then, without judgment for a change, I take a long frank look at a person I haven't seen in a while. Me.

There are many things I dreamed of once that I know now

I'll never do. So many opportunities I missed, situations I failed to grasp, mistakes I made that will never really be righted. I carry some baggage, old ratty parcels packed with disappointment and regret. I've wasted too much time worrying, backsliding into fear, when I could have loved and lived more boldly. I've skimmed the surface of life when I could have been diving deep.

Yet there are also qualities of mind and heart in me that I am grateful for. I recognize, emerging slowly from beneath the layers, the optimism that has always made me me. My faith in other people, my eagerness to trust their motives and extend the benefit of the doubt. The sense of wonder that dawns as fresh in me each day as morning. The idealism that is both my nature and my gift. The creation of a self, it seems, even at this late stage of the game, is more a process than a project, more about opening and allowing than forcing and doing. Perhaps it does not have to be such hard work after all.

What these days at the barn afford me is time—time for this gradual business of settling, clarifying, and paring away, time for steady seeing and quiet accepting. Until slowly, finally, someone I knew once before, long ago, appears. I move into this truth as if it were an old, familiar house, and I walk slowly, quietly, through each and every room, listening, looking, feeling, as if for the first time, what it is to live here, in the body and the spirit of who I am. What a surprise, that in discovering "me" all over again, the plain, unadorned essence of who I am, I suddenly feel, as well, a new, more openhearted friendliness toward the world.

Heading back over the mountain in the late afternoons, on my way to pick up Jack from school, I am always content, fulfilled by the day. And what I begin to think about is something that I've surely known all along but that somehow, in the midst of our small day-to-day crises and preoccupations of the last few years, has been all too easy to forget. Real life isn't out there in the future somewhere. Real life is not going to begin when we move into our own house at long last, or when I figure out what to do with myself, or when we're out of debt, or when our possessions finally come out of storage and we can sit down around our old kitchen table again. Real life is now.

It is the thirteen-year-old son who's at odds with his best friend and takes his frustration out on me. It is the husband bent over the newspaper, glasses sliding down his nose, the dog with a tick in her ear, the carpenter calling to say the bathtub doesn't fit. It is the apple picked from the tree and eaten by the side of the road, the quiet pond, my own stiff shoulders and aching feet. It is my mother and me, side by side chopping vegetables for chicken potpie, our hips bumping in her narrow kitchen. My dad chinking ice into his glass and pouring a drink. The breeze through the screened door, the early darkness.

Real life is all six of us, grandparents, parents, teenage sons, coming together for dinner, passing the salad and sharing news of the day, as we have now for nearly three years. It is the sixteen-year-old asking for the car keys, and it is my sleeplessness until his footsteps finally fall upon the stair. Real life is the midnight call of the whip-poor-will in the lilac bush, remembered from my childhood, repeated now, the same plaintive cry echoing across decades, reminding me of all the years I've laid my head to rest in this house, and of the fact that soon enough it, too, will become a place that we have lived in, loved, and left.

None of this was ever part of the plan, but life so rarely unfolds according to plan. Real life is just where we are, in this moment, and the only mistake we've made so far has been not to pause long enough or often enough to realize that even this odd in-between time is precious, fleeting, and worthy of our attention.

There is nothing special going on here, just the daily comings and goings of one extended family sharing a house and doing our best to get along. But now I begin to view our time together differently, begin to see that stepping up to one's life adventure doesn't necessarily mean doing extraordinary things. It also means coming to understand that viewed in the right light, through the right eyes, everything is extraordinary.

~6~

partners

Perhaps this is the best we can do: to help when we can;
to witness each other with kindness; to offer our presence;
to show the trust we have in life.

—JACK KORNFIELD

$\mathcal{T}$he low point comes in March. We have just returned from a school vacation week in Florida. After a week of balmy days and birdsong, shorts and flip-flops, it is almost painful to return to New Hampshire, to wake once again in frozen darkness, to face the sharp, predatory cold of a record-setting winter. Snow deepened in our absence, and more is on the way. My parents have wisely headed south themselves, and we are alone in their house for a week.

There is no hope of warmth in this drafty antique kitchen, where a long-ago do-it-yourselfer installed the cabinets right over the baseboard heaters, reducing their efficiency by half. Grimly, the four of us jostle for position around the sink and dishwasher, tempers short, our shoulders tensed with cold. We've got all the cupboard doors open in a futile attempt to bring a bit more warmth into the room. The boys shake cereal into bowls and sit down in silence to eat, already running late for school. It is hard to believe that twenty-four hours ago, we were lounging poolside in bathing suits, sipping fresh orange juice and paging through the *New York Times*.

Coming back to reality is a slap, and I'm cranky and peevish, unable to summon any enthusiasm for our return to my parents' creaky old house, long underwear, icy roads, wind-chill factors, and house-building dramas. I'm sick of all of it.

When the first mouse scurries across the floor and into the open pot cupboard, I'm so startled that I scream out loud.

"It's a *mouse*, Mom," Jack points out disdainfully, annoyed by my overreaction. A moment later, a second one pauses mid-scamper and regards us boldly, surprised perhaps to see that the humans have returned. A look into the pantry confirms a full-scale occupation. There are droppings everywhere, cracker boxes chewed through at the corners, bags of pasta opened, trails of crumbs meandering through the dry goods.

It is six below zero, it is March, and we have mice. My to-do list for the day takes shape rapidly—unpack, pick up the dog from the kennel, buy mousetraps, throw away food, clean the kitchen, check in with the builder . . .

All winter, we have harbored the fantasy that our own house will somehow, magically, be finished on time, that school will let out and we'll move in and have a summer like the idyllic one we enjoyed two years ago. But on this bright, frigid day, we must also face the hard truth of the schedule. The house is far from done. There is, our builder finally admits when I get him on the phone, no way that we will be moving in there this summer. If we're lucky, he ventures, the house will be habitable by fall.

The news is as crushing as the cold, almost more than I can bear. Back in our old life, March marked the onset of spring. I used to cut branches from our forsythia bushes and bring them inside for forcing, knowing that by the time they finally bloomed into sunny sprays on the kitchen counter, there would be new life outside as well, the first clenched buds appearing on the maple trees, purple crocuses pushing forth in the garden.

Here, March is nothing but another harsh month of winter. The slog that has become our life seems endless to me, and thankless, the road nothing but rubble, uphill all the way. The sun is an affront in the cloudless sky, offering not the slightest bit of warmth. Everything sparkles, hard-edged, in a frozen, treacherous world. Huge snowstorms this month have been followed by rain, followed by freezing temperatures. Ice rules. Slipping and sliding, chilled to the bone, grumbling under my breath, I run around doing my errands until I can delay no longer. The mice await. In the afternoon, I set out three kinds of mousetraps in the kitchen, begin filling a Hefty bag with boxes that have been nibbled at, take all the food and dishes out of the cupboards. And then I sit down in the middle of the mess and begin to cry.

There must be some lucky, well-adjusted women who cruise right through middle age without ever stopping to ask in dismay and disbelief, How did I end up here? I give myself a savage little kick for not being one of them. Try as I might to discern the blessings hiding right under my nose, I can find no bright spot in this bitter, glittering day. So I look back, in-dulging myself with regret for every decision that led me to this moment, unemployed, far from all my friends, in a house I couldn't wait to leave at eighteen and never expected to return to, and at odds with a husband who, I'm sure, still privately blames me for leading us down this ill-considered path in the first place. It is hard to believe that our bills will ever be paid, that our house will ever be finished, that I will ever feel con-nected to a community again, that life will ever feel normal, that summer will ever return.

The ringing phone interrupts my meltdown. Steve, sounding a little shaky himself, is calling with some news. For weeks before we left on vacation, eQuanimiti's shop across the parking lot from our office had been closed, a cryptic sign on the door explaining, "Off on an art adventure." That note had been followed by one that read, "Taking time to recharge. See you soon!"

We were busy and didn't think to question. Someone in the building had said that she was sick, but no one knew the details.

For as long as we've been renting our own space, eQuanimiti's door has been open from eleven till six, Tuesday through Sunday, without fail, her colorful presence the linchpin of this ragtag coalition of artists and small-time entrepreneurs scattered throughout three old mill buildings at the edge of the river. A shopper or a friend might stop by in search of an offbeat birthday gift or a vintage jacket, but everyone who works at the mill depends on eQuanimiti for something more important, if less tangible, than her merchandise.

Somehow, her colorful, unfailingly enthusiastic presence among us validates all of our enterprises, from the solitary painter who rents a tiny box of a studio on an upper floor to the swimsuit-manufacturing company turning out hand-sewn bathing suits in the building next door.

eQuanimiti is the magnet. Her effusive energy enlivens the whole place, carrying all along these idealistic shoestring ventures on a current of goodwill and unflagging optimism. Without her, the shops and offices feel lifeless. And now three weeks of "recharging" have turned into four.

No one knows much about eQuanimiti's very private personal life, nor have I ever been invited in for a closer look. Her friendships seem to exist in the context of the store where she spends her days, not outside it, in the rented rooms she shares with a tall, thin, distant Vietnam combat veteran named Daniel Two Eagles, a Native American whose taciturn reserve is the antithesis of eQuanimiti's bubbly warmth. As a couple, they are an enigma. Whether they share a home as lovers, friends, or roommates, we have no idea. But eQuanimiti has told us this much: The war is still with Daniel, isolating him from those who can't imagine the atrocities he witnessed and endured. A few years ago, a near fatal heart attack forced him to give up a high-stress job. He has been in a kind of self-imposed exile ever since. Much as we miss eQuanimiti, no one feels comfortable intruding or perhaps offending Daniel by trying to seek out information.

But now, Steve says that he's just run into Daniel at the post office, that they've talked, and the word is not good. eQuanimiti has a horrific case of shingles that started on her face and has since moved into her eyes. She is in agony. Her face is swollen, covered with deep, painful, open sores. She can't keep food down. A doctor has warned that she may lose her sight for good. There is danger that the virus could spread to the brain. There is no health insurance. My husband tells me that he offered help, food, money, whatever they might need.

"Daniel kept insisting that they could manage," he says, "and I didn't know what else to do. But he seemed so alone, and so scared. And the thing is, he had tears in his eyes."

How insignificant a few mice seem in the face of this. Ashamed, jolted out of self-pity, I go into gear, scrubbing pantry shelves and rearranging bottles and cans. And all the time I am thinking about eQuanimiti, her beautiful face ravaged by sores, her wise, dancing eyes swollen shut. Her isolation.

In the prosperous world we left behind, everyone we knew had health care. Serious illness meant good doctors and co-pays, tests and treatment plans, friends arriving at the door to ferry children, deliver meals, take up the slack. Bad things happened; they always do. But money, security, and connections can go a long way toward cushioning the blows. Here, the safety net is not always so well woven, the social contract more ambiguous. We are newcomers, hesitant to overstep in a situation we most certainly do not fully understand. And Daniel, deeply private, quiet, and proud, has already refused our help. But Steve and I have the same instinct. "No, thank you" doesn't always mean "Absolutely not."

The next day, I gather my courage, call Daniel's number, and leave a message, offering food. "eQuanimiti does not care much about eating," he says rather formally when he phones me back. "But thank you for thinking of her." I mail a card, and then another, but there is no word from eQuanimiti. Friends stop by the shop and leave notes for her outside the door; every few days they disappear, but no one gets a response.

Finally, one day, I taste spring in the air, feel the mildest of breezes, gentle as a caress, across my cheek. I crave strawberries, fresh fruits, harbingers of summer. Surely even someone who doesn't care about food could not resist a bowl of watermelon and berries tossed with chopped mint at the end of a long, cold winter. No one has seen or talked with eQuanimiti for weeks, and she is not returning calls. Daniel keeps her well guarded, offering cursory updates when Steve sees him in town. She is no better. She has lost weight. The pain is often unbearable. Medication hasn't worked. But the castle walls, it seems, are impenetrable. They do not ask for help.

I call and leave a message first, then fill a bowl with sliced fruit, write a note, and drive up the long, steep dirt road to their secluded home. Although the day is balmy, all the windows are covered with thick blankets. Daniel meets me at the door, as gaunt and sad a man as I have ever seen. Is he also malnourished? Ill himself? Depressed? I'm not sure, but the darkness here is frightening, palpable.

Daniel explains that even the smallest bit of sunlight is excruciating to eQuanimiti's eyes, and the slightest movement of air across her skin is unbearable on her open lesions. She is too weak to walk, in too much pain to be carried outside. His hand shakes a little as he reaches for my pottery bowl, unaccustomed, surely, to receiving gifts. I do not know this man well, but the depth of his distress stuns me. Suddenly I realize, in a way I hadn't before, that there are two suffering souls within this house and that both of them are sorely in need of love and friendship.

A couple of days later, my cell phone rings. To my surprise, it's Daniel. "eQuanimiti loved the watermelon," he says in a low, hesitant voice. "And anything else you can think of, that might help her, well, we would be grateful."

This is the beginning, a door that's been closed for a long time finally opening, just a crack. I push on through. "Can I talk to her?" I ask.

The voice on the phone is weak, tentative, lacking the effervescence that is eQuanimiti's trademark. It is the voice of solitary confinement and shattering pain, the voice of someone who's afraid she's run out of options, the voice of someone who goes to sleep at night knowing that death is in the bedroom.

"You know," I blurt out impulsively, "you are going to get well. You have to, because I am counting on us being crones together. We are going to have a lot of fun as old ladies, and we're going to start a group, for passionate, strong women of a certain age. But I can't do it without you." There is a tiny, distant chuckle, the slightest acquiescence to hope.

"Look, I'm going to feed you," I tell her then. "And there are a whole bunch of people downtown who are missing you like crazy, and who are just waiting to pitch in."

I can feel her hesitation. In her own way, eQuanimiti is as proud and independent as Daniel, used to being the giver, uncomfortable on the receiving end.

"Remember," I tell her then, returning her own wisdom back to her, "you are not alone in this. There are partners all around, waiting to help you. You just haven't seen them yet."

Within days, eQuanimiti's friends at the mill have rallied to the cause, glad to have the opportunity at last to lend a hand. Steve dives in like a man on a mission. The e-mails fly, and impromptu meetings are held in the parking lot. And then the miracles begin. Money, rides, and remedies appear as if by magic and are accepted with grace. Gifts of books, jewelry, music, and inspiration are bestowed. Steve coordinates with Daniel on the medical front, and I make out meal schedules, shop for groceries, cook and deliver food. An artist friend organizes coverage for eQuanimiti's store and manages, with her blessing, to get the doors open for a few days a week. An old friend of Daniel's finds some unexpected cash in a forgotten fund and feels certain that it is meant to go toward medical bills. Around the hole that is eQuanimiti's absence, a sudden community forms and flourishes. Months of pent-up worry and goodwill translate now to action, to the relief of us all.

A session with an Ayurvedic healer yields suggestions for a warming diet, and the next thing I know, I am in a coffee shop, meeting an Indian woman in a sari, who presses a bag of expensive medicinal herbs into my hands, refusing payment. "Take this instead," she says, and hands me an Ayurvedic cookbook, "and keep cooking for her. That will be payment enough. And remember, use plenty of turmeric."

I call a friend who is a therapist, tell her eQuanimiti's story, and a week later Nancy is there at her side, the first person to be allowed through that well-defended door. Their work together begins at once, that very day, a passionate, no-holds-barred struggle to recommit to life and health. And slowly, slowly, eQuanimiti begins to heal. At the same time, Daniel begins both to soften and to strengthen, as Nancy insists that he has his own work to do, that he must mend his own battered spirit and grow as well. If they are to stay together, survive together, then this journey back into the light is one they must undertake together.

At first, Daniel refuses to eat the food I prepare, convinced that it must all go to eQuanimiti. Finally, I too get tough. "I have some delicious Indian food ready," I tell him over the phone, "but I'm only going to bring it if you promise to eat your share. She needs your company."

For a long time, my world has been contracting, shrinking, to the point that most of my waking moments are consumed by house details. Which kitchen faucet to buy, what width floorboard to choose, what colors to paint walls and trim, what height the toilets should be, and what refrigerator and stove to order. I spend hours considering switch plates and window hardware, drawer pulls and cabinet styles, and before we're done, I change the color of the kitchen walls three times.

Having taken on the day-to-day oversight of every aspect of house progress, I am determined to make good decisions and stick to our budget, but I am equally bent on perfection. It feels as if every finish and appliance is somehow also a reflection of me, a testament to my taste and sensibility and savvy—or lack of it—and the closer we get to completion, the more obsessed I become about the particulars.

But it is taking forever, and it is all about *stuff*. Intent as I am on doing everything right, the pressure makes me tense. I skip meals, lose sleep, and fret about every detail. And the more I seek perfection, the more elusive it becomes. What a long way we've strayed, from our simple, make-do summer in the old cottage to my new habit of paging through glossy home decorating magazines each night in search of the perfect microwave oven, the perfect bathroom sink or showerhead or light fixture.

My task, these days, is shopping. And it isn't lost on me that now that I no longer have any income, I'm the one spending all the money. The choices have to be made, the purchasing done, but I am practically ill from overconsumption and self-absorption. The house is like an insatiable beast, all-consuming, taking up my time, my attention, and my energy, not to mention all the money we've worked hard to save and money we have yet to earn. As the checks flow, my own materialism feels like a trap I can't seem to fight my way out of. "Choose wall sconces," my to-do list reads, and I am off once more to the lighting store, land of a thousand choices.

There is nothing like building a house on one salary that was originally conceived of on two to stoke anxiety and fuel the fear of not having enough. Evenings, Steve and I sit side by side after my parents have gone to bed, adding up how much we've already spent, trying to guess what the rest will cost, and wondering where the money will come from, how we can still scale back. We've already taken out a mortgage we hadn't expected to need; now, backed into a corner, with the house three-quarters done, we don't have enough money to get across the finish line. There is no way out but through, and getting through requires cash; the specter of that family living in the cellar hole is never far from my mind. Reluctantly, we take out a second loan, a home equity line, and agree to account for every purchase made, every dime spent.

It is eQuanimiti and Daniel who remind us that we still have something to share. And just when we're feeling the fierce pinch of privation, it is the simple act of giving that sets us free.

How satisfying it is to spread out ingredients in my mother's kitchen—fresh ginger, garlic, ghee, tomatoes, and mung beans the color of marigolds—and learn to make dal from scratch. Inspired suddenly by a newfound sense of purpose, I embrace my self-appointed job as chef. I read about Indian cooking and healing, search the Internet for alternative cures, and am thrilled to strike gold with an Ayurvedic recipe for warm milk with turmeric and honey that promises to ease the pain of inflammation.

In the end, the grounding, homey work of cooking, caring, and befriending someone else is what finally brings me back into balance with myself. I am done with reading toilet reviews and wandering around southern New Hampshire in search of the ideal door handles. What a relief to turn instead to real work—feeding a friend and serving, at last, some greater purpose than my own.

Releasing my death grip on perfection, I realize that of course our house does not need to be "just so." The quality of our lives within its walls will not be improved by any of my decorating home runs, nor will it be diminished by my strike-outs. Were I to insist on perfection, nothing in the house would ever be finished to my satisfaction anyway.

It seems, in fact, that building a house is a lot like raising a child. It's hard not to get swept up in the frenzy, believing that children ought to look and act and achieve in certain ways and that success and competence must be attained at any cost. I realize I've already wasted months fussing over making the "best" choices, when all I really needed to do was make some good choices, accept them without looking back, and move on to the next. It seems to be a lesson I need to learn again and again.

Just as I must remind myself that my very imperfect sons are in fact perfect as they are, I also need to accept that our "dream" house will have its faults and shortcomings large and small, and at the end of the day none of them will matter. Surely it will be a wonderful, homey place for sleeping, working, playing, and living, even if it is very far from perfect and not anyone's idea of elegant. Home, after all, is so much more than just a building; it is the people who live within as well, and the very nature of our living. We had started with a vision of how we wanted to live, not what we wanted to have. And then we'd imagined a house that might almost be erased by a view we loved, a house where the outside would always be more important than the inside. As long as it is tight to the weather and beautiful to us, who cares if it is perfect or not?

And so, when Henry says he wants his walls painted blue as background for his Red Sox posters, I don't even hesitate. Although I'd dreamed of new furniture, in the end Steve and I gratefully accept my parents' offer of their old maple bedroom set. We decide to furnish the den at the consignment store and to reuse all the porch furniture from the old red cottage. Industrial carpet, cheap and durable at less than two dollars a square foot, will solve the problem of how to cover the floor on the lower level. Someday, maybe, we will get a new living room couch, but for now, our old one will have to do. I relax. None of this is about me, after all. It's just a house. It will be up to us, and the hand of time, to make it home.

"Don't ask yourself what the world needs," advises theologian Howard Thurman. "Ask yourself what makes you come alive and then go do that. Because what the world needs is people who have come alive."

Eager as I am for our house to be finished, it is certainly not the minutiae of decision making and decorating that give me a sense of accomplishment throughout the spring and summer months. What I discover instead is the paradox of giving; nothing pleases me more than coming up each day with some small way to be present for my convalescing friend, a friend I don't really know very well at all but who once tossed a lifeline out to me as I floundered in the rough waters of my own stormy sea.

eQuanimiti and Daniel are grateful for the food that arrives every couple of days at their doorstep, but I doubt they have any idea how much they are giving me in return—the opportunity to reach out beyond myself and a reminder, just when I really need it, that, as Maya Angelou has said, "giving liberates the soul of the giver." Choosing connection, community, and friendship over the exhausting self-defeat of perfectionism, I do feel alive, released at last from the familiar, well-worn territory of my own needs and fears. And I begin, all over again, to recover a sense of myself, simply by giving of myself.

On a perfectly still, perfectly sunny August morning, I drive up the long dirt hill to eQuanimiti and Daniel's house. I am not bringing dinner today, or flowers, or books. This is just a visit, albeit a momentous one. There is no line item in our budget for original artwork, but Steve and I are purchasing two of eQuanimiti's paintings for our house anyway, a transaction of the heart that serves all our practical purposes as well. She needs the income, and we will feel privileged to have her bold, richly colored canvases on our walls.

Although she still experiences moments of excruciating pain

in her damaged nerve endings, the sores on eQuanimiti's face have healed. Most of her vision has returned. Most of the time, she can keep food down. A few lingering scars, she says, are the only visible reminders of her long ordeal. Today, I will see her for the first time in all these months. She is ready, if not to go out and meet the world, at least to let the world begin to come to her.

As I start up the drive, thousands of miniature golden butterflies rise up before my car. I slow to a crawl, inching forward, reluctant to harm a single one. Where did they come from, and why are they here, if not simply to embellish this lovely summer morning with the mysteries of metamorphosis made visible? It seems entirely plausible to me that they have come in honor of eQuanimiti herself, nature's own tribute to her heroic reemergence into life.

When my sons were small, I read them a wise little book called *Hope for the Flowers*. Now, I remember the part that went like this:

> *"How does one become a butterfly," she asked pensively.*
> *"You must want to fly so much you are willing to give up being a caterpillar."*
> *"You mean die?"*
> *"Yes and no," he answered. "What looks like you will die, but what's really you will still live."*

Already, the colors of the field grasses are changing. When I first made this trip six long months ago, bearing a bowl full of out-of-season strawberries and watermelon, there were dwindling snowbanks along the drive, and the meadows beyond were flat and lifeless, still frozen solid. Since then, two whole seasons have come and gone, winter giving way to spring, the blinding greens of high summer softening now to autumn's mellow, wheatlike hues.

Except for doctor's appointments, when she wraps her tender face in silken scarves to avoid any sudden breeze or breath of air, eQuanimiti has been sequestered on this isolated hilltop all this time, like an afflicted princess in a fairy tale. While I have been making dinner, doing laundry, taking a run, driving Jack to a guitar lesson, watching a movie with my husband and sons, shopping for paint and wall-to-wall carpeting, doing the myriad things that make up a life, she was here, suffering so long and so mightily in her darkened room that she nearly lost herself for good, and then slowly, with infinite resolve, giving birth to a new self and a new way of being in the world.

We have had many conversations, raw and heartfelt. Me, hurtling along in the car, eyes on the road, or standing in a hot parking lot somewhere, asphalt softening beneath my feet, cell phone pressed to my ear. My friend, as I imagined her on many an airless afternoon, lying alone on a narrow bed, damp cloth across her forehead, an untouched cup of tea cooling at her side, as she grasped, always, for something to be grateful for.

Some days, bravery gave way to tears of sheer exhaustion. But usually we talked about grace. In her low, musical voice, she welcomed me into the perilous territory of her illness. Together, we mused about the possibility of suffering as baptism and pain as regeneration, a harrowing initiation into a new state of being. As the months have passed, we've grown close in a way we never were in person. And what we've come to share, ironically enough, is a kind of reverence for all processes of transformation and a newfound appreciation for the abundance in both our lives, different as they are.

On a cold winter day with mice in the kitchen, I could not see one good thing in my world. Convinced that I'd run out of blessings to count, I saw instead all that I'd lost, all the tasks that were undone, all that we didn't have, all the things that weren't going my way, all the parts of life that refused to fall neatly into place. Having spent more money than we wanted to on a house that we could no longer afford and couldn't seem to finish, I was sure that I had failed—failed to keep my job, failed to make good decisions, failed in my crazy, romantic vision of a simpler life. The one thing I felt sure of that awful day, as I sat weeping among the cracker boxes, was that I had nothing whatsoever to offer to anybody else.

eQuanimiti and Daniel proved me wrong. What flows out flows in, it is said, and so it was. Giving a little, as Steve and I both came to see, feels like getting more. What we had seen as lack in our own lives suddenly began to seem like enough, more than enough. It had gotten so the two of us could barely look at our construction bills without getting angry, cold, and hardened toward each other. It felt at times as if the house had us in a vise, as if it were squeezing the lifeblood out of us and we were powerless to stop it. Whose fault was that? Both of ours, probably, and nobody's. Yet we wove ourselves a sticky, toxic cocoon of resentment and blame.

Helping our friends saved us from ourselves. We had our health, two growing sons, each other. Soon we would have a house of our own, in a place where, if we so chose, we could watch the sun rise and set every day for the rest of our lives. Meanwhile, we could make ourselves useful. Choosing empathy over fear, our hearts lifted in unison once again and moved in the same direction, toward the fullness of life.

"Why are you guys doing this?" both our sons asked, more than once, as the summer wore on.

"Because eQuanimiti and Daniel need a hand now," we would answer, "and because this is what friends do for one another. If we were in trouble, our friends would be there for us, too."

Sometimes, I tried to take it a little further. "And also because almost everything else we're doing these days is all about us, getting our house done, shopping and planning and getting us all moved in. We have to do that. But you know what? It actually makes me and Dad feel happier when we're able to do something kind for someone else."

Daniel meets me at the door, as usual. Today, though, he steps aside and waves me in with a tiny bow. eQuanimiti waits at the top of the stairs, calling hello. Her hair, usually hennaed the color of rich Cabernet, is all gray now, thick and bristly, chopped short, just growing back where sores and lesions have pocked her scalp. She wears flat, funny sneakers on her narrow dancer's feet and totters a bit nonetheless. Her layers of shirts and scarves and long, loose pants hang on her bones. She is very, very thin. And she is smiling, even as her eyes fill and overflow with sparkly tears. I put my arms around her gently, as if she might break, and place the lightest of kisses on her pale white cheek. It feels amazing to me that she is actually standing here before me, in the flesh. After all these months, it seems as if she ought to wear a sign around her neck proclaiming, "Look! I have come through."

The white walls are crowded with paintings, the old work of an old life. eQuanimiti's shop is closed for good. She is not going back. The flamboyant, artsy businesswoman, who knocked off early one day over seven months ago and drove home feeling a little odd and under the weather, is no more. And the woman who has emerged in her place will lead a different life altogether. I remember a banner in eQuanimiti's bold hand-writing that used to hang over her shop door: "Sometimes you

need to let go of the person you think you are, in order to become the person you are meant to be."

But the letting go, as we must all learn from experience, isn't
just a simple choice between one way of being and another.
Suffering is almost always part of it, and loss. Identities die hard.
And new ones take shape slowly, in increments. Illness forced
eQuanimiti to relinquish her public life, but in return it invited
her to nurture her inner one. A door closed, yet her life has
surely deepened and widened, allowing her, as the Quakers say,
"to proceed as way opens." Now, when her eyes are up to the
task, eQuanimiti is writing, huge words on huge sheets of
paper, so that she can read them herself without strain. To her
surprise, rich, thrilling stories are flowing, stories that have been
hidden away in a dark place inside her for a long time. It is time
to bring them to light.

Daniel serves us herbal tea in pottery mugs and then slips
silently away. He is working, consulting from home, and so
busy these days that he is able to support them both. Their future awaits. Someday soon, he reports, they are going house
hunting.

The late morning sun pours in, illuminating paintings of
pendant moons, textured stone walls at twilight, dark rushing
rivers, black shadowed pines. Before I leave today, I will choose
a pair of these vivid nocturnal scenes to take home and hang
side by side in our own house. But first eQuanimiti and I will
sit for a while and drink our tea. We have a lot to talk about.
Beyond the window, down the drive, clouds of tiny yellow butterflies vibrate in the summer air.

~7~

questions

*The difficulty of the journey sometimes
turns out to be its blessing.*
    —MARIANNE WILLIAMSON

On a late August morning, I wake, reaching for the quilt at the foot of the bed, a new chill in the air. Overnight, it seems, summer has slipped away, and the sharp breeze through the window stirs in me a sadness that time has flown so quickly. As always, the end of summer arrives too soon, our long-awaited week in this rented Maine cabin flies by too fast, and fall arrives before anyone is ready, sending us scrambling for long pants, socks, sweatshirts no one expected to need, still balled up in the bottoms of suitcases.

There is change in the air, this sudden turn of seasons bringing us closer to the threshold between family life as we've always known it and a new one just around the corner. After a long stretch of sultry August nights, the covers feel heavy and strange across my legs, but the weight of awareness is heavier still.

In a few weeks, we will settle at last into the house that has been three long years in the making, the house that my husband and I willed and wrestled into being as our two sons were growing up before our eyes. It seems only yesterday that we imagined a new life elsewhere, sold our house, and moved away without quite realizing how swiftly four years of high school would fly by or that there would be such a long gap between one home and the next. Certainly it never occurred to me that by the time my children would once again have rooms of their own and walls to decorate, it would be nearly time for the first one to pack his bags and head off to college.

Over the next few months, while I work to feather the nest, Henry will be preparing himself to fly—studying for the SATs, visiting college campuses, sweating over admission interviews and music auditions. Meanwhile, his younger brother will begin his freshman year in his new hometown. Each, in his own way, will strive to make his mark. And for a little while longer, our family life will be ruled by the demands of finishing a house and moving in, two different school schedules, music lessons, sports, projects, tests, deadlines, application forms, and fears and hopes for the future.

For nearly a year now, I've been clipping articles about college admissions, most of them apparently written to fuel the anxiety of parents like me, parents who are already wondering just what role we should play in this high-stakes game, as our sons and daughters present themselves on the page and in person to perfect strangers who must then judge them against thousands of other hopeful, ambitious young people all engaged in this same elaborate ritual.

It doesn't take long to grasp just how much times have changed since my classmates and I blithely filled out our own applications to three or four colleges, so many years ago. Recently, a friend of mine shook his head in amazement as he recalled, "I applied to college one night after dinner. Sat down in the kitchen, wrote the essay, typed it, stuck the whole thing in the mailbox the next morning, and didn't give it another thought until my acceptance arrived a few months later."

Now, we are barraged with reminders—in conversations in parking lots, in e-mails from high-priced college-counseling services, in the daily press—that our own children's chances of gaining acceptance to their first-choice colleges have never been worse, the possibility of rejection never higher. "When straight A's are just not enough," read the headline in our local paper in April, above a story about top students being turned down in record numbers by Ivy League schools. "Young, Gifted, and Not Getting into Harvard," was the title of an article that ran in *The New York Times* on the same day.

My husband went to Harvard. We spent most of our adult lives within a few miles of Harvard Square, lived surrounded by neighbors with strong, enduring connections to the school, even chose the name Henry late one night when I was seven months pregnant, as we wandered through Memorial Hall and read aloud to each other the lists of Harvard men who had given their lives long ago on the battlefields of the Civil War.

Perhaps, for a few moments on that crisp October night, I touched my belly and wondered whether the baby I was carrying would one day return to this spot as an undergraduate himself and if we would point to an inscription high up on the wall and tell him, "We named you here." But from the moment two months later, when I finally pushed our first son into the world, the umbilical cord wrapped around his neck, after an arduous twenty-four-hour labor, parenthood has demanded that I let go of most of my first assumptions about success, happiness, and ambition.

The hardest part of being a parent may be learning to live with the fact that there are so many things that we simply can't control, so much of the journey that is not our doing at all, but rather the work of the gods, the unfolding of destiny, fate. We give birth to our children, we love and cherish them, but we don't form or own them, any more than we can own the flowers blooming at our doorsteps or the land upon which we build our homes and invest our dreams. We may tend the garden for a while, take our brief turn upon the land, nurture the children delivered into our arms, but in truth we possess none of these things, nor can we write any life story but our own. It's a truth I had to confront right away, one that I'm still struggling to accept seventeen years later.

Jaundice kept Henry in the neonatal ward for two days after I was released. I couldn't bear to leave him, so, once home, we turned right around and drove back to the hospital, where I sat my sore bottom in a hard chair, hormonal tears of worry and joy rolling down my cheeks, and watched through plate glass as nurses came on the hour to prick his tiny heel and squeeze reluctant drops of blood into test tubes, calmly ignoring his piteous wails.

Success, I knew right then, was a fully functioning liver, a normal bilirubin level, clearance at last to take him home. Happiness, I learned soon enough, was holding this endlessly fascinating, newly arrived infant to my breast. And within days, ambition had contracted to this—a peaceful feeding, a good night's sleep.

So began my initiation into motherhood, a complete reordering of the world as I had known it into a whole new universe in which the health and well-being of first one and then two small humans entrusted to my care took precedence over everything that I had ever yearned for or dreamed of for myself.

At three months, our son developed a runny nose that refused to dry up, a cough that wouldn't go away, a raspy, rattling breath that often caused me to hold my own, as I waited for him to inhale, exhale, inhale again. He was diagnosed with asthma and, three years later, with low muscle tone, sensory integration dysfunction, delayed motor skills.

At eighteen months, he had finally walked, touching his fingertips together in front of his eyes, lurching across the floor like a tiny drunk. But as a three-year-old in morning preschool, he wouldn't jump or climb, preferring instead to sit alone and watch his active classmates. His earnest young teacher called us in for a meeting to suggest tests and intervention. Henry didn't talk or play or interact with the other children, she reported. In the busy classroom, he often seemed lost and overwhelmed. Sometimes he would just tune out altogether, eyes glazed over, mouth hanging open, gazing into space. "Catatonic" was the word she used. He wouldn't walk in snow.

Nebulizers, twice daily asthma medications, and worries about allergies and our son's incessant colds gave way then to graver concerns and a new schedule that included weekly occupational therapy, physical therapy, speech therapy, countless doctor's appointments, one evaluation after another. As our small son's medical file grew thicker, we wondered who he would turn out to be, what he might one day be capable of doing, and how we could best help him. And we tried to come to terms with the fact that this child who brought us so much joy, who seemed almost from birth to call forth what was best in each of us, and whom we loved so fiercely and unconditionally, was different.

We'd had no other baby to compare him with, had no idea he'd already fallen so far behind, couldn't imagine him being other than he was—and yet where we saw a sweet-tempered toddler, those who knew better saw a constellation of problems needing to be addressed. It began to dawn on us that the road he would take through life would no doubt lead us to some unexpected places as well.

Nothing in our conventional experience prepared us for the world we entered now, reluctant immigrants from normality arriving on the foreign shores of reduced expectations and small goals. We didn't know the language of this new land, had no desire to settle here, and yet having entered the system, having availed ourselves of the therapists and specialists and educators whose job it was to help our child realize his potential— whatever that might be—we were expected to play our part, to follow their advice and do the right thing. And so, uncertain and trying, for Henry's sake, to portray a cheer I didn't feel, I now delivered my son each day to a new classroom for "special" children with a wide variety of physical and mental disabilities, from autism to Down syndrome to cerebral palsy.

Henry took his new classmates in stride, adjusted without question to the fact that Jesse needed a harness and a leash to keep him from running away, that Suzanne came to school in a wheelchair, her delicate feet and hands twisted into impossible positions, that some new friends couldn't talk at all, and that others were never, ever quiet. Froot Loops flew through the air, toys and fists and feet banged on the floor, voices were loud, excited, garbled, tears and laughter frequent and often coexistent.

To me, the newcomer, the noise in that classroom was random, chaotic, and crazy. Part of me wanted to linger in the mornings, to chat with the other mothers and learn their stories, to get to know their children. But from the moment I walked Henry through the door, I couldn't wait to get out of there.

I didn't want citizenship in this strange country, yet I couldn't help but be impressed by the pale, determined mothers—

tireless advocates all—who had somehow managed to find
community here, to enter this noisy, confusing world and make
it home. And try as I might, I couldn't bring myself to believe
that this tumultuous classroom was meant to be our son's safe
haven or that while my friends' children were learning to count
and say the alphabet, Henry, who already knew these things,
was meant to sit alone in a corner here, quietly doing one
puzzle after another while the pandemonium of needy children and overworked teacher's aides swirled on around him.

He didn't complain. He liked the children and the teachers,
and he noticed everything. He taught an older boy with Down
syndrome how to fit wooden puzzle pieces into the right spots,
patiently guiding Sam's chubby hand with his own. When a
coiled spring of a boy named Noah decided that every time
Henry built something with blocks, he would kick it over,
Henry handled it; he knew without being told that Noah really couldn't help himself. After a month in his new class, I
noticed that when Henry built castles at home with his wooden
blocks, he placed a ramp in front of every opening. When I
asked him why, he said simply, "So all the people in wheelchairs
can go in." He might not be typical, but he wasn't tuned out,
either.

As first-time parents desperate to do whatever was best for
our son, my husband and I didn't have much confidence in
our gut feelings. Were we in denial? we asked ourselves again
and again. Surely the experts knew far more than we did. Yet
it seemed to both of us that this child of ours was taking in
the world more fully and deeply than any of us could even
imagine.

He might be vulnerable, kind of floppy, and unusually shy,
yet already I sensed in him a way of being, a composure, that
would surely serve him well. There were lots of things that

come naturally to most children that Henry couldn't do. He couldn't stick out his tongue and move it from one side of his mouth to the other, catch or throw a ball, climb a jungle gym, or run. He made no small talk. But he woke up singing to himself in the morning, laughed easily, was content to be alone. He seemed to have arrived on earth with a kind of innate faith in the goodness of life. He was happy and he was kind—and that, to me, seemed like quite an accomplishment for a four-year-old.

Sometimes, my husband and I marveled at the changes parenthood was effecting in us. The promotion he had been seeking at work seemed less compelling to both of us, the idea of running a publishing company less appealing than it always had. Life at home had grown richer, deeper, and more complex. So many of the things that used to matter a great deal— the next book title, the intricacies of office politics and publishing gossip, the making and marketing of the latest best seller or first novel—mattered less.

What mattered more were all the things we'd never even thought about till now. The valiant, tireless struggles of parents whose children don't "fit in" to create rich, meaningful lives for their families. The emotionally demanding work of coming to completely accept the child you have, rather than mourning the loss of the child you might have wished for. The rewards of learning to live into the present moment, rather than always worrying about a future that no one could predict anyway.

Our son lacked hand-eye coordination and had no core strength, the occupational therapist told us as she prescribed exercises to build his stomach muscles and strengthen his skills. But we began to see that nothing was quite that simple, that the labels and diagnoses didn't add up to a person, nor did they begin to tell the whole story—that in fact there are many kinds of strength.

If Henry's outer core was weak and kept him from sitting upright or pumping a swing, his spiritual core was strong, the source of another kind of power altogether, power that seemed much more the essence of who he was than weak abdominals and slow reflexes. Maybe the world couldn't see this kind of strength yet, maybe it would be hidden for a long time or discernible to only a few. Yet I began to set aside some of my worries, began to believe that whatever it was that made Henry special most certainly didn't make him less.

At the end of that nursery school year, the teacher told us gently that in her opinion, our son would always need an aide at his side, to help him negotiate and modify the demands of a regular classroom. We tried to envision that kind of future, so different from what any parent would wish for, a future of lowered expectations and smaller dreams. Yet at the same time, neither of us really believed that she'd got it right.

There *was* something about Henry that was different, but what he lacked in physical strength and coordination was offset by a power of spirit, a way of being in the world that somehow seemed to deepen our own faith in the rightness of things. Perhaps we couldn't expect a harried occupational therapist to see that, but my husband and I sensed it. Our son's very presence seemed to call forth what was best in both of us, cracked open our hearts and sowed seeds of tenderness and acceptance there.

The therapists advised us to keep him moving, so we put on fifties rock 'n' roll and dropped our butts. "Dance party!" we'd call out after dinner, and head for the living room. Chubby Checker entered the pantheon, displaced Raffi, made "Splish Splash" our favorite song. While I waltzed baby Jack around in my arms, Steve would get Henry up on his hands, grab his legs, and wheelbarrow him back and forth across the floor. We'd swing him up onto the window seat, count to three, and yell, "Jump!" until, finally, he did. Then we'd do it again and again, cheering for every leap until he finally overcame his fear and laughed as his feet hit the floor.

We turned the music up louder, twirled around, did flailing jumping jacks and somersaults, danced the twist, the swim, and the pony. What began as therapy for a three-year-old turned into play for a family, a nightly ritual of music and movement and fun.

And slowly, almost imperceptibly, our anxiety over our son's issues and problems was transformed into gratitude for the gifts that made him unique. Already he had led us out of the mainstream and onto an unexpected path; already he had taught us new ways of looking and new ways of seeing. And now he was nudging us two middle-of-the-road, by-the-book people to question the status quo, compelling us to summon our own convictions and to find the courage to stand behind them.

When it was time for kindergarten, we listened carefully to the recommendations of the special ed coordinator as she out-lined her vision—an Individualized Education Plan, OT, PT, speech therapy, an integrated skills classroom, a private aide, regular assessments, more intervention as needed. And then, almost on a whim, we took Henry to visit a nearby Waldorf school, where instead of reading through his daunting pile of test results and evaluations, the kindergarten teacher simply suggested that he spend a couple of mornings in her classroom and see how things went.

"Henry is going to be fine here," she assured us when we came to retrieve him on the second day. "He swept the floor and sang and made bread with us. And he's clearly very musical. When we went downstairs for movement, he stood right next to the pianist and watched her intently for the whole half hour."

Maybe he was musical; it had never occurred to us. But what we did realize was that this wise teacher, with her quiet voice and gentle way, seemed to have a better sense, after just two mornings, of who our son was and who he might yet become than did any of the various therapists and specialists who had been testing and evaluating him for the last two years. She was the first person we'd met who just watched Henry *be,* instead of trying to get him to *do.* The first one who looked at this slight, soft-spoken boy and saw not what was wrong with him, but what was already right, the inner light and soul qualities that truly did make him special.

And so, for the first time, we went with our own intuition and enrolled him in a kindergarten with rose-colored walls and long, soft curtains at the windows, where flowers bloomed and plants and small children thrived. In this serene and lovely place, so different from the brightly colored, highly stimulating classrooms we were used to, there were no weather charts or alphabets on the walls. Instead, a large, faded print of Raphael's *Madonna* hung above the long trestle table where snack was served, the stillness and peace in her painted gaze quieting the heart of anyone who paused long enough to gaze back. Here, all the toys were made of wood and materials from nature, imaginative play took precedence over numbers and letters, children ran free outside in every kind of weather, washed dishes and made applesauce, and listened to hushed stories told by candlelight.

So much of what we had been doing till now, so much of our son's therapy, was about "bringing him up to speed," trying to help him "catch up" to his peers. And every time we held up the yardstick, what we saw was that despite everyone's hard work and three therapy sessions a week, he still wasn't measuring up, not physically, intellectually, or emotionally. Now, it occurred to us that maybe the best thing we could do for Henry was to stop doing quite so much.

We took the yardstick away. We put our faith, instead, in an education designed not to fill a child's head with information and then test what has been learned, but rather to bring forth and nurture that which is already present in every young child's nature—a sense of truth, beauty, and goodness.

What happened next was not an astonishing transformation, but simply the beginning of our son's finding his own way in the world. The homey routines and gentle rhythms of Waldorf kindergarten suited his temperament. Observing the magic that transpired in that classroom—the lively, imaginative play, the simple songs, the pure reverence drawn forth from four- and five-year-olds—my husband and I realized that our child was not the only one receiving an education here. We were learning something, too, learning that in our fast-moving, noisy world, less can be more, silence is precious, and in our daily rush through life, we often sacrifice the very things we need the most—quiet, awareness, patience, joy.

"All the flowers bloom in their own time," my grandmother had said once, when I confided my worries to her. Now, I saw that she was right—but being potted in the right soil helped, as did a simple, steady diet of stories and songs and rituals to feed the imagination and the soul.

I began to understand that perhaps the best thing I could do for both my children was not to grab them by the hand and dive each day into the great rushing river of life, but instead to create for them, for all of us, a protected island, a quiet place from which we could hold the world and its busyness at bay for a while.

We lived in a beautiful town full of large, well-appointed houses inhabited by prosperous families with handsome, accomplished children. Being a good mom, it had always seemed to me, meant taking advantage of the many opportunities and experiences available to all of us. A full calendar, a busy life, a packed schedule, meant that I was doing my job, ensuring that my children were getting the experiences they needed in order to grow up prepared to compete in a complex world.

For Henry, lagging behind physically, there was physical therapy half an hour away from home, swimming lessons and occupational therapy in a pool, structured play sessions and evaluations in which he was asked to stack shapes, solve puzzles, maneuver through obstacle courses. Jack, three years younger, was a natural at sports, so I signed him up for T-ball, rookie rackets, pee wee soccer. Where we lived, there was always plenty to do and never, ever, enough time to squeeze it all in.

By the time Jack arrived in the airy, rose-colored kindergarten classroom, I had begun to wonder if, in the midst of all our comings and goings, we were missing something even more important than any swim lesson or playdate. My children were just five and eight years old, still so young, yet it felt as if our life together had become a blur of activity, our travels dictated by our array of extracurricular activities, school schedules, work schedules, and social schedules.

But what I wanted—more than a five-year-old soccer star, more than an eight-year-old who might finally be pronounced "normal"—was to stop racing around. I began to long, instead, for stillness.

What would happen, I wondered, if we gave up some of our activities—or most of them? If we turned off the television, cleared space on the calendar, made family time—or even alone time—a higher priority than any other kind of time? Trying to live more slowly, more thoughtfully, meant learning to say no to many of the good things available to all of us. Sometimes the choices were hard to make; sometimes we couldn't help but wonder if our sons were missing out on the very advantages we'd always worked so hard to give them.

Slowly, though, my goals as a parent shifted. Instead of filling our afternoons, I tried to empty them, only to discover that out of my own need for, as Thoreau put it, "broader margins around my days," I could give my children a gift of time as well. Instead of feeding my sons a diet rich in experiences, I could offer less and thereby allow them room to figure out for themselves how to produce a puppet show in a closet or organize a game in the backyard with the neighborhood kids.

My husband and I never really adopted an alternative life-style. We didn't eschew team sports and music lessons forever; there were plenty of both in the years to come. We didn't toss the television out the window (although we did unplug it for a very long time) or turn down all invitations that came our way. All we did was try to relax a little. We managed to eat dinner around the kitchen table most nights, to light candles and take time to say grace, to go to bed earlier. Most of all, we reminded each other that both our children were fine, more than fine, just as they were—imperfect, relatively content, sometimes bored, as yet unformed.

I didn't realize it at the time, but making that effort to pull back a bit and to slow down the pace of our family life was a step in my own growing and maturing, a first step, perhaps, in the direction of self-knowledge. Finding the confidence to say no to the culture's siren calls, knowing when to choose quiet time over busy time, becoming comfortable with silence, solitude, and empty hours, meant having some faith that the good things in life are created, not bought, and that my children would get what they needed even if I didn't devote all my waking hours to providing for them.

Growing up in the true sense, I was coming to see, involves more than just keeping all the balls in the air, juggling the responsibilities and details of life as they came at me. It also means understanding that every choice we make gives shape and meaning to the life that is uniquely ours to lead, just as a sculptor's chisel enlivens and shapes, with each tiny stroke, the stone beneath his hands. Thanks to both my sons, my own education was finally under way.

And one of the hardest lessons I was learning was that the answers to the really big questions, the answers we most hunger for, don't ever come to us from the outside; rather, they come from a quiet place within. A place we can reach only when we find within ourselves the courage to pause, to abide for a while in that place of not knowing, to be at peace even with our uncertainties, and then to listen and attend with the ear of our own hearts.

Now, all these years later, as one son prepares to enter high school and the other, unbelievably, to leave it, I often find myself thinking back to the years when they were both still small. Summer days then began with pancakes and just-picked blueberries for breakfast and might end with made-up stories or shadow pictures on a bedroom wall. In between, there were walks to the creek, picnic lunches on the back porch, stacks of books carried out to a quilt on the grass, a plastic wading pool that could enchant two little boys for hours, a shallow red dish full of filmy bubble liquid, and the magic wand that once waved wobbly, iridescent globes into the air, each one carrying an invisible fairy off to a distant sea.

It's still hard for me to believe that all of this has vanished, that those times are truly gone for good. How fresh and green they are, still, in my memory—the intense, constant physical intimacy as well as the countless peanut-butter sandwiches, bedtime stories, earaches and scraped knees, baking soda volcanoes, snowball fights, trips to town for ice-cream cones. Yet I am grateful to have had all of those moments, for they are the ones that have turned out, in the end, to be the most precious recollections of all, though they went unrecorded, unwritten, unremarked on at the time.

Our photo albums from those days are full of pictures of birthday cakes and holiday celebrations, vacation trips and family adventures, piano recitals and baseball games. But the memories I find myself sifting through the past to find, the ones that I would now give anything to relive, are the ones that no one ever thought to photograph, the ones that came and went as softly as a breeze on a summer afternoon.

No picture, or home video, or diary entry can begin to capture the nubbly texture, subtle tones, and secret shades of a family's life as it is from one hour, or day, or season, to the next. It has taken a while, but I know it now—the most wonderful gift we had, the gift I've finally learned to cherish above all else, was the gift of all those perfectly ordinary days.

And so, on this end of summer morning in Maine, I look around the dim bedroom and try to memorize the ordinary moment that is now—the chill in the air, the cold metallic smell of damp beach and deep lake water, the week's worth of limp newspapers piled on the dresser, the golden, knotty-pine walls of this cabin we love so much. I pull the blankets up to my neck and prop my head upon the pillows so I can glimpse the tall pines beyond the windows.

In the half-light of early morning, my mind leaps to the future, and, as usual, to questions only time can answer. Will this life we've envisioned for so long turn out to suit us after all? Will Jack finally begin to feel that what he has makes up for all he's lost? Is Henry really up to the job of applying to college? Will I possess enough self-restraint to let him find his own way? How will we deal with the unprecedented financial strains of tuition and two mortgages, the stress of moving yet again, the long-awaited task of settling into a house that's only partway finished, the end of childhood, our sons' uncertain and unknowable futures, the emptying nest? I don't have answers to any of these questions yet, but each one reminds me—as if I needed reminding—how swiftly time is passing.

We have a year left. One more year in which we two parents and our two nearly grown sons will still sit down to dinner together, negotiate morning showers, discuss who gets the car and who deserves the last ice-cream sandwich in the freezer. One more year to forge a new, more adult relationship with our older son, a relationship intimate and resilient enough to survive the challenges of distance, freedom, and all the preoccupations of college life.

A year from now, I'll awaken again in this cabin, hear the high, mournful cry of loons across the lake, feel a cool breath of autumn through the screened window, and count on one hand the days we have left together. I'll try to prepare myself for what's just ahead—the bittersweet finale of one more summer, a summer that will end with a flurry of packing, an empty bedroom, a first trip to college, a bittersweet good-bye—and the knowledge that the second farewell, just three years away, will follow all too soon.

And then, with one last turn of season, our family will shift and change shape irrevocably. We will go from a houseful of four to a quiet house of two, and my work as a mother of children at home will come to an end.

For now, though, I am called back to the present, the transitory challenges of the here and now. Somehow, in these next months, I must find a way to invoke the power of home all over again, to transform a raw, new space into a haven for all of us, invest it with love, and at the same time accept the fact that my real job now is not to hold my children close, but to prepare them, as best I can, to move away from us and into lives of their own.

Figuring out how to mother these two tall, hairy, taciturn teenagers who are, for the moment, still very much with us is humbling work. Many days this summer I've taken a long, deep breath and asked myself, How could I do this better? I haven't come up with a very satisfactory answer, but I have learned this: Every time I'm able to let go even a little—of control or judgment, of my need to be right or my inclination to worry—I'm rewarded. Life suddenly seems a bit sweeter, and easier, for us all. My sons relax, we find humor in the moment rather than the urge to redraw our old battle lines, and I'm reminded once again that a simple change in focus can improve the tone of a day.

If motherhood has taught me anything, it is that I cannot change my children, I can only change myself. Try as I might, I can't shape either one of them to my desires or designs, but I can choose, moment by moment and day by day, my own reaction to who they are. So perhaps my real job now, and in the year ahead, isn't to direct my sons' lives, but to work on becoming more thoughtful and deliberate about my own.

It will be enough, I think, if I can help my older son approach the months ahead not as a final push toward some holy grail called college admission, but as an essential rite of passage, an opportunity for his own growth and self-discovery. It will be enough, too, if I can support my younger son's transition into a new community, a new school, and new expectations, not by trying to orchestrate and oversee his life, but by being strong and sturdy myself, so that his new freedoms can be explored within clear boundaries and on solid ground.

And it will be enough if I can begin to learn the art of letting go by practicing it in the present, brooding less about what *could* happen and paying close, grateful attention instead to the small pleasures of our life together now: shared meals, a few words at bedtime, the four of us squeezed on the couch to watch a movie, a late night walk up the road with the dog.

What I aspire to is nothing more or less than to learn once again—even when they're pushing my buttons or ignoring my good advice—to have faith in my children. Faith in them and a little more compassion for myself.

On this unseasonably cool morning, I am grateful that there are still four of us here, tucked into the green-and-white cabin that has become, over the course of our many annual August weeks in these rooms, a home away from home. Through all the changes of these last years, this remains one place that seems never to change at all, the place from which we always mark another summer's passing.

As always, with one quick turn in the weather, we're transported from the stillness of an August afternoon to a morning like this one, when the lake water is suddenly, briefly, warmer than the air, and the mountains, blurred in steamy haze just yesterday, stand out in sharp relief against a sky that's dawning paler, clearer than before.

The wind in the pines sings insistently of September and of

change. No one will swim today. For the first time in weeks, I curl tight against my husband's body, seeking warmth. Our sons are still deep asleep on the other side of the thin pine wall, their long adolescent bodies sprawled across the too-short twin beds in the room they've always shared here.

For a few more idle days, we'll paddle kayaks along the shore, play Scrabble after dinner, doze in lawn chairs with books in our laps. One son will spend hours on the porch glider, teasing jazz riffs from his guitar. The other will work his way through the last chapters of *Anna Karenina*, his summer English assignment. My husband will indulge himself by reading two newspapers a day. I'll take my long solitary walks up the hill to the rambling white farmhouse and its wooden roadside stand, where snapdragon bouquets are arranged in old tequila bottles and sold on the honor system. And then, at week's end, we'll gather up the dirty laundry, the stacks of books, the tennis rackets, the jumble of sneakers, and head for home—home being a place we have yet to create, in a house that is still full of sawdust and unfinished edges, its light-filled, empty rooms awaiting their baptism, the familiar sounds of everyday life.

8

applying

The hero's will is not that of his ancestors nor of his society, but his own. This will to be oneself is heroism. Life is a desperate struggle to be in fact that which we are in design.

—José Ortega y Gasset

The man is fifty or so, with a ponytail of long, thin gray hair. He wears a leather bomber jacket, Timberland boots, jeans, a worn messenger bag slung across his shoulder. He's chatty, overly so, and clearly has a lot invested in being a cool dad. He's certainly having a good time today. Our tour guide at Berklee, the college of choice for many an aspiring young jazz musician, is a vivacious young Latina singer whose work-study arrangement includes taking groups of high schoolers and their parents through the city campus, answering questions about everything from auditions to graduation requirements. There are twenty-six or -seven in her charge this morning, a diverse international group, all of us listening intently as Neena describes her singing career at Berklee, her months touring Europe with a band made up of friends from school, her plans for the future. It is late August, hot again, and the air is thick with humidity. This morning, my son and I drove through rush-hour traffic from New Hampshire to Boston, parked a few blocks away from the admissions building, took a look at the overcast sky, and decided to leave our raincoats in the car. It had rained steadily all the way down, but suddenly the clouds lifted. Warm steam rose from the pavement; surely the sun was about to shine.

Now our wet, bedraggled group has taken refuge from a downpour in a black-and-gray Berklee lobby, where we drip puddles on the floor as sheets of rain slide down plate glass windows. A kiosk by the entrance, stuffed with CDs made by students and alums, seems to promise future recording contracts to all who pass through these doors. Posters advertising concerts and private lessons, notices seeking band members, housemates, and used instruments line the walls. Out of the chaotic mess of papers emerges a remarkably coherent message: This place exists to train and launch musicians.

We've seen the recording studios and rehearsal rooms that are booked twenty-four hours a day, seven days a week, twelve months a year. We've been awed by the huge digital screen outside the admissions office that continuously flashes details about gigs all over the world, the Berklee equivalent of Wall Street's giant ticker-tape screen. We've pushed our way through the crowd of students smoking cigarettes on the littered stretch of asphalt on Mass. Ave. known as the Berklee Beach. We carry brochures and catalogs emblazoned with the Berklee slogan: "Let Us Discover You." The energy swirling within this musical bubble in the heart of the city is intense, infectious; the whole place seems to hum and spin on a combination of noise and adrenaline, aspiration and attitude. Even on this humid, rainy late summer morning, everyone is moving fast.

The prospective students on our tour are quiet for the most part, stunned, perhaps, as they take in the scene. We have learned a great deal, however, about the gregarious, ponytailed dad. He lives in Maine and plays guitar. He's in a band. He writes a little music himself and sings. And he wonders what opportunities exist here for getting one's own compositions heard. How do bands get formed? He is working hard to draw Neena out; clearly, he wants to get to know her, is even more intent on making sure that she notices him. Where has she performed? he asks. Where does she live, and how did she find her off-campus apartment? Does she feel safe on the city streets? Where, he inquires now, lowering his voice and stepping up to the front of the group so he can address her more intimately, will she be singing next? He'd like to catch her act.

Henry and I exchange a look. We're both thinking the same thing: There is at least one person among us who would really like to go to Berklee. Unfortunately, he's missed his chance. I glance at the man's silent wife and son, hanging back at the edge of the group, and can't help but feel for this boy whose father is so eager to live his life for him that he's knocking himself out trying to impress a twenty-year-old tour guide. No doubt the boy will hear quite a bit on the ride home about his dad's impressions of the school. I wonder if he'll have a chance to form any of his own. Yet in a way, I know exactly where that overzealous father is coming from.

One night last spring, toward the end of Henry's junior year, I found myself at eleven-thirty, alone in my parents' kitchen with my laptop, cruising college Web sites the way a prospective home owner might look through the online real estate ads—a bit obsessively, greedily, with a combination of anxiety and covetousness that shocked me.

There is no escaping the fact that my son happens to be a member of the largest group of graduating high school seniors ever, part of the much documented two-million-plus cohort of

applicants who are expected to break records this year at colleges and universities across the country. We had thought of
high school as a time for our son to grow up. Now I wondered
if we were about to pay the price for not having pushed him
harder, for not demanding more of ourselves.

Had we been too unrealistic, I asked myself, in believing that
this quiet, unassuming boy of ours would somehow be able to
find his own way when the time came? Too lackadaisical in not
thinking, all along, of his high school career as a crucial proving
ground for college admission? And even worse to contemplate,
had we deprived him of his chance for a successful future by
allowing—no, supporting—his decision to attend a small, idealistic high school where learning to build and sleep in a leaf
shelter in twenty-degree weather is considered at least as essential as precalculus?

We had moved away from a town where all but 2 percent of
high school graduates go on to college to settle, instead, in a
town where only half do. There was no question that both our
sons would one day go to college, but now I was overcome by
doubts about the path we'd chosen. Had our approach to family
life, education, and our own parental responsibilities been
lacking? In our desire to reject some of the pressures and competitiveness that so often make modern life feel overstuffed and
overly stressful, had we in fact compromised our children's
chances to get into good schools, reduced their options for the
future, and narrowed their opportunities?

Several months earlier, a good friend from our old town had
confided over dinner that she and her husband had hired a
consultant to guide their son through the maze of college admissions. At the time, nothing could have surprised me more.
What reason, after all, did they have to worry about the prospects of their smart, responsible seventeen-year-old, a boy who

had enjoyed every advantage a loving, privileged upbringing could confer? My friends are thoughtful people who have never bought into the notion of competitive parenting. They tap the maple trees in their yard each spring, raise bees and chickens behind their suburban garage, grind wheat on the kitchen counter, run a loose, freewheeling household. So I wondered what, all of a sudden, were they so afraid of? Of course, what I was really asking myself was, Should we be worried, too?

That conversation marked my introduction to the angst and insecurity that have come to surround the college application process in the middle- to upper-middle-class milieu that is, for better and for worse, the only world I know. Since then, I've seen many other friends, most of them otherwise sane and thoughtful adults, become obsessed with which schools might accept or reject their children.

Unsure what stance to take, I finally asked Henry if he felt he needed professional help figuring out where to apply to college and how to go about it. He considered for a few minutes and then answered, as if he knew what he was talking about, "I think I can do it myself."

I wanted to take him at his word. It seemed to me that he should indeed be the owner of this process, that the experience itself would prove to be a crucial part of it, no matter how it all turned out in the end. Yet I couldn't just dismiss my friends' fears or ignore the discouraging statistics in the newspaper articles I'd filed away. I suppose it was just this kind of anxiety that had launched me on my solitary midnight journey through college Web sites, into a world that appeared both surprisingly enticing and all but impenetrable.

Eventually, that night, I turned off the computer and leaned back on the old plaid love seat in my parents' kitchen. The dishwasher finished its cycle and clicked off. The dog dozed at my feet. The house was quiet but full, the way a house is when all its occupants are present and accounted for—both my parents just down the hall, my husband and two sons asleep upstairs.

My son was seventeen. In a year, he would graduate from high school, and three months after that, he'd be gone. In that instant, I understood that where he might go was much less important than the stunning, unavoidable fact that someday, in the not too distant future, he would no longer be *here*, playing the piano, leaving the bathroom light on, asking for the car. Sitting there in the hush of midnight, I was struck by the realization that this time of all four of us living together under one roof is really just a single chapter in our family narrative, not the whole story after all, and that each day brings us inexorably closer to the final page.

On the September evening a year from now, when I set three places at the dinner table instead of four, my husband and I will find ourselves in a new chapter, one in which we're awaiting news from a son in college and adjusting to the reality that before long Jack, too, will leave us to embark on a life of his own. How quickly we'll go then from a life that is filled with children to one that is suddenly our own to shape. How strange it feels already, to realize that our sons' complete dependency has evolved, right before our eyes, into a relentless, inexorable quest for freedom and autonomy.

Sometimes, as Henry and I visit college campuses these days, I almost forget that what we're doing here is laying the groundwork for a life he'll lead away from us. Sometimes it's hard for me to remember that I'm not the one heading off to college; that in fact these trips are not about me and my dreams at all.

Peeking into a vast, light-filled library or strolling through a leafy quad, I feel my heart quicken in excitement, part of me wishing that I could step right back into this chapter of my own life, do it all over again, and get it right this time.

At the same time, I can't resist the idea that at the very least I'll get to experience college again vicariously. So I chatter on about the beauty of this campus, the opportunities in that program, the impressiveness of this department, as if by expressing all of my enthusiasm to my son, I can also share in his experience, get a taste of college by proxy, just by virtue of being his mother and being part of his process of dreaming and envisioning.

But then I catch myself. We are not on this mission, after all, to find the college that I love most, or even the one I think would be best for my son. The point of these visits is to find a school that feels like a good fit to *him*. I bite my lip, force myself to wait for Henry to tell me what he sees in a school rather than blathering on about what I do. My role, as I must continually remind myself, is to drive the car and be quiet, to listen rather than talk, to remember just whose life this is anyway.

And so today I'm oddly grateful to the hardworking, overbearing, ponytailed father who so clearly yearns to relive his youth at Berklee and whose avid hunger for attention has overshadowed his son's very presence here. He makes it easier for me to remember my place. If it weren't so sad, it would be funny.

Henry is halfway through his own school-visiting agenda, and I'm finally realizing that it takes a while, and visits to several different kinds of schools, before a seventeen-year-old high school senior can be expected to have any sense of where he belongs or what he's really looking for in a college. My son has come up with a couple of criteria, the first of which is that the school not be too far away. He wants a good music department, and he also wants to be able to come home easily, any time and for any reason.

Though I try not to make too much of it, I'm all for proximity; New England offers plenty of good options. Somewhat to my surprise, though, he's firmly ruled out a couple of colleges I'd thought would be sure bets, because they seem to him too tiny and insular, too loose and eccentric, too much, as he explains it, like High Mowing. Too safe. He's lived and thrived for three years in an intimate community on a country hilltop. Now, a little startled, perhaps, by his own emerging self-confidence, he wants to spread his wings.

Last spring, Henry took it upon himself to meet the chair of the music department at Bowdoin College. We had taken a tour months before, because we happened to be nearby and thought Bowdoin was as good a place as any to begin the process of looking. On that cold November day near the beginning of his junior year, I think my son began to picture himself, for the first time, as a college student. The campus was intimate and inviting, the students welcoming, our affable student tour guide enthusiastic and encouraging. It was easy to feel at home. Easy, too, to be seduced into believing that this small, elite college was, just perhaps, within his reach. Certainly my son—in no great hurry to make any decisions—had never expected to get excited about the very first place he visited. Yet everything he saw that day enchanted him, from the venerable oak tables and chairs in Massachusetts Hall to the bearded student who grinned and called out, "Come to Bowdoin, man," as he passed him on the path.

That afternoon, as we were offered glimpses of tidy living suites, a stunning new concert hall, and exquisitely timeworn classrooms, I found myself falling under Bowdoin's spell as well. It was not an altogether comfortable feeling. For I knew, in a way that my still innocent son did not, that admission here was at best a long shot, with the odds already stacked against him. He'd never taken an AP class, was terrible at standardized tests, and would graduate from a high school that refused to track or rank its students.

On the other hand, in fine hovering-parent fashion, I could rustle up a few arguments in his favor. He would be an All State jazz pianist in a school full of biology and psych majors. He was a straight-A student, had a list of unusual extracurriculars, could surely count on glowing recommendations.

Did he stand even the slightest chance? Did I have the heart to suggest he didn't? And who was I to make such a call, anyway? It was so tempting to picture him in this prestigious, picturesque, not-too-far-away place; to imagine future family visits to Maine, trips home on the spur of the moment, the easy security of the well-known and highly esteemed. In one day, it seemed, college had gone in my son's mind from being some vague and distant future destination to an imminent reality—a small, academic, highly competitive school called Bowdoin. His conviction surprised me. He couldn't wait to come back.

And so, the week before Bowdoin's commencement, we'd returned to the campus. Henry had written ahead and arranged an appointment for himself, and I remember wondering, as we drove, whether this long trip was a waste of time. Three and a half hours each way, just to meet with one music professor who had agreed to give my son a few minutes of his time, at a school where his chance of admission seemed highly unlikely. It was a gorgeous spring morning, and I wished I weren't spending it behind the wheel. It was in this negative, twitchy frame of mind that I looked over to the passenger seat.

"Do you have your music résumé?" I asked. Henry smoothed out the grubby piece of paper he'd been folding and unfolding for the last hour or so. "That's it?" I said, incredulous. No folder, no envelope, no pristine copy for the music department chair. It was then that I noticed how long his fingernails were, and saw, too, that they were none too clean. If I'd had to grade the job he'd done shaving that morning, I might, in a generous mood, have rounded up to a B minus. But my mood was heading south. I launched into a little lecture about facial hair and fingernails and general grooming principles, then proceeded to list the reasons that papers belong in folders and folders in backpacks. I began to grill my unkempt seventeen-year-old child about what he hoped to accomplish with this visit and how he intended to do it.

The tension in the car was thick by then, and we were both miserable and angry. I was mad at Henry for obviously not having a clue about how to present himself, at myself for not checking him out more carefully before we left home and for being so negative and critical now. It wasn't helping. The truth was, he looked utterly unimpressive to me. How would he ever manage to impress anyone else?

We rode into town in silence.

A block from the college, I pulled up outside a Rite Aid, went in, and bought nail clippers and a single yellow file folder. My son cut his fingernails in the parked car, and I wished him luck. By then, I knew, the best thing for me to do was to get out of the way. There was no reason for me to meet the chair of the department and make nice; Henry would sink or swim by his own lights. As well he should. I took my book and headed for a bench in the quad.

Twenty minutes later, I heard a laugh and looked up to see Henry and an older man strolling by, talking easily. And half an hour after that, my son was practically skipping toward me, a huge smile spread across his face. "That," he exulted, "was great."

He and the professor had hit it off "totally," he'd played a few pieces on Bowdoin's new concert grand piano, they'd talked about music, the department, the possibilities, and opportunities in store. Professor G.'s kindness and encouragement had ignited a bright spark of self-assurance in my son; he was flying, exhilarated, certain now that he'd found the perfect school for him. "They want me here!" he exclaimed.

Heading home, he began to talk about applying early to Bowdoin. It didn't feel out of reach, he assured me, but rather like a place where he'd already been welcomed, by a teacher he'd love to work with for the next four years.

I learned a couple of things on that trip last spring, but the most important was that applying to college really was going to be Henry's process, not mine. Someone who knew more about the intricacies and competitiveness of admissions might steer him elsewhere, might suggest another approach or urge him to present himself a certain way. Someone else might tell him to be more realistic, advise him that his chances at Bowdoin, which admits about 9 percent of its applicants, were slim at best. But I doubt any of that would truly be helpful. First, he needs to be allowed to dream his own future—borne aloft, as he was in that joyful moment, by a half hour of music making with a kindred spirit who saw him, heard him, and made him feel wanted.

It could very well be that, in the end, whether Henry is accepted at Bowdoin or Berklee or at some college he has yet to see is less important than that he go through the long, revealing exercise of applying. For better or worse, the job he must now undertake—of looking at schools, choosing a few that feel like a good fit, and getting himself accepted at one of them—is going to be more rigorous, more time-consuming, and more merciless, than anything he's ever tackled. As one friend in academia put it, applying to college these days "is not for the faint of heart."

I could make the process even harder, on myself and on my son, by getting depressed about the odds, being annoyed with him for not being more put together, and getting attached to some idea of the best result. But if I can manage to back off and give Henry his space, then this rite of passage might actually mean something to him. This is his chance to prove to himself, and to the world, that he's ready now to be recognized as a young adult.

There is an opportunity here for both of us—for me to begin the work of stepping back and letting go and for him to gain in competence and maturity as he's called on to make grown-up decisions about where he wants to be, how to manage the process, and how to devise plans C and D in case plans A and B don't work out as he hopes. Each step will deepen his self-sufficiency, self-knowledge, and self-confidence—the very qualities, of course, that he needs as he moves from childhood into adulthood.

That said, it also seemed clear, as Henry and I drove home from Maine last spring, that he had learned something that day, too. We were sailing down the interstate then in high spirits, singing along to Earth, Wind & Fire on his iPod. We'd had a delicious lunch outdoors, a stroll through downtown, and time to talk. The judgment and disapproval I'd felt heading north in the morning was history now, replaced by pride in the way my son had managed this meeting. The validation he'd experienced would surely serve him in the months to come as he began to look at other schools, wrote his application essays, and prepared himself for interviews and auditions.

Now, having discovered that he could show up somewhere and make a good impression, he was motivated, eager to take on the many other challenges ahead. But the trip had also served another purpose. By trial and error, Henry would learn to be his own admissions counselor. I doubted I'd ever have to check his fingernails again or buy him a folder en route for his résumé. Next time he headed out the door for a college visit, he'd know how to get ready.

And next time, I promised myself, I'd be ready as well. I would know enough to relax and enjoy the journey. To savor our brief, rare time alone. To ask my teenage son what's on his mind rather than get caught up in the urge to polish and package him into someone he's not. How much better, for both of us, if I could support and encourage him in this process without getting too involved myself.

In the end, surely, he will end up where he's meant to be and will learn whatever he most needs to know at this stage of his young life. And a big part of that education will be figuring out how to get there. Someday, no doubt, he'll look back on this intense, challenging time and recall how difficult it was to live for so many months with so many unknowns.

But what I hope Henry will remember even more than how hard it was to "get in" is how much he figured out about himself while trying. I hope he'll remember, with some fondness, our road trips through New England, the music we listened to and the meals we ate, and the pleasure we found in each other's company. And I hope he'll feel that at each one of these schools he learned something worthwhile just from going to have a look, from setting foot, if only for a day or two, on new paths, meeting new people, entertaining all sorts of new ambitions and ideas about the future.

•   •   •

At the end of our Berklee tour, Neena wishes everyone luck with their auditions, says, "I know you'll love it here," and bounds out into the rain. Henry and I seek refuge in the tiny college bookstore, jammed floor to ceiling with more music and books about music than we've ever seen in one place, a smorgasbord of possibility that is at once enticing and overwhelming. Hard to believe that Berklee and Bowdoin share the planet, let alone the East Coast, so different are these two worlds. Hard to know what my quiet, inscrutable son is thinking as he browses through a shelf full of texts about improvisation. No doubt he's comparing these two wildly divergent environments, wondering where on earth he might be headed. For the moment, both roads seem to beckon. It is all I can do to keep my mouth shut.

A week or so later, on a lovely end-of-summer morning, Henry asks if I have time to look over his first college application. He's spent the last few days filling out a detailed, exhaustive form intended to shine a light into every nook and cranny of his life and musical experience, beginning with his first piano lesson at age seven right on up to the advanced theory textbook he labored through on his own time last year. Three or four months from now, he'll join a thousand other applicants from all corners of the world for interviews and auditions at Berklee; by the end of January, he'll know whether he measures up. Not so long ago, Berklee accepted almost half of the students who applied, but as the school has gotten increasingly popular, it's also become far more competitive. The number of applicants has risen, admissions rates have dropped, and requirements are tougher; it is harder than ever before to get in.

On this day, however, a week before he begins his senior year of high school, Henry is not even sure that he wants to go to a music school. For months he's been weighing the pros and cons of conservatory training versus a liberal arts education.

Since his earliest childhood, the piano has been his refuge, music a place where he could at once challenge himself and seek safe haven. Now, somewhat to his own surprise, he's waking up to other hungers, suddenly curious about literature and politics and computer science. He isn't certain he's ready to forgo all this unexplored territory in favor of moving to Boston to immerse himself for four years in jazz theory and performance . . . but then again, he might want to do just that. Right now, he thinks, the important thing is to cover the bases, to do what he can to try to ensure that when the time does come to decide, he has some choices.

That means that his last two weeks of summer vacation have been all about essays and applications. It is an odd exercise for both of us, putting dates on the calendar months in advance, as he schedules interviews and music auditions for December, February, March. No one in our family is accustomed to planning so far ahead, and the dates and places don't seem quite real, even as I write them down. But this application form in front of us on the computer screen, with its requests for the names and addresses of every piano teacher he's ever had, is certainly real enough.

For the first time, my son has been required to try to put into words what he's sought, and what he's found, in all those hours spent at the piano over the last twelve years. Now, as we sit at the kitchen table, sunlight streaming through the window, I get my first glimpse of how he sees himself these days, how he wants to be seen, the future he's just beginning to envision.

It is so hard to offer ourselves up to scrutiny at any time, but most difficult of all, perhaps, for an adolescent who is only beginning to wrestle with the complexities of identity, ambition, and desire. How much do you tell about yourself? How much, after all, do you really even know? Do you dare reveal your grandest, deepest dream? Do you confess if you don't yet have any dream at all?

The lists of teachers and books, show tunes and jazz standards and sonatas, that constitute my son's musical autobiography cannot begin to suggest the real depth of his journey, from the timid kindergartner who once stood transfixed by a jazz pianist in a hotel lobby to the dedicated seventeen-year-old who for the last year has risen at six every Saturday morning to immerse himself in a full day of jazz classes at a Boston conservatory an hour and a half from home. Nor do his carefully worded answers begin to tell the whole story of who he is.

There is no place on this form to explain, for example, that when Henry first began pleading at age six to play the piano, it was my father and brother who made his wish come true, appearing at our house one Saturday morning with our family's plonky old upright wrapped in blankets and lashed into the back of my dad's pickup truck. Or that at the end of his first lesson, the teacher took me aside to whisper that she didn't think my son was going to be able to play the piano because his fingers were too weak to press the keys. There is no space here for the story of how a long-ago trip to New York City to see *Beauty and the Beast* gave an impressionable eight-year-old his first look at a Broadway orchestra pit, a glimpse into a magical world that seemed even then to hold a promise for the future. Certainly there is no way to include the fact that in addition to knowing Rachmaninoff's Prélude in C-sharp Minor by heart, this particular applicant is a person who carries in groceries from the car, cleans up a kitchen better than anyone in his family, writes beautiful notes on birthday cards, and secretly aspires to manage the Red Sox.

Looking at him now, this stoop-shouldered, earnest son of mine, I see also, of course, the boy he's been at every step of the way. I remember asking, after that very first lesson more than a decade ago, "How much should he practice?" And I remember Mrs. Katsuki's sage reply: "As much as he wants to. If this child is going to be able to play piano, it will be because he has to, and because he loves it. So why not just let him own this?"

And I remember marveling, as the weeks and months and then years went by, at the dedication that was born of that love. No one ever did tell Henry to practice. What motivated him to sit down at the piano was his own desire for the music, not any schedule or agenda imposed by someone else. A budding concert pianist he was not—that kind of virtuosity was never in the cards—yet the story of his life so far is above all else a story about the maturing and ripening of a passion that could be expressed only through the development of a will. Over time, I came to see that my son's growth as a musician was thoroughly, inextricably intertwined with his growth as a person. The piano gave him his life, and in return he gave it the best of himself.

It may be that we all carry the source of our gifts deep within us, that they lie like seeds in the dark, awaiting their moment to grow and flourish, dormant until there is water and sunshine enough to coax them forth. And as these gifts begin at last to unfold and bloom, whether early in life or late, we come into ourselves, discovering in the process that we have even more gifts than we ever could have imagined.

The young man sitting beside me at the table this morning has come so far from that long-ago corner where he sought his own silent refuge from the noise and chaos of preschool. He learned that what is impossible one day—be it pitching a baseball, swimming underwater, or memorizing a Beethoven sonata—becomes possible if you believe you can do it and take the time to try. Yet, as I look at my son, I realize that I know something of who he was, and who he is in this moment, but nothing at all of who or what he might yet become.

So all I can do, as I read my son's attempt to condense his seventeen years of existence on the planet onto one page, is wonder: Is it too much to hope that an overworked admissions officer will somehow read between these lines, will see here not just one more aspiring music student, but also the precious treasure of a young life, poised on the threshold between childhood and maturity? This, I suppose, is where faith comes in. We try so hard to prepare our children to go forth and meet the world, even as we try, perhaps in vain, to prepare ourselves to release them to their destinies.

Then the time arrives, and no one feels quite ready. Suddenly our children—and wasn't it only yesterday that they were just children?—must prove themselves as young adults, on the page and in person, to perfect strangers. Meanwhile, we parents must try to summon the good sense to stand back and trust them to find their way.

Easier said than done. As an involved, committed parent, my own impulse has always been to leap in on my sons' behalf, to smooth the way for them, to help them look good. More than anything, I want them to do well, no matter how they eventually define the concept. I want their ambitions to be realized, I want the schools they set their sights on to say yes. I want them to be happy. I want to help. Stepping back, when every synapse of my being is urging me forward, is turning out to be quite a challenge.

A month ago, my husband and I heard from the father of a former classmate of my son's, who called to ask, "How are you two handling the whole college admissions thing?"

Caught off guard, I answered, "Well, I guess we're not handling it. Henry is." Silence. So I inquired, "What about you?"

He told me that he'd recently taken a course on how to get his daughter into an Ivy League college; now he was busy calling admissions officers with his list of questions, enlisting the services of well-connected friends, traveling far and wide visiting schools. It sounded as if he and his wife had turned their daughter's college application process into a small cottage industry; it was turning out to be a full-time job for everyone involved. The idea that their intelligent, high-achieving seventeen-year-old might have undertaken any of this on her own seemed not to have occurred to them. Securing admission to a top school was clearly way too important to leave up to a teenager.

Yet I know that if I really want to encourage my own two children to follow a course in life more purposeful than accumulating wealth, power, and prestige, I must first acknowledge the value of such a life myself. I need to show, by my own example, that the path to fulfillment has but little to do with mastery and conquest and much to do with coming to know oneself, finding pleasure in everyday events, doing work that matters, living in community with family and friends, being loved and loving in return.

Giving in to fear—fear that can easily come to permeate every aspect of our existence—we close down to gratitude. We lose our ability to appreciate life's small gifts in all their form. Worse, we pass on our anxiety to our teenage children, who worry in turn that perhaps they really aren't quite good enough, or smart enough, or capable enough, to step up to the challenges of their own lives.

And perhaps that is just what my own son is wondering this morning as he looks to me to judge his first attempt at writing a college essay. Do I have what it takes? Will I be noticed? Do I measure up? The temptation is strong, of course, to jump in here, to rewrite, to recast, to advise. Yet what my son needs right now is not my help, but my belief in him. He needs to know that I do think he has what it takes, that I'm confident he'll pass through this long rite of initiation and come out the other end victorious—which is to say, with an acceptance to a school that will be a good fit for the person he wants to be, a school where he will undertake the deep learning and growing that is really what a college education is all about. So I resist the urge to touch my fingers to the keyboard and start "improving" on my son's work. Instead, I'm quiet, reading.

What I realize is that the story told here in my son's own words is just the first chapter, the prelude to a much larger, unknowable tale that's only now about to unfold. The lists of dates and names give rise to memories, of course: Here is the fierce teacher who sent him to the bathroom to wash his hands before letting him touch her piano, insisted his pencil have a perfect point, and once hissed in his ear before a recital, "Now, don't mess up!" And here is Harvey, the kindhearted jazz pianist who first encouraged a lonely third grader to "stretch out" as he played, to find the joy and magic in every melody, recognizing in his young student not only the soul of a musician, but a child in desperate need of a friend.

From the time he was six years old, Henry has played piano not to compete or to impress, but simply because that's who he is. Along the way, saying yes to music has meant saying no to other possibilities. Choosing one path always means rejecting others. In the end, all these choices, the big ones and countless little ones, add up just to this: a life in process, a work in progress. Now, the job of applying to college requires that he stop for a moment, look back, and take stock of the passions and people and decisions that have shaped him thus far. Viewed this way, the task truly is a rite of passage, not merely a means to an end, but an integral, valuable part of the journey into selfhood.

Suddenly, my eyes filling with unexpected tears, I begin to see the year ahead, and all these trials, from a new perspective. A transformation truly is taking place right in our midst, from the hesitant little boy who once looked to his parents to organize his days and give direction to his life, to a young man charting a course for his own future. The years of school and lessons, practice after dinner and Sunday hymns in church, commitment to an instrument and striving for excellence—all of that is finally coalescing here, the disparate bits and pieces of one young life coming together in a vibrant, multilayered collage of emerging identity.

So I remind myself to tread gently into this mystery and to pay attention to the moment at hand—the worn wooden table still scattered with breakfast crumbs, the breeze coming through the open door, the stillness of late morning, my nearly grown son sitting at my side, awaiting my response to his work.

"Your children are not your children," writes poet Kahlil Gibran. "They are the sons and daughters of Life's longing for itself. They came through you but not from you and though they are with you yet they belong not to you."

The initiation is already under way. The quest that begins today, with these pages on a computer screen, will lead just a year from now to a silent piano in our living room and a son making his way someplace else. My role isn't to manage the details of this trip, but rather to support its unfolding, to trust in the rightness of the route, to encourage my son to have faith in his own dreams—faith that may sometimes have to transcend reason.

Life is precious, I want to tell him, and every hour of time that you spend now thinking about how you want to live your own is worth the effort. How strange it feels, this weighty mix-ture of pride and sadness, yet I suspect both will grow familiar in the months ahead. Already, my heart is stretching. Already, I've begun the long, wrenching work of this good-bye.

We add a forgotten piano teacher to the list, change the order of things around a bit, correct a few typos in the essay. "It's really good," I say. We read the whole application together one last time. And then, holding his breath, my son hits "send."

"Well," he says with a grin, "I've applied to college."

~9~

transformation

. . . it is necessary
to reteach a thing its loveliness,
to put a hand on its brow
of the flower
and retell it in words and in touch
it is lovely
until it flowers again from within, of self-blessing . . .
—GALWAY KINNELL

*I*t is eighty-two degrees outside and a lot hotter than that in the airless gymnasium. Tomorrow, my son Jack will begin his freshman year in this room, in a high school that is ten times bigger than the small private school he left behind in June. Will he feel as small and alone, I wonder, as I do now, making my way through the crowd of parents arriving for orientation night, every one of them a stranger to me? In our old town, I'd recognize half the people streaming through the door, would be hugging friends I hadn't seen all summer, asking about teachers and fall sports.

But no one knows me here, anonymous and invisible in the midst of this chatty, friendly group. I take a seat by myself, high up in the old wooden bleachers, and watch the latecomers arrive, watch them wave to friends, call out greetings, squeeze over on the narrow benches to make room for yet one more body.

Above us, felt banners pay homage to champion seasons long past—basketball, lacrosse, baseball, golf. The air smells old and stale, of locker rooms, ripe sneakers, and sweat, as if all the heat and exertion of last spring and winter and fall has been bottled up within these cinder-block walls and cooked over the course of the long, hot summer. Parents who picked up forms and brochures on the way through the door use them now to fan themselves, creating the illusion of breeze in the sweltering room. Sweat trickles down my ribs. The principal, a solid woman in a green suit too heavy for this steamy late summer night, steps out onto the scarred wood floor to welcome the assembled crowd to the start of a brand-new school year.

Four years ago, we went in search of a high school that would be a good fit for our older son, allowing our move from suburb to country to be driven, in part, by a desire to find a school that put a higher value on a balanced life than on GPAs and test scores. How hard it was, back then, to imagine the day when Jack, our baby, would be ready for high school himself.

He was just eleven, still small enough to be carried upstairs to bed on his dad's back after a long day. To cut his toenails, I'd scoop him up and heft him onto the bathroom counter, then try to make him laugh while the small crescent moons fell upon a bath towel. He was so little, still a child, and the big decisions about his future seemed a long way off, bridges to be crossed much, much later, when we came to them. Somehow we'd convinced ourselves that Jack, wiry and impulsive, bright, social, and always quick to make friends, would thrive just about anywhere. As long as we were happy, surely, he would be happy, too.

Yet it was Jack who begged, from the very first mention of

the word *move,* not to go. Once we'd survived the upheaval of packing and leaving, I assured him, he would very soon feel at home again. Home didn't have to be a physical address, I explained, or a building or a town; home was, and always had been, wherever we were as a family, wherever we did the things that had always made us feel safe and secure—holding hands, saying grace, making pancakes on Saturday morning, throwing tennis balls for Gracie to fetch.

Home is more than a house, my husband and I had repeated to ourselves and our children as we packed boxes and prepared to say good-bye to ours. Certainly we needed to believe that in order to go. But Jack never did buy it.

It was Jack who gave voice over and over again to our own doubts and fears, who said through tears of anger, and sadness, and finally desperation, that we had the best life possible right where we were. Jack who had lain in his bed, in the only room he'd ever known, the room with the cloud wallpaper and a view of the garden and the swing set in the backyard and his best friend's house across the street, and said, "Think about how terrible it will be to spend the very last night in this house, knowing that we will never, ever sleep here again. Think how terrible it will feel when some other family is living here, in our house, the house that we should have lived in forever."

On Jack's bedroom windowsill at my parents' house, there are four hollow shells, shells that used to be inhabited by his hermit crabs. And though the shells have been empty now for almost three years, each time I look at them, these humble relics of our former life, my heart clenches a little, with an old sadness that still comes when I wonder if, at a tender and vulnerable time in his life, we let our younger son down by trying so hard to do right by our older one.

Jack bought his crabs when he was eight or so, at a street fair in our old town, a day the two of us spent together, visiting each and every booth and trying out every activity. Jack had devoted a blissful hour to hand painting a ceramic dinosaur in carefully chosen shades of green and orange and gold. He had entered the Twinkie-eating contest, been a roaring lion in the kids' theater performance, watched a game of human chess.

At the end of the afternoon, after much consideration, he'd decided that he would spend his allowance money, saved for weeks, on two hermit crabs, whom he named Ben and Jerry. We took them home and settled them into his old fish tank on top of his dresser. Jack installed tubes and toys for them to explore, dishes for food and water. A few weeks later, a friend who was moving away asked Jack to adopt his hermit crabs, so there were four. Those shy, mostly nocturnal creatures turned out to be pretty good pets, low maintenance, fun to play with and to challenge in mazes made of blocks, fascinating to watch as they scuttled sideways around the edges of their glass home or dug themselves into hiding beneath a rock.

When we moved out of our old house, the end came in stages. The boys had three nights of sleepovers across the street at their best friends' house while my husband and I doggedly tried to finish up the packing. On the August day the moving trucks came, Steve and Henry drove to New Hampshire, leaving me behind with a blow-up mattress and a change of clothes so I could finish cleaning. On that very last night before the closing, Jack decided that he wanted to stay in the house with me rather than go with his dad and brother or sleep next door with his friends.

All the furniture was gone, the house was completely bare except for that one mattress, my cleaning supplies, and the hermit crabs, who would ride with us in the car the next day, part of the final load.

Jack and I sat on the floor of his empty bedroom that night with a flashlight and talked about life and growing up and heartache. I had told him that if he was going to spend the night there with me, he had to promise, truly promise, that we wouldn't hash over all the old stuff again about how he didn't want to move. I knew, in my own fragile state, that if Jack got started, we'd both spend the night crying, and I was too exhausted and raw to bear that.

He kept his word. We talked instead about how hard change is for everybody and how sometimes, even when we're sure that our sadness is more than we can bear, we get surprised and discover that we are stronger than we thought. I promised him, for the hundredth time, that his dad and I would do everything we could to make sure that our new life would be good.

At some point, we took out the four hermit crabs and set them down on the floor of Jack's empty bedroom, and then for an hour or so, we watched them make their slow, exploratory way around, inching along the blue carpet, back and forth around our feet. Sitting there, leaning against the wall in the darkness, we were quiet together at last, letting our good-bye to the house be what it was. Emptiness, silence, full hearts, memories.

Finally, we lifted the crabs back into their fish tank, walked down the dim, bare hallway, and curled up together on the mattress on the floor of the playroom. We shone the flashlight on the ceiling and made our favorite hand shadows, the wolf and the rabbit, for old times' sake. I kissed his forehead and tousled his hair. And then the two of us went to sleep in our house for the last time.

All summer, Jack had anticipated and dreaded this moment. "Think what it will feel like to sleep here for the very last night," he'd say. "How could we ever do that?" Now we were doing it. And I was grateful, more than I ever would have guessed, for his company.

The hermit crabs took up new residence in Jack's bedroom in my parents' house in New Hampshire. My mom and I did everything we could to make his little room in their house feel cozy and homelike. But our efforts were for naught. Jack missed his old classmates and his old school. He missed his friends in the old neighborhood, basketball in the driveway with his pals, his baseball team, his bedroom, Joe's Pizza, and riding his bike downtown. He missed everything he'd ever had and lost, everything he'd always known and taken for granted. And while the rest of us had lived long enough to know that over time we'd grow used to our new rituals and routines, Jack knew only that nothing felt right or good anymore and that life in this new place had nothing on life in the old.

We could point out the fact that we had everything we needed—a roof over our heads, food on the table, even a Ping-Pong table in the basement—but that wasn't going to change the way he felt or ease the sorrow in his heart. He wanted to go home. And home as he had always known it did not exist anymore.

There were many days that fall when I felt the same way, bereft, as if some essential part of me had gone missing. Which is no doubt why I was so enamored of the small red cottage when I saw it first and so blind to its deficiencies. Like a newly single woman falling too hastily in love on the rebound, I was hungry for connection, eager to sink new roots into a place of our own. In those first weeks we spent back in the house of my childhood, home seemed farther away with each passing day, as if we'd embarked on an impulsive, open-ended trip without knowing the itinerary or the destination. Could it really be here, with my parents, in these rooms I thought I'd left for good decades ago? Or was it somewhere else, a dream still waiting to evolve—hazy, elusive, and just out of reach?

Sometimes, setting the table for dinner, pulling potatoes out of the oven, greeting my dad as he walked through the door, I felt like a child again myself, as if all the years of my own grown-up life had vanished right along with our house and our mortgage payments and my own sturdy pots and pans, now packed away in storage.

On the day I saw the "For Sale" sign beside the road, pulled over, and wandered up the driveway to the red cottage, to its view of twin mountains and fields crisscrossed by stone walls, all my old romantic notions of home came instantly into sharp, clear focus again. I thought I knew what I wanted, and here it was. I would attach myself to this hilltop, would create a life here with my husband and sons. Suddenly, home once again became a real place, one that I could smell and touch and begin to inhabit in my mind's eye. I thought about nothing else.

About two months after school started, just a week or so after we'd bought the cottage, I was straightening Jack's room at my parents' one afternoon and reached down into the fish tank to pick up Ben. As I lifted the green-and-white speckled shell, the lifeless body of a crab tumbled from it. Dry-mouthed, I searched for the other three and as I touched each shell, a tiny corpse dropped out.

I sat on the edge of Jack's bed, put my head in my hands, and wept. The pain I felt wasn't really about the crabs; it's hard to form an emotional attachment to a hermit crab. What I was mourning, really, was their story, our story, and the fragment of our family's history that they had carried along with them inside their shiny shells. The crabs, so easily cared for all those years, hadn't survived our move. How long had they been dead?

I wondered, realizing that we'd all been too distracted even to notice.

How small and insignificant and naked they looked. Seeing them for the very first time outside of their protective homes, it occurred to me that they were as vulnerable as our own bare selves as we struggled, each of us in our own way, to move from one home, the big solid vessel that had held and protected us for so many years, into another, temporary place that didn't feel like home at all. The death of Jack's pets, their suddenly vacant shells, seemed symbolic, somehow, of the death of our old life, the loss of our own sheltering house. And the crabs' desiccated little bodies pointed up my own failure to live up to the promise I'd made—to uphold and honor the idea of home no matter where we were. In fact, returning to live in my parents' house had unmoored me. Preoccupied by my own sense of displacement and my fantasies of the house that might await us in the future, I'd neglected the life that was ours to live in the here and now.

There was no way to know for sure what had caused the hermit crabs, all four of them, to die, but I felt responsible. It had been a long time since we'd taken them out to play or cleaned their box, days since I had given them a thought at all. Perhaps Jack had forgotten to feed them, but I had forgotten to ask. Their water bowl was dry.

When Jack got back from school that day, we buried the crabs beneath the apple tree in the field, alongside all the dogs and cats of my childhood. We washed the empty shells and put them on the windowsill, so that Ben and Jerry and Oscar and Meyer would not be forgotten. I cleaned the fish tank and carried it down to my parents' basement. For now, anyway, home was right here, and it needed tending. Or rather, the crabs' demise had reminded me, home is less a location than a discipline.

It is a way of being, a domestic, considered attention to familiar routines and the small, essential details of everyday life. From now on, I promised myself, home would be wherever I was, not the place that I one day hoped to be. I would create it by being present. I would try to do better.

In a month or so from now, our own house will be finished, and the boxes we packed so carefully more than three years ago, without knowing where they would finally end up, will be opened at last. The eleven-year-old who begged to stay forever in his bedroom with clouds on the walls is nearly fifteen. At five feet ten inches, he towers over me. Yet every once in a while, I catch a glimmer of that little boy who didn't ever want his life to change. Eager as he is to get on with things now, to move into our own house and to begin high school in a new town, he's a bit apprehensive, too.

"Do you think I'll do well in high school?" Jack asked me a few days ago. I considered for a moment, not wanting to answer too quickly. For while Henry found his own home away from home right away, in a high school he embraced wholeheartedly and that returned the gesture, Jack has flailed and fought his way into adolescence. At times, it has felt as if he might drag the rest of us right down into the pit with him, so pervasive was his sense of loss and injustice, so infuriating was his descent into the black hole of puberty, and so dim, at times, seemed our prospects of ever finding our way back to a normal, reasonably harmonious family life.

But as I sit on the bleachers of his new high school and picture him running a basketball up the gymnasium floor, imagine him charging in for a layup or high-fiving a teammate, I allow myself to hope.

There have been times over the last two years when daily life with my younger son has been so difficult that I've wanted to scream, or give up, or pack a bag and run away from home. The truth is, I have screamed. I've despaired, at moments, of both my children's futures and worried that their adolescent short-comings portend disastrous personality flaws for their adult selves. But it is Jack's struggles to grow up that have kept me awake at night, wondering how to move beyond our dispiriting battles over clothes on the floor, the inappropriateness of certain movies and video games, endless showers, undone chores, general rudeness, laziness, and apathy. I've seen and railed against the worst in my brilliant, funny, relentlessly oppositional teenage son. In the process, I confess, he has brought out the worst in me.

One grim morning, when Jack was thirteen, I hid his huge black sweatshirt rather than watch him head off to school one more time in that sinister garment with its dangling arms and knee-length hem. I pointed out that his closet was full of perfectly good, right-sized shirts and sweaters, never worn. He was outraged. The only acceptable apparel was the baggy, beloved sweatshirt, the sweatshirt I refused to surrender to him. The lines of battle were drawn then, and the two of us went hard at it.

Perhaps there were weeks of pent-up tension and frustration being released that morning; I couldn't honestly say now. I've blocked much of the scene from my mind, so painful is this memory. I do know that we both slammed doors, threatened, hurled vicious insults and ultimatums. When Jack shouted through sobs, "You can't hide my clothes, Mom, that is totally sick," I knew he was right, but I didn't cave. What I mostly remember is this: We both went completely crazy over something utterly innocuous. A sweatshirt, for heaven's sake. I remember how scared I was by how awful we were.

Somehow, Jack went to school that day, bruised and fragile, eyes still swollen with tears, wearing the hideous sweatshirt that I finally pulled out of the paper bag in my parents' laundry room where I'd hidden it. But no one won the fight. By the time I picked him up that afternoon, we were ready to call an exhausted, wary truce. We drove to Target and he found two new oversize sweatshirts that he could bear to be seen in, one green, the other gray.

During the year of the sweatshirt, Jack also refused to cut his hair. He grew himself a large 'fro, and he, his father, and I fought bitter battles over that, too, as his sweet little-boy cowlicks grew into wiry, ever longer corkscrews that stuck out wildly in all directions. All through the second half of seventh grade, he nursed his head of outrageous curls, protected them, was hugely offended by the mere suggestion of a trim. And it seemed to me that his smile, always ready, grew fainter as his hair grew longer. Sometimes I wondered if it was gone for good.

Meanwhile, he covered the walls of his room with posters featuring skulls and words that dripped with blood, musicians with pierced, carved, tattooed bodies, black-rimmed eyes, and shaved heads. He drew weird symbols in ink all over his arms and the bottoms of his shoes. He spent hours in his bedroom with the door closed, listening to music that made my teeth ache. His favorite band was Disturbed; his favorite song, "Stricken." That seemed to describe all of us pretty well. One day, in a rare amiable moment, he said without inflection, "It's really amazing that you and I are related, since we have absolutely nothing in common." I had to agree.

Playing out this drama under my parents' watchful eyes only made it worse. Although they were for the most part sympathetic, all my antennae were up, alert to the slightest hint of their disapproval. Much as they tried to stay out of the fray, as their lively, precocious grandson molted into a defiant, sullen adolescent, they could not have been deaf to the voices raised behind closed doors or oblivious to our silent fury at the dinner table. And all the while, I was certain my own mother and father must be wondering, Why on earth can't they manage their son?

Perhaps what I loved most about being with my sons when they were small was the daily opportunity to witness their blissful relationship with the universe, that unconscious, wide-open connection with the sublime that is the special realm of childhood. Young children have precious little awareness of themselves in relation to the world at large; they are just in it. And if we're lucky, and paying attention, we parents get to reexperience some of that innocence and freedom ourselves, seeing the world anew through their eyes.

The year Jack turned twelve was the summer we lived in the red cottage, the summer we found ourselves first reluctant to commit to the place and then, in spite of ourselves, surprised and enchanted by its dilapidated charm. Among the house's many peculiarities was the minuscule flamingo pink bathroom off the kitchen, with its antique claw-foot tub. For the rest of us, the tub was an annoyance. Every time you wanted to shower, you had to arrange half a dozen large chip clips to hold the three plastic shower curtains closed and then hunch under the spray while washing with one hand. But for Jack, still a regular soaker, the tub was a nightly treat.

All that halcyon summer, he rode his bike to town, hit golf balls off a tee in the yard, drew pictures, read comics and Stephen King novels on the screened porch. At night, while I cooked dinner just steps away, he'd steep, sloshing off the day's dirt in the tub. Sometimes he'd ask me to come sit and keep him company. It's what we had always done.

One night as he chatted happily away, I looked down at his long, smooth body in the water, deeply tanned and still utterly childlike, and suddenly I knew—this could well be the last time. Surely he was on the brink of self-consciousness. Any day now he would demand his privacy, and this old ritual, too, would end. So instead of dashing back to the kitchen to wash salad greens, I settled myself on the toilet seat and listened. When the long bath was done, I dried my son's pruney skin, his body as familiar to me as my own. I rubbed his head, smoothed sesame bath oil into his thin shoulder blades, down his brown arms and legs, bundled him up in a huge towel, wrapped him in my arms, and kissed his damp forehead. This is it, I thought, the absolute sweet spot of motherhood—these unguarded moments of pure intimacy, love assumed, the delicious hour when time slows at the end of a day and parents and children come together, reweaving their connections with one another. It was just a child's bath, one of hundreds I'd presided over, but I was blessed that night with the prescience to stop and be grateful, to notice and cherish every detail.

The very next day, an older girl asked Jack's best friend to go out with her, and the axis of his world tilted. The proposed date never happened, but the question itself, much discussed among the boys, catapulted my son from innocence into awareness. If he and his buddies were old enough to get phone calls from girls, then by extension he was definitely and absolutely too old to take a bath in front of his mom. The bathroom door swung shut for good. By the time school started that fall, he was under full hormonal assault.

Waldorf high school teacher Betty Staley observes that as children grow up and lose their unconscious connection to the world, they experience a powerful shift in identity and withdraw into themselves. "They lose the world to find themselves," she says, "and with this loss they experience loneliness." At the time I couldn't see it, but of course Jack and I both lost something precious and irrevocable in his passage from childhood into adolescence.

My days of mothering young children were really and truly over, and that was hard to bear. His life as a little boy was over, too, and that was also hard. Neither of us slipped easily into this new way of being. Perhaps it is the rare mother and son who do. But for us it seemed as if all the old ways, our intimacy, the very essence of our relationship, had to shatter first and lie in pieces. We were raw, and each of us was hurting. So I didn't grasp then what seems so obvious now, in hindsight: The intense need for solitude, the black, oversize clothes, the brutal music, the general withdrawal from life as we'd always known it, were essential to my son's survival through a period of enormous physical and emotional change.

Caterpillars spin cocoons in which to metamorphose into butterflies. Teenagers, it seems, need to create for themselves the same kind of transformational space in which to do the hard, private work of growing up. They can't retreat into a tough, hairy case, but they do find their ways, leaving behind all that once was beloved and disappearing for a while into a place that is, for all intents and purposes, out of our reach.

Our older son, always quiet, arrived on the threshold of puberty and simply turned away from us, as if in a kind of self-imposed solitary confinement. Taciturn as a monk, he didn't disrupt the rhythm of our daily life so much as vanish from it, spending hours alone in this room, initiating conversations with no one, emerging only to go to school, play piano, or watch a baseball game on TV. We worried that he was depressed, wondered if something was wrong, asked in vain if he was happy, found ourselves at a loss to do anything but wait him out.

Writer Anne Lamott says that when her funny, mellow son Sam turned thirteen, the plates of the earth shifted, and suddenly in her heretofore peaceful house "there was the Visitor, the Other. I called him Phil. Phil was tense. Also sullen and contemptuous." Desperate, she taped a card to her wall to remind herself: "You can either practice being right, or practice being kind." What I found was that being right didn't do a bit of good and being kind was really, really hard.

Most days, Jack wrestled with the existential tension between himself and the world by posting a "Keep Out" sign on his door and crawling into bed. Unbeknownst to his father and me, he watched three entire seasons of *Lost* on his iPod that winter, making quite a mockery of our limits on TV, which of course were well-known to him. The general mess and grisly decor he effected in his bedroom succeeded in making it feel off-limits to everyone else. The deafening, dissonant music was an affront. Nightly back rubs and bedtime chats stopped. The intimacy we'd always enjoyed evaporated, replaced by anger and hurt feelings and separation. His temper was unpredictable. School sucked. Everything hurt.

The boy who had always run fast, couldn't. His ankles were gimpy, his legs ached. He lost interest in sports and had no strength for them anyway. He was growing so quickly that his ligaments, stretched too far, couldn't keep up. Even the slightest task seemed to demand too much energy. He lay around all day, wasted time, stayed up too late, talked back, tunneled through boxes of cereal and tubs of ice cream in the middle of the night. He snuck onto the computer after we'd all gone to bed, played video games, and left every school project to the last possible minute. He lost his homework or forgot to do it. He drove us crazy.

These were tense months. Furious as I was at my younger son, I was even angrier at myself for failing so miserably at every attempt at effective mothering. One day, at wits' end, I confided to a friend that my son had turned into a stranger to me, a person I could barely stand to be in a room with. "He's thirteen!" she said with the knowing smile of one whose children are grown, "it's his job to be an asshole." And then she advised, "Just say yes as often as you can, and save your no's for when you really need them. And keep a sense of humor. It will be easier on both of you."

Slowly, finally, I started to get it: Though subtle from one day to the next, the transformation my son was undergoing during that year truly was astonishing. Bones, hair, muscle, lips, teeth, eyes—it was as if he were being remade from scratch into a completely new human being. And who wouldn't be scared and undone by that? I began to see that in fact this passage was as hard on Jack as it was on the rest of us. That perhaps my husband and I weren't the only ones who were afraid, worrying about just what kind of person our cranky, difficult son might turn out to be. He was probably worried, too.

And once I started to figure that out, I also started to soften up a bit. I did try to say yes more often. I practiced being kind. Old rules, clearly outdated now, came up for renegotiation. The fourth season of *Lost* emigrated from the bedroom and onto the family TV, where Jack and his dad could watch together and then talk about it—more satisfying for both of them.

When I looked at my son, I suddenly began to see beyond the black knit hat pulled low over his forehead and into his beautiful dark eyes instead. Instead of objecting to his clothes, I reminded myself that beneath those huge, dark, ugly layers beats a fragile heart, as vulnerable and frightened as my own. Rather than steering clear of his presence, I began deliberately to seek him out and to reclaim him, bit by bit, with back rubs and tenderness. To my surprise, I grew rather fond of his hair.

A week before his graduation from eighth grade, Jack said it was time for a haircut, and then he went and got his head buzzed. Most of the other things we'd fought over so bitterly for months seemed to vanish in pretty much the same way. Or else they just didn't seem to matter so much anymore, to anyone. We had all moved on.

Jack has grown a startling five or six inches in the last two years. For the first time in his life, he outgrows his clothes before he wears them out. Yet the real growth is mostly invisible. Over the last few months, the angry, miserable fourteen-year-old has turned into someone else altogether.

The boy who will arrive for his first day at school tomorrow is a tall, handsome freshman who favors close-fitting T-shirts that show off his newly developed physique. (When someone gave him a black sweatshirt for Christmas last year, he said politely, "Black isn't really my color. It's a little depressing. But maybe I can exchange it.") He favors lively colors, jeans that aren't too distressed, short hair. He looks fantastic.

Certain that his path is not the same as his brother's, Jack has made his own choices—public school, the most challenging schedule possible, a full load of freshman honors classes, cross-country running in the afternoons. And so, when he asks in all earnestness if I think he will do well in high school, I tell him the truth. "That's really going to be up to you. You've grown up a lot over the last couple of years," I say. "You've changed. And now you're lucky to be getting a fresh start, in a school where no one knows anything about you. If you're willing to work hard and do your best, I'm sure you will do well."

Every morning for the last week, Jack has risen at seven, pulled on shorts and a pair of sneakers, and subjected himself to two and a half hours of conditioning and running. When he hobbled home, exhausted, after the first day of practice, I was sure he'd never go back. He did. A few weeks ago, Jack spent a day at my computer, loading music onto his iPod. Classic jazz—Wes Montgomery, Miles Davis, Herbie Hancock. When we went to pick out a cell phone for him, he scanned the expensive models, then said that the basic one would be fine and programmed it with a Count Basie ring tone. These days, we have a few things—actually, more than a few things—in common.

The emotion I most remember from that very difficult year and a half of black clothing and blacker moods, in addition to the anger and helplessness I often felt, is fear. It seemed as if the boy we'd known and raised had disappeared. The teenager who moved in to take his place was a stranger, and not a likable one. I think my husband and I were both terrified that the person who sulked down to breakfast every morning was it, the alien replacement we were doomed to live with forever. Looking into the future, I saw nothing but long, bleak years of fighting with a surly individual who let it be known daily that he could not endure our company. So miserable were we that the whole idea of "family life" began to seem like a cruel joke, an idealized past now lost to us for good. Some days, though Steve and I struggled to uphold the illusion of civility, barely a kind word was spoken in our midst.

Life with Jack is not all sweetness and light now, but it does seem as if we've come out the other end of a dark tunnel into a little patch of sunshine. I wish I could say that in a flash of wisdom we suddenly figured out how to relate to a teenage boy or that our son woke up one day and found himself back in sync with the world. But life is never that simple. All I'm really certain of is that communication between the generations in our family got ugly and confusing for a time, we made one another truly miserable, and none of us handled it very well. For the moment anyway, we're doing better. And along the way I think I've at least learned something about how very imperfect parents and their very imperfect adolescent children can coexist under one roof.

When we focus on what is good and beautiful in someone, whether or not we think that they "deserve" it, the good and beautiful are strengthened merely by the light of our attention. When we choose to see and appreciate what is good and beautiful in our children, that goodness can't help but grow, and their beauty blossoms forth.

Sometimes it is a long, slow flowering. Sometimes it is necessary, as Galway Kinnell has written, "to reteach a thing its loveliness, to put a hand on its brow of the flower, and retell it in words and in touch it is lovely until it flowers again from within, of self-blessing."

I keep a copy of Kinnell's poem under the stack of bills and papers on my desk. A friend of mine, who has struggled for many years with her daughter's panic attacks and mood swings, does the same. "It reminds me," she says, "not to yell. It reminds me to put a hand on the brow instead." I know exactly what she means. Whenever I think of it, I slide the poem out onto my own desk, to help me remember: Everything "flowers again from within, of self-blessing."

It is always a relief to be reminded that my job is not to control, or judge, or change my son, but simply to help him

remember, with words and touch, who he really is. Loving him
this way, I am better able to find within myself the faith and
patience necessary to survive his painful transformations. I
know to hold a space for his beauty, even when it slips from
sight. And I come a little bit closer to understanding his true
essence, to remembering the goodness that resides just beneath
the surface of even his very worst behavior, behavior that is
usually rooted in fear and confusion and self-protection.

Not a day goes by that Jack and I don't disagree about something, for he is a teenager and I am his mom. Often, he feels
confined, and that I'm the one confining him. He wishes that
I would just quit setting limits and insisting on consequences.
What I see as protection he easily mistakes for punishment. Yet
I would also say that we have more to talk about now than ever
before. He sees into the hidden depths of things, and I like listening to his take on the world, which is always totally different
from mine. He knows I'm interested. Most of the time, we get
along.

This week, our family has split up, Steve and Henry still at my
parents' house for Henry's first week of his senior year, Jack and
I spending nights at a vacationing friend's condo around the
corner from his new high school. For the next month or so, until
our house is ready for us to live in, we'll be juggling these conflicting schedules and commuting fifty miles a day to get everyone where they need to be. But for now, Jack and I have a
place to ourselves just minutes from his school. I've stocked my
friend's kitchen with teenage-boy fare—bagels and cream cheese
and chips and juice, cereal and orange sherbet and peanut
butter.

But more than that, I've cleared a space around the beginning of his high school career, arranged things so that even in

the midst of house finishing and moving preparations, these first important days will be free of distractions for both of us. I want him to know that I take his life, and this new beginning, seriously. He has been trying hard to be nonchalant, but we both know it—tomorrow is a big day.

When the parent meeting is over, I slip out of the steamy gym and drive up the hill to my friend's small condo, where Jack is waiting for me. "Come look at this," he says, leading me downstairs to a basement storage room. There, my friend has a bookcase crammed full of children's books, saved from her own son's childhood and all well-known to Jack and me. "They have all our favorites," Jack points out, pulling books from the shelves—*McElligot's Pool*, and *Thidwick the Big-Hearted Moose*, and *Frog and Toad*, and *Owl at Home*.

It's been three years since we packed up our own cache of beloved picture books, longer still since any of us so much as looked at them. But finding this treasure trove of dear, familiar titles on a basement bookshelf is like running into old friends on a dark street in a foreign city. We're delighted. What happens then is one of those miracles of mothering, completely unexpected and, to me, at least, magical.

Jack suggests that we take a few of these "old chestnuts" upstairs and give them a read. We're here alone, and there is nothing else to do, so my teenage son and I spend the last evening of his summer vacation side by side on my friend's small, high-backed sofa with Dr. Seuss and Arnold Lobel for company.

Tomorrow, he will walk away from me and into his new life as a high schooler. But for a little while tonight we are just a mother and child, reading aloud. It is so rare and unexpected— as if a bird had suddenly come to alight on my finger—that at first I barely dare to breathe, for fear of breaking the spell. But by the time we've laughed our way through a couple of Dr. Seuss classics and turned to Arnold Lobel's *Grasshopper on the Road,* we're playing our old roles, switching off to read the way we used to do when Jack was first learning to sound out the words, each of us coming up with our own funny voices for all the characters—the insistent mosquito, the busy housefly, the butterflies who insist that every day be exactly the same as the one before.

If change has been the theme of our family life over these last few years, it has also been our challenge. And no one has found that challenge harder to meet than my younger son, who mourned the loss of each familiar foothold and fought his way through his own painful transformation from child to teenager.

One thing we've all learned along the way is that reinvention seems always to require some painful elements of rejection and tearing down. But as we change, so do all things change. To hold on tight is to miss out on opportunities for growth and movement. Letting go, stepping forward into the unknown, we discover our capacities for resilience and faith, and we begin to glimpse our unique potential, to realize it in ways we couldn't have begun to imagine just a short time ago.

Now, as Jack and I read *Grasshopper on the Road,* I wonder if he's getting the message. When the adventurous Grasshopper meets a trio of butterflies who do exactly the same things every day, he is incredulous.

"Don't you ever change anything?" asked Grasshopper.

"No, never," said the butterflies. "Each day is fine for us." And then they insist that he join them in their unchanging routine.

"Grasshopper," said the butterflies,
"we like talking to you.

We will meet you every day at this time.
We will sit on this mushroom.
You will sit right there.
We will tell you all about
our scratching and our flying
We will tell you all about
our napping and our dreaming.
You will listen just the way
you are listening now."
"No," said Grasshopper.
"I am sorry,
but I will not be here.
I will be moving on.
I will be doing new things."

"I think kids' books are really as much for grown-ups as for kids," Jack says when we finish reading this one, "because most of this stuff is just lost on you when you're little." I know exactly what he means. And I feel lucky that, poised here together on this threshold between my son's childhood and a new chapter of his young adulthood, we have found some useful spiritual guidance in the pages of an I Can Read Book.

At seven-fifteen the next morning, I drop off my freshman son in the parking lot of the high school, then watch till he disappears with a crowd of other teenagers through the front door. I don't expect to cry, but as soon as he's out of sight, I do. I remember as if it were yesterday how I slipped his small hand from mine at the nursery school door and tiptoed down the hallway, leaving him behind. I cried in the parking lot that day, too, for the end of his babyhood and the loss of our day-in, day-out time together, though at the same time I was ecstatic to finally have two school-age children and a few hours each morning to myself. Now, a decade later, the good-bye feels just as wrenching, this change as poignant and bittersweet—and as necessary—as every other. I know now how quickly four years of high school pass, know that it won't be long at all before this brief chapter, too, is over and my younger son will be heading off for freshman year at a college away from home.

We've had more than our share of struggles, this boy and I, and no doubt there will be more to come. Certainly we've said and done things that we've both regretted later. Right now, though, what I feel is not regret for all those past mistakes, or even apprehension about what's around the corner, but gratitude that we've come this far together and ended up here, sharing this step into his future by pausing long enough to reclaim some cherished moments from his childhood.

During his first week of high school, Jack writes all his assignments in a notebook, gets up early, runs seven miles through the woods each afternoon. He goes through three T-shirts a day, eats hugely, and struggles with the rigors of honors math. And then, just before bed each night, we grab a few more old children's books from the basement and read aloud, his big curly head on my shoulder. Surely he would die if anyone knew. Yet these intimate moments at the end of the day are balm for both our souls.

By the end of the week, Jack knows his way around the building, has made a few friends, has a regular lunch table crowd. He likes his classes and his teachers, senses that whatever they ask of him this year, he'll be up to the challenge. That's all good. And so, in high spirits, we pack our bags after school and running practice on Friday afternoon and head back over the mountain to my parents' house, where it's time at last to begin packing for real, sorting through three years' worth of accumulation and an enormous pile of boxes—and deciding just what bits and pieces of our old life will have a place in the new.

On Sunday afternoon, I poke my head inside Jack's bedroom to see how he's coming along. The music is loud, the floor is littered with clothes and candy wrappers, and the old Disturbed posters are coming down from the walls. Jack rolls them all up together and snaps a rubber band around the tube.

"I don't want to put anything up on my new walls for a while," he says, dropping the posters into a storage box labeled "Jack's Old Stuff." I invite myself in and sit on the bed, to watch for a few minutes as he takes the room apart, this place that has been both battlefield and cocoon over the last three years. He's not an orderly packer, but he's getting the job done in his own way. After a little while, he comes to the hermit crab shells, lined up in a row on the windowsill.

"Remember Ben and Jerry and Oscar and Meyer?" he asks. We look at the shells for a minute, trying to recall who lived where. And then, these too go into the "Old Stuff" box, to be packed away in our new basement along with all the other relics of a past that Jack no longer needs to revisit every day, but that is still, and always will be, a part of who he is. It seems pretty clear now that he, like Grasshopper, is ready to be moving on.

~ 10 ~

home

A voyage to a destination, wherever
it may be, is also a voyage inside oneself;
even as a cyclone carries along with it the
center in which it must ultimately come to
rest. At these moments I think not only of the
places I have been to, but also of the
distances I have traveled within myself
without a friend or ship; and of the long
way yet to go before I come home within
myself and within the journey.

—LAURENS VAN DER POST

*Y*ou arrive at our front door through a tangle of garden. And
this is how I, too, first make my way to the threshold of our
nearly done house. While carpenters finish nailing baseboards
to walls, while painters brush second coats of Windham Cream
on window trim and stair risers, I am on my knees outside the
kitchen, digging in the dirt. Eager for something to tend, I
begin the work of housekeeping here by weeding and thinning
what remains of the old fern-choked garden bed along the
stone wall.

When questions arise about the final dimension of a chair
rail or the delivery of the stove, I'm close by enough to answer.

But mostly I am here because I can't bear to be anyplace else. As each mild September day brings us closer to our long awaited move, I run errands for the carpenters, try to spur them on with coffee and homemade muffins, and pick up construction trash from the yard. Inside, the empty rooms beckon, filled with light and promise.

Soon, we will return for good to this spot, lay our heads to rest for the first time in the upstairs bedrooms, and begin to etch new scenes of family life upon the empty canvas of pale green walls, bare pine floors, and tall blank windows. Until then, I find the sense of purpose I need, and a kind of emotional sustenance as well, in the creation of a garden.

Home, as Wendell Berry points out, is not just a building but an enactment. It is the alchemy by which wood and glass and stone, field and mountain and sky, are transformed by domesticity. Home is the sharp-scented rosemary plant by the front step, the view from the living room window, a friend's painting propped upon the mantelpiece. If these three nomadic years have taught me anything, it is that only a small part of being home is the house itself. It is also how we choose, over time, to imbue a place with meaning, how we inhabit the spaces we claim—making the beds, cleaning the refrigerator, and adorning the walls; offering dinner to a friend, sweeping the garage, staking the peonies in May, shoveling the walkways after snow.

Home, I know, will emerge slowly in the months to come. It will be revealed as we live in this stark, new space, soften its edges and make it our own, the small details of ordinary life accruing, day by day and night by night, into new family stories, myths, and memories.

But now, as we await the finishing touches and the building inspector's final nod of approval, the landscaping is my project. More than our weary, overextended builder is willing to take on, the outdoor work is something I can oversee myself in order to keep things moving along. The goal is to make the new house, built on the same spot where its predecessor stood for the last two centuries, look as if it has been here forever. The plan is to bring in enough dirt and fill to get the house hunkered down low to the ground, so that a casual passerby might not even quite notice the switch.

Two years ago, I found the demolition partner we needed in the very nick of time. Since then, just as eQuanimiti predicted, the partners we've wished for have always appeared—at times, it seems, as if by magic. The house has emerged not just from our vision, or even from the architect's graceful design, but from the efforts of a small handful of craftsmen I've come to see as our creative partners in this enterprise—the right people, heaven-sent, I sometimes think, showing up at just the right moment.

There was André, who spent a cold November Saturday in the woods behind my parents' house, choosing each piece of granite for the fireplace. For weeks afterward, with crowbars and ropes and boards, chisels and hammers, he shaped each stone by hand to create a massive, elegant jigsaw puzzle made of rock. Granite slabs harvested from my childhood home found their place alongside foundation pieces saved from the old red cottage, resulting in a hearth that tells its own story of home through pieces of stone. When I showed up midway through, lugging canvas bags full of rocks from our favorite cove in Maine, he worked those in as well.

Romeo, the master carpenter who originally turned down the job, arrived unexpectedly on a gleaming white motorcycle one afternoon just as we were wondering who might have the expertise to build the stairway. He'd changed his mind, he explained, quit his new desk job, and wanted to know if he might still be helpful here. Over the next months, he not only crafted stairs with mathematical precision, but also devised fine, subtle solutions for every carpentry problem that arose.

In the humid heat of July, Steve Graves returned as promised, dripping sweat and full of enthusiasm, his black pickup truck bristling with battered scraps of trim and molding scavenged at the dump. He had our old cupboard doors in the back, a few filthy, rough-hewn barn boards we'd hauled out of my parents' shed, bags full of rusted black hardware saved from the red house, a pair of tall, narrow windows crusty with ancient layers of paint.

No one else saw the makings of a pantry in this heap of bits and pieces, but we'd learned to trust the partners when they appeared, so we gave him free rein in the cramped storage nook near the kitchen. What he created there, working alone in the middle of the night when the house was quiet, is a most fitting homage to the old red cottage, yet supremely practical as well, with its multitude of hooks and shelves and cupboards, every-thing old yet ingeniously resuscitated in service to the new.

A few weeks ago, looking at our house so garishly pro-claiming its newness from atop a tall, gray cement foundation, I wondered how we could possibly coax this present-day con-struction into harmony with the two-hundred-year-old stone walls that surrounded it. All the landscape designers I called were booked into next year, way beyond our budget, or both. Finally, on a friend's advice, I phoned Jimmy R., a mason spe-cializing in New England fieldstone walls. He, too, was sched-uled for months to come. But the next day, Jimmy called me back with second thoughts. "Why don't I come on over to your place and take a look," he suggested. "Maybe I could help."

There are many days of house building that I choose now to

forget, mistakes made along the way that never did get fixed, crises that weren't resolved to anyone's satisfaction, and a few people we hired to our later and lasting regret. But when I meet Jimmy one early morning, and he says that he'll juggle things around so that he can work with me here, starting two days from now, I know that we've been blessed yet again with a good partner.

Jimmy arrives each morning with the sun, just in time to watch it slide silently into view from behind the mountains. He likes that time here all by himself, he says, so that he can look at the stones, walk the land, and think through the day's work in peace. By the time I show up an hour or two later, he is on his blue tractor, pushing dirt around or moving boulders.

Our landscape design is intuitive, originating not with sketches on a piece of paper, but with whatever inspiration the day brings and then growing out of what's already here—the contours of the earth, the piles of stone and foundation pieces saved from the old house and a barn that vanished long before our time. For doorsteps, we return to my parents' place, where over the years my father has excavated long slabs of granite from the edge of the stone quarry in the woods beyond his house.

With the help of neighbors down the road, Jimmy lifts these venerable, lichen-encrusted trophies out of my parents' dooryard and nestles them into permanent spots here in ours. From there, he works outward, spreading truckloads of dirt and sand to bring the grade of the land up to meet the house, moving and rebuilding the old stone walls and creating new ones, re-shaping and smoothing the earth so that, at last, our house begins to look less like a job site and more like a place where people might live.

All through September, I drop Jack at school and then head to the house to confer with Jimmy on the day's agenda, which we make up as we go along. I imagine low-growing blueberry bushes right beneath the kitchen windows, so he digs a trench there and fills it with rich, dark dirt. One day, as he fits large, flat pieces of stone into place for a walkway to the front door, we realize that the kitchen door needs its own path and that the small space between the two entries would be a perfect spot for a garden.

It is late in the year for planting, but there is nothing I can do inside the house until the carpenters are finished, so I order a few yards of compost and begin to work it into the ground. I beg plants from friends' abundant gardens, cruise the end-of-season sale at the hardware store, and let the new kitchen garden emerge by serendipity—nothing fancy, nothing that would have surprised a gardener here a century ago, phlox and bee balm and purple salvia, coneflower and black-eyed Susans dug from a field across the road.

From the edge of the patio at my mother's house, I scoop small clumps of creeping thyme, to press between the stones on the kitchen path. Pleased by the continuity of gardens, and the idea that her garden will help give birth to mine, I help myself to some leggy, late summer stalks of mint and oregano as well. I buy the very last of the blueberry bushes from a roadside nursery, at a bargain price, dig mounds of catmint from beneath a friend's window, and transplant old peonies that have no doubt bloomed here for decades into new spots more to my liking.

It feels like a homecoming. Choosing plants for the new garden, thinning the ancient lilac bushes by the side of the road, settling our old, weathered Buddha into place beneath a low-hanging branch, I fall in love with the idea of working in concert with the land. Learning to live well in a place is a subtle

vocation, but I suspect already that it may be work for a lifetime. To begin, at last, is a great relief.

And so, impatient as I am to settle into our house, I try to
see these last few weeks as a gift of time in their own right.
The heavy lifting of moving in and setting up housekeeping
will begin soon enough. For now, though, that timetable is
beyond our control. The big decisions have all been made,
school has begun again, the weather is beautiful. And there is
plenty to do.

Day by day, season by season, I want to learn to read this
landscape, to grow familiar with each aspect of the abiding,
ever changing view, to know each rock and tree and fragile
flower. There is, I remind myself, no more direct pathway to
peace, no simpler way to encounter beauty, no better way of
slowing down, than to try to practice devotion right where I
am, doing each day's tasks as they come and building a life
around what is already here.

Out of respect for the tenacious plants that have thrived
along the edges of the old yard for years without benefit of
human care, I enter gradually into my new relationship with
this land, regard the patch of fresh black dirt outside the kitchen
with humility and a bit of hesitation. There is a casual, overgrown character to the original garden beds that have survived
along the crumbling stone walls, and having razed the old
house, I am reluctant to wreak any more havoc here. It seems
important to preserve the sense of timeless, incidental serenity
that drew me so powerfully to this spot three years ago.

I set about these first chores slowly, dividing the thick, inter-
laced roots of lilies and moving clumps of fern, pruning out the
dead, dry underbranches of a gnarled laurel, allowing the yellow
stalks of goldenrod to abide, for now, exactly where they are.
Someday, maybe, I will exert more dominance over these wild,

neglected beds, but amid all the newness here, I am inclined to spare every modest survivor from the past.

One afternoon, the architect shows up, casts a dubious eye upon the scraggly little blueberry bushes beneath the kitchen window, and suggests that I call a garden designer he knows for some professional help. I've already sensed that he's less than enthusiastic about Jimmy's improvisations with the backhoe, his spontaneously executed retaining walls and casual approach to following a plan. Now, as I explain my vision of a garden right outside the door, filled with kitchen herbs and old-fashioned perennials, I realize that he's pretty certain I have no clue what I'm doing. Clearly, he'd been hoping for something more sophisticated, at the very least a few orderly foundation plantings to complement his spare farmhouse design. I take the number he offers and, my confidence shaken a little, promise to make the call.

I should be used to partners showing up by now, but Maude catches me by surprise. Tiny as a wren, she is a sinewy, sun-browned wisp of a woman in baggy blue jeans, with a kind, sweet smile and dark, gentle eyes. For an hour one morning, we wander around the dusty, torn-up yard together as I de-scribe my intentions. Mostly, she listens, nods her head, and agrees. She is quiet, knowing, the opposite of pushy. Her gen-erous presence and wise observations remind me how much I've missed the easy, everyday companionship of women. If I had a teapot, running water, and a cup, I would invite her in for tea.

Instead, we circle the house, musing about what might be. Her passion for form and texture, her deep understanding of color, rhythm, and mood, belie an artist's sensibility. When she tells me that she has been a weaver, a painter, and a bookmaker, I'm not surprised. At midlife, after years of working in a bookstore, raising a daughter, trying to carve out time for art, for gardens, for the gardens of friends, she'd realized that it was time to allow her calling to become her livelihood.

Gardens are more than living tapestries or temporal canvases, she'd come to see, more than a means of earthly sustenance or self-expression—they are doorways into spiritual growth and healing. We are standing in the shade of the maple tree, lost in conversation, having gone way beyond the hour consultation I'd requested. Now, regretfully, I explain that we don't really have any money to hire a garden designer at the moment but that someday I truly hope we can work together.

Yet it seems that we aren't quite finished. Before long, we're talking about books we love, writing and reading, hiking trails, and the tiny cabin she and her husband built by hand on a lake in Maine. I am wishing that I could hire Maude to help me create a garden, just to enjoy her company, to learn from her, and to continue our conversation, which feels as if it's just getting started. And then, as we walk slowly back to her car and I dig in my pocket for cash to pay her, it suddenly occurs to me—the two of us could be friends. In fact, it feels as if we already are.

I've often wondered if I would ever find deep, enduring friendship in this small, close-knit country town, where it seems that everyone already knows everyone else, bound by common memories and a local history that I was not a part of and can never hope to absorb. With no babies to pave my way at mothers' groups or playgrounds, no small children to draw me into school committees or chaperone duties, I've worried that I might be too late, that no new midlife connection could begin to match the intimacy of our old suburban neighborhood or the passion and urgency my friends and I once shared through the daily struggles of motherhood, comparing notes on our efforts to juggle jobs and kids and spouses while still making time for our own intense, confessional relationships with one another.

But as Maude's blue car disappears down the road, I suspect that this partnership won't be a professional one after all, that we won't need garden designs to bring us together again. I turn and walk back toward the house with a light step, aware that my life here is already deepening, acquiring new layers, resonant as a poem. The early September sunshine warms my bare arms. I have lavender, thyme, and sage to plant outside the kitchen this morning, and years and years' worth of work ahead. I'm alone, but far from lonely. In fact, it feels as if the universe has just extended its hand in welcome, to offer the most lovely housewarming gift I can possibly imagine. A friend.

There is one last piece of granite left in the tall grass, and now, more certain of my own instincts, I know exactly where it should go. Jimmy sets two large rocks side by side in the kitchen garden and lowers the long, rectangular piece down upon them. Just the right height for sitting, angled just so toward the broadest view, the bench looks as if it has been there always, a place to pause and watch the clouds drift by, to listen to the drone of bees on a summer's day, to tune in to the steady, eternal rhythm of the universe.

Day by day, the work in the house winds down. There are still bookcases and cabinets to build, a hundred small jobs to complete, but we'll gladly share space with the carpenter; now our goal is simply to meet the building code and get in. We call and postpone the movers four times, but finally, at long last, the end is in sight. Henry's senior year is well under way, Jack has grown used to the long commute early each morning from my parents' house to his new school, the autumn leaves have already turned

color, and the baseball postseason is half over by the time we finally have a certificate of occupancy in hand.

And then, as so often happens in life, the great day turns out
to be somewhat less than glorious. After all the years of dreaming
and pushing toward this moment, after weeks of packing and
preparation, Steve and Henry have, against all probability, won
lottery tickets to a Red Sox playoff game in Boston. Steve offers to sell the tickets, and if it were any other time, any other
thing, I would probably insist.

But we are all too aware that we have begun a year of lasts
and that next year at this time, our baseball-loving son will be
living somewhere else altogether. Any opportunity not seized
now is an opportunity lost for good, so it is easier, easier than
ever before, to know what matters and what doesn't.

It was Henry who made his dad into a baseball fan, his childhood passion for every nuance and detail of the game igniting
a flame in his father. Ask either of them where they've most
enjoyed being father and son over the years, and there's not a
moment's hesitation: Fenway Park. So now the question seems
moot—skip a crucial World Series game in order to lug furniture and sleep in our new house amid the chaos of moving
day? Not likely. Just as the long truck pulls into the driveway,
loaded with every stick of furniture we own, my husband and
son hop in the car and head for Boston, for a baseball game and
a sleepover with friends.

So it happens that Jack and I will spend the first night in the
new house alone, just as we did the last night in the old. Then,
we labored together through the painful, emotional work of a
final parting; this time, the task is physical, but it seems just as
daunting. The finish carpenter is still hammering away, and a
team of burly, fast-moving men are hustling chairs and tables
and boxes in through the door faster than I can think about

where any of them should go. It is unseasonably hot and humid for October, there are still no screens on the wide-open windows, and the whitewashed wooden ceilings teem with opportunistic hornets, drunk on tung oil and sunshine. Fat bluebottle flies bat aimlessly against the freshly painted kitchen walls.

Soon every room is piled high with boxes and jumbled furniture. There are drifts of sawdust on the floors, construction grime coating every surface. Suddenly, stuff we've lived without for so long that we forgot we ever owned it is popping up everywhere, overflowing through the beautiful bare rooms. In the course of just a few hours, we have gone from emptiness and order here to chaos. Hot and panicky, unsure what to tackle first, I haul out the vacuum and go for the top layer of grit.

In the afternoon, salvation appears in the form of my mother, armed with good cheer, sponges and buckets, and ready to assault sinks and toilets and bathroom walls. Jack arrives from school, surveys the mess, and disappears. It's hard to imagine that we'll have bedrooms ready for us to sleep in tonight, but I start opening boxes, hunting down sheets and towels and shower curtains.

A long time ago, when I first began to imagine a different kind of life in a different kind of place, I bought an old-fashioned dish drainer at a flea market, made of heavy dark wire, with a removable trough for silverware. There was no place for this relic on my efficient suburban countertop, so I stashed it on a basement shelf, in the hope that someday, somewhere, it might prove useful. To me, that dish drainer seemed to symbolize simplicity, a gentler pace, the kind of home I aspired to. I imagined a simple kitchen, a farm sink full of soapy water, a view from the window that would lift my heart, and time enough just to stand there, fingers softening into wrinkles, slowly swirling a sponge across a china plate.

My mother had laughed when I told her about this odd purchase; surely I was the first person ever to buy a dish rack in anticipation of a house. But she understood it, too, knew without my saying so that what I was really seeking was not a new way of doing dishes, but a way to live more attentively, with a pause in each day to be still and know the taste of quiet.

There is no real rhyme or reason to the unpacking; I have no idea where anything is. Yet one of the very first things to surface is the brown paper bag containing the dish rack, wrapped in old newspaper, tucked away and forgotten all those years ago. I set it on the grooved, slanted surface of the drainboard beside the sink. The kitchen countertops are made of soft gray soapstone, as is the rectangular country sink, with its gently tipped front and wide, deep bowl. The view of mountains from the window is the view that inscribed itself on my soul the first time I ever saw it. For the first time in our new house, I run cold, clear well water from the kitchen faucet into a coffee mug and drink.

Hundreds of feet below the ground here, water courses along the fault lines of a ledge. In the field below the house, springs send rivulets of water pulsing up from the silent earth, creating patches of mud that last all year. In spring, bobolinks converge upon the weedy, green dampness; come late fall, the first crusts of ice appear across these shallow indentations. It astonishes me to think that the water splashing now into my kitchen sink is drawn up from the ground beyond this very window, its bracing mineral taste a reminder that we will live as dependents on this land, supported by it, and in daily relationship with its mysteries. I rinse the cup, set it upside down in the wire rack, and step back to appreciate this one small thing, a fleeting, seemingly insignificant moment born of a dream from long ago.

Somehow, a change that had its first subtle stirrings years earlier in my imagination has become manifest. A blue pottery mug drips water into furrows of smooth, smoke-colored stone. A shaft of afternoon sunlight turns the kitchen to liquid gold. Dust motes dance and shimmer in the air. The dish rack belongs here.

As darkness falls, I realize that I can't make one more decision, lift one more box, or empty one more pail of filthy water. And that's when my dad shows up with flowers, a bottle of champagne, and an offer of dinner out. My parents, who thought they were giving us a room for a couple of months, have instead shared their house with us for more than three years.

They have attended our sons' school plays and science fairs, Jack's basketball games and Henry's piano recitals. They have helped out with rides, held their tongues when our teenagers were acting like teenagers and through many evenings of late night TV, raucous Ping-Pong games, dropped juggling balls, and loud music pounding through the floorboards. They've seen us through a seventeen-year-old's first car crash, an eighth grader's suspension from school, one window shot out with a BB gun, bruising battles over video games and movies and social plans. Living with my parents through these years of my sons' adolescence, I have a new appreciation of what they went through in the course of mine.

But what also amazes me, as I move out of their home and separate from them all over again, as a middle-aged woman this time rather than as an eighteen-year-old, is how easily they take in stride so many things that used to drive them

nuts, how mellow they are now compared with what I remember. How mellow they are compared with me.

My parents love the two boys who have eaten at their dinner
table night after night as much as my husband and I do, but
they worry about them far less, correct their lapses and mistakes without judgment, without concluding that because our
kids screw up, we have failed to raise them well. They seem
certain, even when Steve and I are full of doubt, that the dark
moments will give way to light and that in the end their two
grandsons will both turn out fine.

I suppose they remember that my brother spent his adolescence sprawled on the couch, watching reruns on TV, while
my father railed at him to get off his butt and make something
of himself. In his own good time, he did, but not before both
of my parents had nearly given up hope that he would ever
turn in a homework assignment on time, let alone earn a living.
At sixteen, I couldn't have imagined ever being as happy to see
my father as I was when he walked through the door of our
new house tonight. I certainly wouldn't have believed that I
would one day, of my own free will, return to live under his
roof, enjoy his company, or feel a pang of regret when it was
time to move out again. By the same token, he might have
been surprised, thirty years ago, to know that I would not always be the evasive, judgmental teenager who skulked past him
every night on the way to her room.

And yet, critical and self-absorbed as I was at seventeen,
furious as he was when I defied his attempts to control what
I wore and where I went, we get along just fine today. So I
suspect that my parents' simple faith in my sons' futures has it
roots in our own family history. They've been through all this
before and know the arc of the story, having learned firsthand
that the long view is usually the better one. Living with them

these last few years, I think I've finally begun to absorb that lesson, too.

It occurs to me now, as Jack and my dad chat over steak dinners on this balmy October evening, that I would do well to take a cue from my older, wiser parents. This afternoon, Jack's idea of unpacking consisted of finding his Xbox, setting it up, piling his video games on a shelf, and plopping down on the sofa to play. For an hour, I felt my irritation building. Couldn't he see how much there was to do? When would he learn to think of someone besides himself? Didn't he know enough to pitch in, instead of waiting for me to insist on it?

And then, although my teenage son didn't suddenly leap up to lend a hand, another kind of help did come my way. I drank that mug of water in the kitchen. I gazed out at the solid, silent mountains beneath a broad expanse of sky. I took a slow, deep breath and stood still, allowing the feeling of being in the right place at last to sink in.

Take the long view, I reminded myself, looking out across the fields to our own long view. Life finds its balance. Children grow up. Second chances come along. In the meantime, I could choose to savor this moment. What good would it do to allow annoyance to interfere with gratitude? My own dear mother—the bane of my existence at seventeen—was downstairs right now, on her knees, scrubbing a bathtub. My son Jack—who surely considered me the bane of his—was just being a teenager, no more or less self-absorbed than I had been at his age.

"We can always choose to perceive things differently," Marianne Williamson has written. "You can focus on what's wrong in your life, or you can focus on what's right." Standing at last in the messy, light-filled kitchen of our own house, surrounded by all the stuff my husband and I had accumulated in the course of twenty years of married life, I understood the truth of these words. My life, all of it, is what it is—today's hornets and over-flowing boxes, my sweet, generous mother and my impassive teenage son, tomorrow's hours of cleaning and unpacking, the bills we have to pay and the debts we somehow have to manage, the many more changes in store, the joys and losses just around the corner. And how I feel about this life, what I make of it in this moment and in all the moments to come, is up to me.

Jimmy had shaped the land around our house by beginning right at the front door and working slowly, deliberately, outward from there. The first day, all he did was fit two huge stones into place, level and straight, good for a hundred years or more. From that step, all the rest of his work followed, until new grade levels blended seamlessly with old, new stone retaining walls met those built two centuries earlier, and slowly, day by day, the house settled into its spot on the earth as if it belonged here and nowhere else.

Watching him at work, I had come to see that what had at first seemed random was in fact wise. Faced with the challenge of a house sitting too far above ground level, a pile of boulders heaved up by the excavators, mountains of construction rubble, and a yard that had been ravaged, he started by placing one stone step in front of the door. He didn't rush. He took the time to do it right.

Later, as I began to think about a garden, I came across some words of advice in an old book on permaculture and sustainable ecosystems. "If you want to know how to control your site," the Australian homesteader wrote, "start at your doorstep."

It is just another way of saying, Narrow your focus and start where you are. Take a good close look at what's right in front of you, and then set to work from there, using what's already at hand. This is what Jimmy had known intuitively about landscaping, even when it came to a couple of acres of raw dirt and a pile of six-hundred-pound pieces of granite. Now I see it makes sense not just as a philosophy for gardening, but as an approach to my own everyday life.

According to my old gardening book, the key to any sustainable system is to be realistic about what you have to work with, and then figure out how to use everything positively. Rather than try to impose our own human will on the landscape, it suggests, observe it closely instead and then learn to work in harmony with what already exists. It occurs to me that such thoughtful observation is a blessing we can bestow not only on the place in which we live, but on the people we love as well. How much better things are when I take the time to work with a son in an obstinate mood rather than against him; when I accept whatever's offered in the present moment rather than turning away or trying to shape it into something else.

"It is easy to love the people far away," as Mother Teresa famously said. "It is not always easy to love those close to us. It is easier to give a cup of rice to relieve hunger than to relieve the loneliness and pain of someone . . . in our own home. Bring love into your home, for this is where our love for each other must start."

If we are going to live the life I've dreamed of in this house, if it is to become a home built not just of walls and beams, but of love and peace, then both the house and the people in it will require steady care and attention. Peace, tolerance, patience, and understanding will have to grow and be nurtured here first, if ever any of us are to carry peace and compassion out into the world beyond our door.

And so, as I stood there by the kitchen sink on moving day, the first thing I did in our new house was make a small, deliberate choice for peace and for the present moment. True, the

setting an intension

day hadn't gone as I'd hoped, with all four of us working shoulder to shoulder, cheerfully setting up beds and celebrating this great milestone. Life would go on. The boxes and piles weren't going to disappear; we'd be unpacking for weeks. There would be time enough for Steve and both of the boys to do their share, time tomorrow to make a schedule and give out to-do lists.

Meanwhile, I could attend to what was right in front of me. I could be thankful that we were here at last and pay attention to all that was good about this day. I could look out the window and heed the mountains' silent reminder: Take the long view, it's almost always better.

Maybe this is the knowledge that time and age bestows. Living in close quarters these last three years, my parents, husband, sons, and I have all been called to summon our best selves, to learn not to sweat the small stuff, and to cultivate tolerance for one another's lapses and idiosyncrasies: Steve's habit of leaving doors and drawers and cupboards open, my father's insistence that the newspaper be folded just so and tucked behind a particular sofa cushion, Henry's way of ripping his bread into tiny pieces, Jack's grouchiness in the morning, my choice of dish towels over paper ones, my mom's preference for dinner at five.

Somehow, we've managed. More than that, we've all learned a thing or two about keeping perspective on our everyday struggles and shortcomings. Now, as my mother and father, my son, and I clink our glasses together at a small outdoor table aglow with candlelight, I realize that the completion of a house is only one of the things we're celebrating here. We are toasting the family we've become as well. The time we've spent together, the stresses and strains of the last few years, have knit us all closer together, shaped us into a different family from the one we were three years ago. We are both more reliant on one another and more generous with one another. More closely connected. Easier, or so I like to think, to live with.

I don't say so, but I can finally admit it to myself—I'm glad the long odyssey from one home to another included a detour, a twist in the road that allowed my parents to watch my sons grow up, that gave my husband a chance to grow closer to his in-laws, and all six of us an opportunity to share the ups and downs of daily life for a while.

After dinner, Jack and I drive up the long, winding hill from town to our dark, silent house. The building is pitch black, looming. We feel our way in through the back door, groping for light switches. Everything is strange. Our voices bounce off the walls, too loud. We find toothbrushes in our overnight bags, run water into the dusty bathroom sinks, rummage for pillows. The desk lamp sitting on Jack's bedroom floor casts weird shadows across his new coffee-colored walls. Someday, this house will comfort us with its well-worn familiarity. Tonight, though, it thrusts us headlong into the unknown. Unsettled, bereft of ritual in this new place, I sit on the edge of my son's bed to say good night.

"I love this house so much," he says, surprising me. "It rocks. And it is going to be really great here when we get it all fixed up." I realize then how long I've waited to hear these words, how much I've hoped that Jack, perhaps more than any of us, would finally feel glad to be here.

Later, in my own bed, I open all the windows, breathe in the cooling night air, and listen for the noises that I remember from our summer on this hilltop, the steady pulse of crickets, the midnight owl, the *shush* of wind through the trees outside the window. Above the bed, a skylight, like an open, unblinking eye, affords a glimpse of stars. I am way too excited to sleep, alert to the house's every creak and click and sigh.

We are here. And I am only too glad to lie awake in this room, to turn my face toward the smattering of stars outside the window, to observe the subtle play of light and shadows on the walls, and to mark every passing hour of this long first night. Slowly, deliberately, I tune my ear to the low, distant night voices of those already living upon this land and to the unfamiliar sounds of the house. It is so new and bare, this untouched, uninhabited structure, an empty vessel that holds no secrets yet nor carries any history of its own, only the unknown shape of the future, the unwritten stories of all the years yet to come and all the families who will follow in our footsteps here.

~ 11 ~

gifts

The only trust required is to know that when there is one ending there will be another beginning.

—Clarissa Pinkola Estés

$\mathcal{D}$eath startles us to attention. When a loved one passes on, when the person we spoke to on the phone last Sunday slips quietly out of the world on Thursday, we are reminded: Everything is transient. Life hangs by a gossamer thread. Today is a gift; tomorrow, not a guarantee.

Steve's father had never been keen on our plan to renovate a crumbling summer cottage, but he was thrilled beyond belief when we decided to tear it down and build from scratch instead. In his own long lifetime, he'd overseen construction of four well-made houses; it pleased him when we finally came to our senses and decided to build one, too. On visits to Florida, we rolled out plans for him to look at, and even after emphysema had robbed him of breath and made it difficult for him to speak, he studied them carefully and grilled us about our choices. Why were the bedrooms so small? Why weren't we treating ourselves to two sinks in the master bath? Why didn't we have a dining room? Our rustic post-and-beam house, with its reclaimed pine floors and paint-streaked old doors, is not his idea of style, but he's glad we have what we want, proud, too, that we've spent our money on good insulation, a sturdy oven, tight windows and doors.

Week after week, we apprise him of the progress. Sunday means a phone call, all four of us chattering into the phone in turn, knowing he can't possibly make sense of our various dilemmas and construction delays but that he's hungry for news, eager to share something of our busy, scattered lives. As his own world shrinks—as he resigns himself to an ever-present oxygen tank, more meals in his room, shorter visits with Steve's mom, muted by Alzheimer's—he continues to cheer us on, sending generous checks at Christmastime, poring over every photo we send. "Hurry up and get that house finished," he shouts into the phone, "before those boys go off to college!"

Finally, Steve dials his number one brilliantly sunny morning and announces, "Well, Dad, we're here. We got ourselves moved in. We've got pancakes on the stove, it's a beautiful October day in New Hampshire, and we've still got lots of work to do. But I sure do hope that we can get you up here for visit."

Two days later, a nurse at the health center where my father-in-law lives tells my husband that the family should come quickly. His dad's systems are starting to shut down. There follows a flurry of phone calls, airline tickets, hotel reservations. And then, an hour after his four children and oldest grandson have arrived at his bedside, he struggles up, grips their hands with fierce strength, looks intently at each of them in turn, and dies.

Steve's voice is unsteady when he calls moments later, just after five in the afternoon. I am standing in the kitchen, surrounded by boxes of pots and pans, and I mouth the words to Jack as I take them in myself: "Granddad has passed away." It is getting on toward dusk, but we haven't turned lights on yet.

The room dissolves in shadow. Tears roll silently down my son's cheeks while I listen to my husband describe how it's been, the first of our parents to die. I hang up the phone then, put my arms around Jack, and hold him that way, silent in the dark-ening kitchen, for a long time, both of us realizing that the world feels different now, with one less person in it.

"I don't even remember what I said to Granddad on the phone on Sunday," Jack says at last, choking on tears. "And I don't remember what his last words to me were, either. I don't know if I told him that I loved him." After a little while, Jack climbs the stairs to his room and closes the door, and I slip outside, into the ephemeral opulence of an autumn sunset.

The evening light is low and rich. The mountains, washed in shades of pink, deepen imperceptibly to purple as the sun slips away. The tall grasses thrum with the relentless, ringing pulse of crickets, the sound of urgent, fleeting life. The chilled air is scoured clean, fresh and clear as water. Slowly, a pale orange disk of a moon emerges from behind the mountains, breath-takingly fat and full, a numinous, sacred presence. I run back to the house, up the stairs, to find Jack lying facedown on his bed, shaking with sobs. "You must come outside," I insist, "there's something you need to see."

Together, we walk slowly down through the north field be-yond our house, straight toward the moon. When we get to the stone wall down at the bottom of the hill, we stop, entranced, in a sea of waving grass, and turn our faces heavenward. It is as if, for this moment, anyway, a curtain has been drawn back and we are being offered a glimpse into the deep, beating heart of things. I take my son's hand and squeeze it tight.

Just an hour ago, the great life force that was my intense, irascible, loving eighty-eight-year-old father-in-law departed the earth with a sigh, eyes wide, as if in surprise at what was coming next. Now, here, as the moon climbs above our heads, growing brighter and more luminous as the last light drains from the sky, some vast spirit is most certainly present. Surely we have been called here, Jack and I, led to this place of stunned, absolute quiet where, for a few brief moments, anyway, we seem to find ourselves on both sides of the veil, caught somewhere between life and death, straddling mystery.

"That's Granddad's moon," I whisper at last. And truth be told, it does seem as if he's close, has somehow joined us here in the lowering darkness. My son is a month shy of fifteen, questioning everything, so I hesitate a moment before I speak. "I think that when a person dies, God sends a message back to all the people who are left behind," I say, "to let them know that the soul is already on its journey, and that the person we loved is being held, and carried on into the next place, just as we are being held and carried right now, here on earth."

This is the first time Jack has ever had to wonder, When life ends, where do we go? "I just talked to Granddad the other day, and now I don't even know where he is," he had said. "It feels like I didn't even realize how much I loved him until he was gone, and now I'll never have a chance to let him know." But as night falls around our shoulders, as our tears cease to flow and we are wrapped in peace beneath a benevolent moon, I assure my son that I have a sense that somehow, somewhere, he does know.

We eat a quiet dinner, Jack and I. I talk to Henry, who's worked late at school and is spending the night at a friend's, and we try to watch a little of the World Series on TV. But the sober truths of death keep intruding on these ordinary activities. There is no pretending normalcy on this night.

In the end, the moon, high overhead now and gleaming white as a pearl, is our only solace. Sleepless at midnight, we put on sneakers, and jackets over our pajamas, and go back outside, the moon so bright that it sends our shadows dancing across the damp grass. We tip the lawn chair backs flat and lie down side by side out on the edge of the hill, beneath the infinite, reaching expanse of sky. We don't say a thing. I wonder if Jack is thinking now that this first family loss is just a beginning. I wonder if, holding the new, unfamiliar weight of death, he has come to understand for the first time that, one by one, the people he loves will depart this world, and he will be left like this, again and again, with a heart full of all the loving words he wished he'd said but didn't, all the gestures he wishes he'd made but hadn't.

"I wish I could have said good-bye," he murmurs at last.

"Me too," I say.

We lie there together for a long time, until our hands and feet ache with cold, listening to emptiness.

And so we begin to ensoul our house by grieving here. Our first memory of our new life is death. But it is also grace. As I begin in earnest the work of unpacking and making our house livable, I carry within me the imprint of that indelible moon, and with it a new awareness that this hilltop is also a place where, inevitably, hearts will break and then begin to heal again.

The raw, sharp smells of tung oil and fresh paint still hang in the air, and fine, floury dust filters down from between every ceiling board. It is a warm October, and I keep the windows open as I slice into boxes and confront our life in layers. There is so much stuff here, more than we need, more than will ever fit in these simple rooms, this house we designed to make use of every inch of space—no attic, no dark basement where the detritus of outgrown pastimes and unfinished projects might pile up, out of sight and out of mind. Three years ago, emptying out our old house, I'd had a system that deferred decision: When in doubt, pack it. Now, the moment of reckoning has come. At seven-fifteen every morning, Henry and Steve head over the mountain, to school and work. I drive Jack to his school, five minutes away. By seven thirty-five, I'm home again, face-to-face with our possessions.

I come across a small green pottery pitcher, bought at a crafts show the year we married, that used to sit on the windowsill above our sink, filled from June until first frost with jewel-toned nasturtiums. The smooth, black, heart-shaped rock, picked up on a beach in Maine when Jack was a baby, then placed on the kitchen table, where it stayed for ten years. The small reclining Buddha, whose languid posture of repose reminds me, each time I glance her way, to slow down and breathe.

These familiar, cherished things are easy to place in their new homes, grounding me here in the unfamiliar, untried spaces. I unwrap a small red china fox, a curio Steve loved as a child in his grandmother's house in Kentucky, and see its tail has shattered. My guess is that after all this time, my husband will never notice the little fox's absence from our living room, yet it still makes me sad, this fragment of his past disappearing for good with the day's trash.

Reluctantly, I start to fill a box with things that will never fit in this house, and then a second and a third. There is no place to store, and no way to use, the piles of damask tablecloths and monogrammed napkins that have been passed down to us; no need, in this efficient, casual house, for extra china, an inherited silver coffeepot, cut-glass vases and candy bowls. The burden of these beautiful old things seems suddenly too heavy to bear, the need to edit our lives, our belongings, our attachments, at once liberating and terribly painful, as if with each load carried out to the car and delivered to the consignment store, I'm severing a part of who we've been, who we may one day wish to be again.

In the small corner office off the kitchen, I begin to arrange the tall, narrow shelves with the books I consider "mine," the ones that have always been special to me. But here, too, I am surprised to realize how few of them seem essential now. For years, my office bookshelves held copies of every book I ever edited, the first novels and biographies and essay collections by which I defined myself, throughout my twenties, as a literary editor in New York and Boston. And then, sixteen years' worth of short-story collections, multiple copies, which I once arranged upon the shelf in chronological order, each the product of a year's worth of reading and culling, testament to my productivity, to my carefully balanced life as a working mother.

Now, I realize that the conversation I once had with all these books is long since over; we are done with one another. And I am reluctant to give up precious space to any book that has no bearing on my life as it is right now, or on the work that may one day be done in this small room with its view of sloping fields, woods, and quiet road. I take a few of the short-story volumes in my arms, carry them up the stepladder, and push them onto the highest shelves, out of reach. And then I fill the lower shelves with all the books whose voices seem to call out most urgently from between their covers—the poetry, memoirs, journals, and reflections of fellow travelers and observers, yearning souls whose lives change somehow midcourse, who leave familiar truths and places in search of unforeseen wilderness, only to discover instead, in the words of Wendell Berry, that "the world cannot be discovered by a journey of miles, no matter how long, but only by a spiritual journey, a journey of one inch, very arduous and humbling and joyful, by which we arrive at the ground at our feet and learn to be at home."

When I come upon my own journals scattered among the boxes, I set them aside in a pile. Before long, I'm astonished to see, there are eight, ten, fifteen notebooks, all filled with my own dense handwriting, hundreds of pages recording the details—the delights, the despair, the rambling dreams—of hundreds of days. When did I write all this? I wonder, incredulous, as I pick up one at random and begin to read.

I open to a morning in July, ten years ago. A dream I'd had the night before, in which my grandmother, long dead even then, begs me, as I dash out her door, to come back and have a cup of tea with her. In the dream, I turn to hug her, insisting I must rush off, but that I'll come again soon and stay longer. Looking over her shoulder, embracing her frail, tiny body, I notice for the first time a row of luminous, multicolored glass birds on her windowsill. And I realize that in all the countless times I've visited my grandmother, all the nights I've spent in her house as a child, I have never once noticed her beautiful birds. I awake from this dream weeping and admit to myself in a spill of words on the page that in my daily dash through life, I am giving all the people closest to me—myself included—short shrift. Slow down and pay attention, I know my grandmother is telling me, before it's too late.

"I feel so overwhelmed by things to do," I wrote to myself on that forgotten summer morning, "that I'm desperate, trying to keep us all afloat, trying to take care of everyone I love, but never having enough to give, or enough time to be fully present anywhere, with anyone. I want to change the way I am. I need to change the way I live."

The overwrought journal entry brings me up short, the way a mirror held just so can suddenly reveal an unknown aspect of your own face, a piece of who you are that you've never glimpsed before. By the time I've finished unpacking the book boxes, there is a shelf's worth of notebooks, years' worth of my own forgotten writing. The woman who lives and breathes within these private pages is someone whose existence I've scarcely acknowledged, let alone appreciated or tried to get to know. I have never gathered these notebooks all in one place before, have never once gone back to read the record of my own everyday life. Yet as I page through the journals now, one after another, I discover not only my own younger self, but also a solitary, reflective, questioning self, someone, I realize, it is time to befriend.

I have to laugh, taking stock of her output. For years, it seems, I've been moonlighting as a writer, pouring my heart out onto the page behind my own back. Now, like precious gifts left behind by a stranger, I find in the forgotten pages of my journals descriptions of my sons at every age, recorded bits of conversation with little boys waking up from naps and on autumn walks in search of horse chestnuts and acorns. I find an intimate, revealing portrait of my husband and all the ups and downs of our years of marriage—the easy roll and swell of the everyday landscape of our life together; our inevitable descents into valleys of pain, anger, and misunderstanding; the relief that reconciliation always brings, as we make our slow, careful steps back into each other's arms.

"Life flows on, and it's ok," I wrote in a small black notebook at the very end of our time in the red cottage. "We create our own happiness by choosing it, even as the very things we hold most dear change and transform before our eyes. Today is unfurling, already slipping away, with nothing at all to make it memorable or special. But maybe that is why I'm so content on this lovely fall afternoon. The best days, sometimes, are the days when nothing happens to ripple the calm surface of life. No big surprises, no great ups or downs, no regrets. Instead, time just to notice what is. Time to linger over dinner, to take a walk, and read in bed. Time to ask Steve, and both of the kids, How are you feeling about things? And time to listen, my heart wide open, to each of them in turn. Who wouldn't wish for days like this?"

I close the notebook and stare out the window. This, I realize, is what I've wanted all along: to be more attentive, to honor the flow of days, the passing of time, the richness of everyday life. Some part of me has always known it, known it well enough, apparently, to write it down, over and over again, year after year. Finally, there is another part of me that's ready to stop and listen to what I've been telling myself, ready to pay attention to what I know.

"Let the beauty you love be what you do," Rumi advises. "There are a thousand ways to kneel and kiss the ground." I think of my husband, my two sons, myself, just a year away from fifty. We have all been so busy—doing our work, growing up, being a family. Soon, it will end. All this striving, accommodating, juggling, will be the past. No more leaving dinner dishes on the counter in order to race to a son's basketball game in a distant town. No more fingerprints to wash from the piano keys or stacks of music to pick up from the floor. No more midnight treks in winter coats thrown over nightgowns, cold eddying around bare ankles, driving icy roads to pick up a teenager who needs a ride. No more college applications to proofread or loads of sweaty T-shirts in the hamper. No more enormous sneakers to trip over as I walk through the back door.

And I will miss it all. The beauty that I love is the life that we live, the four of us together, now, this moment, with all its cluttered complexity and inconvenience. The beauty that I love is the gift of every ordinary day that's left to me. I want to center my life on the things I'm grateful for. I want to pay attention to what's worth caring about, to read the sacred in everyday life, to develop the spiritual sturdiness I need for that simple, endlessly challenging practice.

The desk in my office is L-shaped, built onto the wall, a scant eighteen inches deep. Sitting here, I can reach my arm across the Formica, through the open window, and touch the sky. I look out across the field to a stone wall lush with ferns, the woods beyond. It is a place of solitude and silence. A place where I might finally take the time to get better acquainted with the woman in my notebooks, draw her into conversation with the woman I feel myself becoming. A place, too, where I might begin to write a story of midlife longings and discoveries, of lessons learned in the search for home and a new sense of purpose, and the bittersweet intensity of life with teenagers—holding on, letting go. A place where the new beginning I sought may just turn out to be a return to what I already understood most deeply.

I don't remember the pleasant, unremarkable day I wrote about in the little black notebook, but I do remember very well what life felt like that summer in the red cottage, the way contentment snuck up on us and took us by surprise. Letting go, living with less, expecting less, we experienced abundance. And therein lay the paradox.

Now, as I sort through our belongings, trying to decide what is worth keeping, I remind myself—choose beauty, but don't hold on too tight. As I envision new work, I wonder if perhaps what I am meant to do next is simply what I most want to do. My journals tell a story that I never bothered to read. Now, I see that my soul has been hard at work in those pages, writing the journey that brought us here. "I want to change the way I am," it cried out years ago. "I need to change the way I live." And then, while I was busy taking care of children, driving car pools, tending to the demands of life and work, my soul took up the task of envisioning something different. Surely it was an act of imagination, as much as anything, that brought us here. And surely imagination is still required, as we undertake to create a home that in time will resonate with memory and fulfill our longings for love, security, and connection.

I know I can't make time slow down, can't hold our life as it is in a freeze frame or slow my children's inexorable journeys into adulthood and lives of their own. But I can celebrate those journeys by bearing witness to them, by paying attention, and, perhaps most of all, by carrying on with my own growth and becoming. "Perhaps," May Sarton wrote in *Journal of a Solitude*, "we write towards what we will become from where we are." Now it dawns on me that the only way I can figure out what I'm meant to be doing is to try to understand who I'm meant to be.

I put the journals on a shelf, slide the computer into place between the windows, and start filling desk drawers with file folders, paper, and pens. The day stretches before me like an invitation. The house awaits a hundred finishing touches. Everywhere I look, there is something I need to clean, hang, unpack, or put away.

Yet what I feel is not the burden of this work, but all the hope and promise and possibility beyond it. My heart ascends into rare, unexpected elation. I will not waste this life, not one hour, not one minute. I will not take for granted the blessing of our being here, together still. I will give thanks for the first tinges of orange in the maple tree outside the window, the silence of the house at noon, the clouds scudding across the sky as I lean against the kitchen counter and gaze out toward the mountains, hands wrapped around a mug of steaming tea.

And then, later, I'll welcome the sound of tires crunching on the gravel drive, the thud of a heavy backpack hitting the floor. I will notice the way my younger son walks, tilted forward a bit, just like his dad and like his dad's dad before him. I will lift my husband's glasses off his nose after dinner, kiss his tender eyelids, try to imagine what it feels like to be him, the oldest son of a father gone. I will listen to every note that sings forth from our piano tonight, will let my heart overflow with music, knowing that next year, we will keep the piano closed. I will proofread an English essay on Thoreau, make biscuits from scratch, watch a few innings of the year's last baseball game, just because. I will run my palm across a bristly cheek, give a back rub, put ice-cream bowls in the dishwasher, remember to say good night. It would be so easy to forget to love this life, to just go through the motions, doing what needs to be done, as if it's all going to last forever.

But I need only open any one of fifteen dog-eared note-books, to any page at all, to realize that the past is nothing more than an infinity of moments, all come and gone in the blink of an eye. And I need only look into my sons' faces, changing still from the boys they were to the men they are becoming, to know that time rushes on, whether we pay it any heed or not. So I try to memorize the curve of a shoulder, the tilt of a nose. I inhale the grassy, familiar scent of my husband's neck, then squeeze in close on the sofa and call out to the boys to come join us. I tune my ear to the excited dog-dreaming whimper Gracie makes in her sleep after a long day of chasing squirrels and tennis balls. And I remind myself: The life we have right here, right now, is the best life there is.

This weekend, Steve and Henry and Jack and I will scrub

the screened porch, and then we'll carry in the ancient, squeaky glider and all the old wicker furniture we saved from the red cottage, spray-painted now a soft shade of gray. We will put our old kitchen table out there, with the blue wooden chairs my mother and I bought at an auction years ago. We'll light some candles, carry dinner out on trays, and watch the bats materialize out of the darkness. I hope it will be warm and that we'll linger around the table, in the candlelight, for a long time, getting reacquainted with this hilltop. There won't be many more of these mild days. Already the trees have begun to turn, and it is dark by six.

I haven't written a word at my narrow desk in the corner office by the kitchen, but somehow it feels as if I've already taken a step—over the edge of my old boundaries, away from where I've been, and into new territory. I feel something moving toward me, too. I have an idea of what I need to write about, of how I want to live, of how to kneel here and kiss the ground.

~ 12 ~

tests

A pearl is a beautiful thing that is produced
by an injured life. It is the tear [that results]
from the injury of the oyster. The treasure
of our being in this world is also produced
by an injured life. If we had not been
wounded, if we had not been injured, then
we could not produce the pearl.

—STEPHAN HOELLER

The concert begins as a joke, Henry and a friend fooling around at the piano in our living room one weekend afternoon. Jeremy loves singing in languages not his own—French, Spanish, Italian—and Henry will sight-read anything. I hear them laughing, noodling through snatches of music, running up and down scales. Then, suddenly, Jeremy's clear tenor rides a wave of piano chords, crests, and pours through the house. I tiptoe to the living room door, startled by this breathtaking voice and the beauty of the music, a plaintive, achingly tender French love song. How can it be that the two scruffy teenagers who clomped through the kitchen moments ago are capable of this? Such unself-conscious expression, such joyful noise?

The magic of this unexpected collaboration, if not antici-pated, is not lost on the boys. By the end of the afternoon, the two of them are excitedly planning a two-man show, envisioning an evening of unabashedly romantic music, none of it in English. So it is that Henry's long list of senior-year projects grows longer still. His early decision application for Bowdoin is due November 15, and he wants to record a CD to round out his portfolio. He's gathering recommendations and still needs to revise the essay. In addition, he has a job managing the school store in the afternoons, is working on assignments for his Saturday conservatory program in Boston, and is arranging Broadway show tunes for his senior project, a musical revue with six classmates, which he'll rehearse all winter and produce in the spring.

Most nights, as Steve and I head down the hall to bed, a thin rim of light still shines from beneath his door. Long ago I gave up suggesting that homework be done in silence; there is always a sound track for his late night exertions, usually jazz, low and private, something that will keep him going through another page of math problems or a German translation.

One day he shows me his calendar, a testament to diligence, all organized and compartmentalized within a software program called Entourage—every deadline, audition date, and school assignment a click away. The college applications, each with its own labeled folder, are a job unto themselves, a long, slow trek through an uncertain landscape. Surveying the crowded screen on his laptop, the multipart to-do list, I think how glad I am not to be him, carrying the weight of my own unknown future in my hands. At the same time, though, I can't help but marvel at his steady, industrious calm in the face of it all, this relentless race to a succession of finish lines.

At the end of October, we drive north through resplendent fall foliage for his interviews at Bowdoin and Bates, stopping en route at a Gap outlet to buy shirts and pants that might strike the right note: not too dressy, just casual and understated enough. We've gotten pretty good at these college road trips now, having discovered that they offer us the secret bonus of escape from our everyday routines, a legitimate excuse to disappear for a while, catch up with each other, and live lightly in the world, as only travelers can.

Still, at Bowdoin I sit outdoors under a hot fall sun, recording positive thoughts into my journal, obsessively checking my watch. Why not yes? I wonder. Why not him? Why not here? Wouldn't any admissions officer be happy to give the nod to such an applicant, to offer this kind, smart, hardworking young man a place in next year's freshman class?

But of course, what no college interviewer could possibly know, and what Henry could never begin to explain, is how far he's come. The part of his past that makes his present most remarkable is not a story he can tell himself. I think back to my son's fourth-grade year, the first paper he ever had to write, four pages of facts about the African elephant. Side by side we sat, at a desk in the living room, cleared specially for this major undertaking and surrounded by the colorful books about animals and their habits we'd carried home from the library. Slowly, painfully, I tried to guide him through the process. Reading, thinking, writing.

He seemed frozen within himself, overwhelmed, so daunted by the challenge, so afraid of failing, that he couldn't begin. Behind my patient, simple questions, I despaired. Where was the switch that would turn the light on here, awaken curiosity, engage the mind, the will, the desire to learn and know and do?

Later that same year, a tall, strong, vicious girl chose Henry to torment at school, teasing him so mercilessly in gym class that he finally confessed to us, in tears, that he couldn't endure one more day of it. We spoke to the teacher, urged our small, uncoordinated little boy to ignore the taunts. But the malicious girl only bore down harder, drawing other classmates into her sly assault. Finally, Steve and Henry made a deal. Steve would drive to school at gym time, bring Henry home for an hour, and then take him back. They would have their own gym class in the yard.

Have I ever loved my husband more than I did that spring, watching from the window as he tossed ball after ball after ball into his son's outstretched glove? There was nothing Henry wanted more in the world at that time than to be on a baseball team and nothing for which he had less natural talent. "Glove up!" Steve would call as, a second too late, Henry would lift his arm and close his hand around . . . air.

Hour after hour, day after day, they went at it, early in the morning before school, during the private "gym class," every single night after dinner until dark. Sometimes Jack would dash out with his own little glove, join in for a while as if born to the game, and then, bored, wander off. But for Henry, every motion had to be learned, every reflex trained by endless repetition. He hung in there, determined to catch, determined to throw, willing his body to react and respond. My husband, he of seven varsity letters in high school, natural athlete and former state champion swimmer, tried in vain to imagine what it must be like to live in a body with so little connection between hand and eye. While Henry doggedly learned to pitch and catch, Steve learned a kind of patience he'd never before been capable of. Together, they stuck it out.

And by the time baseball season began in our town that spring, our son, the world's most dedicated ten-year-old student of the game, was ready to play. The determination, the hours in the yard, had paid off. To his, and our greater, astonishment, he became a pitcher on his team. The coach was amazed at his concentration, not to mention his ability to stay calm in the heat of battle. He could throw strikes. He could win games. We spent a lot of time over the next few years watching both our sons play baseball, but the highlight for me was not a great play at home or a seventh-inning save. The best moment of Henry's brief baseball career, as far as I'm concerned, happened on the sidelines, in his second year of pitching, when the mother of a small, shy benchwarmer watched Henry coolly strike a guy out and then turned to me and asked, "Has your son always been athletic?"

Baseball taught Henry that he could do anything he wanted to; that with enough time and effort and dogged will, he could achieve the goals that mean the most to him, and that impossibilities are just the things he hasn't mastered yet. If he could learn to throw a ball across home plate, then he could certainly learn to read music, memorize a Bach prelude, write a research paper, drive a car.

The last week of summer vacation before his sophomore year of high school, Henry sat on the screened porch at the red cottage, highlighter in hand, and read a book called *Feel the Fear and Do It Anyway*. A week later, on a camping trip with his class, he stuffed his fear of heights into his back pocket, clipped a harness around his hips, and climbed to the top of a sheer rock face. My guess is that he didn't choose to tell anyone that he'd spent days summoning his nerve, or that as a child he'd never once set foot on a jungle gym.

Now, watching him confront the demands of senior year, I realize that my son has been shaped as much by the obstacles he's surmounted as by any accomplishment listed on his résumé. Yet I know that his newfound confidence depends, in part, on being seen at last as just a regular guy, a strong student, a gifted musician. He has no interest in the backstory, at least not yet. But I, after all these years, find myself recalling his long uphill battle in a new light, surprised by gratitude for his challenged life and all its lessons, for the struggles that have taught him humility and faith. I don't need to worry about this kid anymore, I realize. He already knows so much more about who he is than I did at that age, already understands the ways that adversity can be turned into strength. Most important, he realizes that he alone has the capacity to shape his own life, to undertake the kind of growth and learning that will allow him to become the man he wants to be.

When I look up from my notebook, he's standing in front of me, blocking the sun, looking down, grinning. "Well, I think I aced it," he says. "Let's go get ice cream."

By November, the landscape is stripped bare, brittle and frozen, awaiting the softening contours of snow. Slowly, we settle into our house and learn what it is to live here, growing accustomed to the sounds that, over time, we'll come to associate with home—the relentless rooster next door, rousing his flock each day in the darkest hours before dawn, the whoosh of warm air rising up through black iron grates on the floor, the eerie, eager yip of coyotes circling in the lower field, the thrum of rain on the metal roof.

Mornings, I come downstairs first, brew coffee, slice bread for the toaster, and watch the sky. The sun arrives in the kitchen just after I do, casting pale light across the black stone countertop, illuminating every crumb and Cheerio and errant poppy seed. Steve heads out the door with Gracie for their morning game of fetch. By the time the boys clatter downstairs for breakfast, we are shielding our eyes; the kitchen is filled with light.

The mountains are the left-hand line against which the story of our new life is written, the start point for every day. We are drawn, each of us in turn on these frozen fall mornings, to stop, gaze out across the valley, and allow ourselves to be absorbed by beauty. They are never the same mountains twice. Every sunrise is different, each bearing its own shifting palette, its constellation of shadows or cloak of obscuring mist. A month ago, the hills blazed with color; bare now, their dense fabric of trees leafless, they still absorb the colors of the sky, set the tone for the day. And yet, changeable as they are, the mountains are also the solid, calming presence I return to hour by hour, the omnipresent backdrop against which everything else happens here—life, weather, breakfast, lunch, and dinner, time passing, seasons changing. No matter where I am, no matter what I'm doing, I feel them, immovable and eternal, and I find myself accepting, again and again, their invitation—to pause, look out across the valley, and allow my life to slowly begin to bind itself to the place where it's lived.

During my hours at home, I clean, organize drawers and closets, and spend hours on the couch, notebook in my lap, gazing into space, lost in thought. I try to write, try to finish putting together a room, and am abashed by my own slow progress on both fronts. I'm used to being productive, to getting things done. One morning, I stare at an empty wall for an hour before summoning the certitude to pound a nail and hang a picture there. The house is simple, spare, still an almost blank canvas, and I am so loath to fill it up with clutter that I find myself mulling over every decision—and then, often as not, choosing light, or empty space, over old objects and possessions that now seem drained of life or meaning.

So it is with the book that I find myself thinking about night and day. I long to write about simplicity, yet each attempt to organize my thoughts seems overambitious and too complex. I take long walks alone, return to my spot on the couch, pick up pad and pen, stare into space for a while longer, and start over, again and again.

Meanwhile, we settle into new schedules, spread ourselves out through the rooms, and resuscitate some of our old habits—early morning walks, candles at suppertime, tea in the kitchen before bed. We begin to remember which cupboard holds the waffle iron, where the extension cords are kept, to latch the door so the wind won't blow it open. As everyone rushes off in a flurry of hasty good-byes each morning and then comes home, tired and hungry and full of news each night, the rhythm of everyday life works upon us all. With each morning's departure and each evening's return, the magnetic pull of home grows stronger. And yet, most of the time, I'm alone here. The task of igniting the spirit of this house, breathing life into our daily routines and tending the hearth, falls to me.

Senior year of high school, I now understand, is really just a prolonged dress rehearsal for the separation to come, an extended exercise in letting go. The son whose company I cherish is home less and less. When he is here, he's busy. Most of the time, life is already calling him elsewhere. Jack, too, stays late at school. As soon as running season ends, he's in the gym every afternoon, practicing for basketball tryouts, having a blast. Afterward he brings friends home, two or three ravenous boys who kick off their shoes at the door and then sweep behind him through the kitchen, downing huge glasses of orange juice, bags of chips, English muffins, bunches of bananas. Sated, they troop into the basement like a pack of animals in retreat, to discuss plays, strategies, who "owned" who at the hoop today.

The tryouts for the freshman team are one night only, the

Monday we fly home from Steve's dad's memorial service. For Jack, certain of his skills on the court, the only question is whether he has a shot at JV; either way, he says, is fine with him, he just can't wait to play. High school basketball has been his goal for as long as he can remember, through a childhood of shooting around in the driveway, through two seasons of junior high ball, through the last two months of daily running, which, truth be told, he endured only to build speed and get in better shape for basketball, *his* game. Now, at last, the life he's always wanted, the life of a serious high school athlete, is about to begin.

Our plane touches down in Boston, and we drive hard and fast, shaving time off the two-hour trip to New Hampshire, swinging by the house for sneakers and shorts. Five minutes later, he arrives at the gym door in high spirits, just a little bit late. "Good luck," we call to his back. He turns, waves, gives a confident thumbs-up, and disappears inside.

When he calls for a ride two hours later, his voice is barely recognizable.

I realize that my son is not the first high school freshman to have his athletic career, and all his youthful hopes and dreams, expire in a moment. The scene is all too easy to imagine, as it must surely play out in gyms and locker rooms everywhere: You hold your breath, every muscle in your body frozen in time and space, as the coach reads the list of names, the list that your entire future depends upon. Then, heart suddenly pounding as if to escape your chest, you break out in a sweat as he comes to the end and looks up over his half-glasses, done. The coach is already calling out the time for practice tomorrow, but you're in shock, barely aware of your best friend there in front of you, his awkward, "Sorry, dude," because you're still thinking maybe there was a mistake, or maybe, just maybe, you missed it—for even now, surrounded by guys high-fiving one another, you can't quite believe what you didn't hear, can't quite absorb the fact that the only name that matters, the one you are still straining your ears toward, your own, wasn't on that list at all.

Jack is devastated. There is no way I can assure a fifteen-year-old boy whose dream has just collapsed that life will go on. There's no way his father's shock and disbelief can be translated into useful action. And there is no way that Jack, who'd never entertained for an instant the possibility that he wouldn't make the team, can pretend that this wasn't the most important thing in the world to him.

Our suitcases and bags are all over the floor, the mail in a scattered pile on the table, the house still in disarray from our hasty departure two days earlier. In the last forty-eight hours, we've listened to eulogies and shared our stories; we've wiped away tears, blown our noses raw, kissed and hugged aunts and uncles and cousins, remembered Steve's dad and said our final good-byes, flown hundreds of miles and driven a hundred more to get to this all-important tryout. And now it is ten o'clock at night and we are hollowed out, at a loss for words. There is no hope of putting this new pain into perspective tonight, no way at this hour to sort death from disappointment or to come up with a plan that might make it easier for Jack to get up in the morning and go back to school.

Two boys, Jack tells us, asked right away if they could be managers and practice with the team. Two others were cut, and he was one of those. Is there a chance the coach might allow a third manager? I ask, though I already know what his response will be. "There's no way I'm going to be the stupid water boy for all my friends," Jack says angrily, slamming his bedroom door behind him.

Steve and I lie side by side all night, exhausted and sleepless, crushed by the burden of our son's disappointment. Should we write to the coach? we wonder. Would it be appropriate to intervene? Or is it time for Jack, for all of us, really, to confront reality, to accept that rejection and dashed hopes are always going to be part of the picture, no matter how much our hearts may desire a particular outcome? The only thing we can know for certain about life, I want to tell him, is that whatever he's going through now won't last forever.

When I go into Jack's room at six-fifteen the next morning, it's clear that he's been awake most of the night, too. And it turns out that he's made his own decision about what's next. "I'll do anything," he says now, quietly, "to get to practice. If the coach will let me be a water boy, I'll do it, if he'll just let me practice with the team."

And so Jack finds his own way into basketball practice, subdued and humbled, willing to keep score, round up basketballs, play any role he's offered. After a couple of weeks, the coach says he should go ahead and bring in a check for a uniform, but then he warns: There will be no promises about playing time. For Jack, it's enough, more than enough; he is willing to earn his spot, and he's grateful to his teammates for pulling him in wholeheartedly, for never once bringing up the fact that he arrived through the back door and on bended knee.

The days dawn, ripen, and pass, growing shorter, colder, grayer. We are all learning humility this season, it seems, getting jostled by life. How naive I was to have ever imagined that settling into our own house would mean that everything else would settle as well, that all the scattered puzzle pieces of our days and dreams and desires would finally snap into place, and that the picture would be complete. Instead the opposite is true, I finally admit to myself as I throw away dismal chapter drafts and scribble notes into my own calendar, trying to keep track of who needs to be where when. These are not settled times, and nothing is easy.

Yet hard as it was to lose my job and then watch our savings disappear into a house it was too late to back out of building, I am finally glimpsing the slender silver lining in that dark cloud. We are here, after all, living in this house at last. And now, with no paying job to do or house-building tasks to complete, my time really is my own. Beyond my window, the austere landscape invites reflection and offers stillness in return. It is what I've always dreamed of—time simply to walk in the rain, to sit on the kitchen doorstep on a mild day with the warm afternoon sun on my face, to watch the sky grow dark and the moon rise. Time to meditate alone, in silence, and reflect on the last three years, the mistakes made and the lessons learned. It has taken a while, but I've finally come to understand that the true journey, the one that will engage my soul and bring me face-to-face with myself, couldn't really begin until I stopped moving. Now, there's no avoiding it. I am ready to sit, to listen, to allow some long dormant part of myself a slow, quiet awakening, an unfurling into new life. As with any journey, this one poses its own challenges, as I seek at last to choose patience over activity, acceptance over judgment, faith over doubt.

And hard as it was to see our son suffer the humiliation of not making the team, my husband and I also realized this: The resolute young man who shoved his basketball shoes into his gym bag the next morning, in the hopes that the coach would allow him onto the court to practice, was a stronger player, and a more resilient person, than the boy who'd flashed that cocky thumbs-up the night before. The blessing that came out of not making the team had nothing to do with the fact that he finally did get to play and everything to do with the resolve he summoned in himself as the sun rose the next morning. Grace happened when he realized that he loved the game so much, he could swallow his pride for the sake of his passion.

Here, in the crucible of everyday life, it seems that we are all being tested. My sons' days and nights are filled with activities—music lessons, school, practice, homework, sports, tests, college interviews. My husband and I vow to keep a healthy distance but find ourselves pulled into the fray instead, trying to anticipate what's next. We wonder if Jack will finally get to start in next week's game, why his room is always such a mess, and if he will make up his mind to work hard enough to turn his B's into A's. We wonder if Bowdoin will say yes, whether Henry will get the top spot in the All State Honors Jazz Band, whether he can bring up his miserable score on the SATs. There is so much riding on the future, it seems, that I can barely manage to pay attention to the present.

And then, one blustery November night, the hidden beauty of the moment just sneaks up on me. Everyone is home for a change, and we have gathered around the kitchen island for a late dinner. I dim the overhead lamp and light candles, dish up pasta and sauce from the stove, and sit down across from my sons and husband. I look at these three faces, the two younger ones still changing daily in subtle and surprising ways; the older one etched with age, gentler than it used to be, so very familiar. Gracie sits at my feet, as usual, waiting patiently for some small morsel to fall her way. Outside, an unseasonably fierce wind whips through the trees. In the kitchen, the clink of knife on plate, sudden laughter, the grind of the peppermill. There is nothing much going on here, nothing of importance being discussed, just the events of the day, the weather, a teacher's comment, the plans for the weekend.

Yet what I feel is a profound sense of thanksgiving, so glad am I for the food before us, our warm, sheltering house on a cold night, and our own flawed, often frayed little civilization of four. We are just a family gathering around a table for a few minutes at the end of a day. But the scene itself feels hallowed, sacred, as if my own awareness has suddenly illuminated us all with a shaft of holy light.

Maybe this is what I'm meant to understand during this slow descent into winter and all the changes that lie just around the corner. That there is no such thing as a charmed life, not for any of us, no matter where we live or how mindfully we attend to the tasks at hand. But there are charmed moments, all the time, in every life and in every day, if we are only awake enough to experience them when they come and wise enough to appreciate them. Sitting at dinner with my husband and sons, I realize that there is nothing I want more than what we have right now—the simple fact of us, here, all living together, for a little while longer.

My challenge is to hold on to that awareness, even on days when everyone's stress runs high, when one or the other of my children needs more than I can give, or when I'm simply overwhelmed by the demands of life with adolescents or saddened by the idea of life without them. The challenge, too, of course, is to remember that none of the things that seem to preoccupy us this year, as the application homestretch looms—the grades, the scores, the interviews and auditions, the early admission decision—really matter much at all in the grand scheme of things.

One day, I page through a book Henry's been reading by a top college counselor, about how to play the admissions game, and am surprised by the author's suggestion that eighth grade is not too young for students to be working on their résumés and plumping up their schedules. The admission successes of tomorrow, she insists, are built upon the extracurricular activities and accomplishments of today.

This emphasis on competition has become so much a part of the application process that it's almost impossible to keep any real perspective or to remember that my son is just a seventeen-year-old boy, not a product that needs to be packaged in order to stand out from the pack. As one of my friends, the mother of a sweet, intelligent high school senior, said not long ago, "It's not enough just to be normal anymore."

And yet, as I watch my own two sons, so different from each other yet each wanting so desperately to be seen and known and loved for who he is, I know that what they need most of all is not a strategy for winning at the high-stakes game of life as envisioned by that college admissions counselor, but simply encouragement and understanding as they begin to give shape to their dreams, come to know their own strengths, and learn to make peace with their shortcomings.

"Do you have agendas for your children that are more important than the children themselves?" asks William Martin in *The Parent's Tao Te Ching*. He continues, "Lost in the shuffle of uniforms, practices, games, recitals, and performances can be the creative and joyful soul of your child. Watch and listen carefully. Do they have time to daydream? From their dreams will emerge the practices and activities that will make self-discipline as natural as breathing."

Over the years, I've returned many times to my well-used copy of this book of ancient wisdom, distilled for modern-day parents. When my children were small, it was easy to protect and honor that daydreaming space. Now, with so much on the line, it's harder than ever to have faith that, given space and time, each really will find his way.

And letting go of my own agenda for my sons seems to be the hardest kind of letting go of all. So when Henry tells us one day that he wants to check out a school he's read about in Minnesota with a great music department, and that, by the way, he's also decided not to take the SAT test again at all, because it turns out to conflict with the date of his Berklee audition, I go back and read William Martin's reassuring words again.

I've never been quite sure if Henry has kept his college search within a three-hour drive of home for my sake or for his, but he certainly knows how much I'd love to keep him close. Now, on the advice of his guidance counselor, who's urging him to look beyond New England, he suddenly wants to book an interview halfway across the country.

The test is another issue. For months, my test-averse son has studied online for the SATs, locking himself away for hours over the summer doing practice tests, all in the hope of pulling up a lamentable math score before the final application deadlines. Now, for the sake of one music audition that he's loath to change, he proposes to blow off the SATs altogether.

There is part of me that's proud of him for having the courage to opt out of continued membership in the all-powerful College Board club, a club he never had any interest in joining anyway. But there's another part that goes immediately into panic mode—everybody takes the SATs, and most colleges still require scores, and he's worked so hard to get ready for it. My worries fall on deaf ears. "I've done some reading about the ACT," he says reasonably, "and I think it might be a better test for me, so I'll just take that."

So it comes back, as it so often does these days, to my own fear and anxiety as opposed to my son's increasingly self-aware perceptions about who he is and what he should be doing. If I can give up my agenda, if I can remember that my own hopes and dreams do not belong on his shoulders, then perhaps I really can offer him the kind of support he needs. And if I can let go of my own idea of what success might look like for him, then I can encourage him, instead, to discover and treasure in himself what is unique and internal and truly valuable.

Each step he takes on his own now is not just a separation from us and our ideas, but a move in the direction of his own life's possibilities, part of the necessary, ongoing process of self-discovery that growing up is all about.

"Watch and listen carefully," Martin advises. And I promise myself to try. I look for the creative energy that comes from being entrusted with the job of charting your own course, and I see it—in my son's excitement about visiting St. Olaf College, in the enthusiasm with which he looks into plane fares and flights to Minnesota, in his certainty that an SAT score has no real bearing on his future. I look for the joyful soul that makes Henry Henry, and I'm relieved to see that, too. He is in love with his life, with all his ambitious, half-done projects, his unfinished applications, his new ideas about what might be just around the corner.

So what if he doesn't take the SATs? By choosing not to take this test, he truly is making his own statement about what matters most to him. "You know," he says to me, "I think that any school that's going to judge me by my SAT score isn't really a school I'd want to go to anyway. I'd rather be at a school that's more interested in who I am." His words hit home. He wishes to be judged on his own terms, not by a number on a piece of paper. And that, I suddenly realize, is exactly what I've wanted for him all along.

Henry and Jeremy decide that they will perform their concert not in the small performance space at their high school, but in the large auditorium at the school across the road, and that the evening will be a fund-raiser for the music scholarship at High Mowing. They create a poster, draft a press release, and do publicity, and as the date approaches they practice every day, honing the program. Although I don't say so, I have my doubts that two earnest young boys can attract much of a crowd for an evening of romantic music sung in languages that no one in the audience will understand. But the two of them are determined. No English. No compromises. Do they want any help getting ready? I ask. No, thank you.

And so, on the night of the concert, we have friends to our house for supper for the first time and then show up at the auditorium door along with everyone else. In his own gentle way, Henry has made it clear that he doesn't need or desire a backstage mom. "I just want you to come and enjoy yourself," he'd said in the afternoon when I asked what he planned to wear and if they had thought about flowers for the stage.

The large theater is nearly full, with teachers, classmates, parents, and friends. Looking around at so many faces, both familiar and unknown, I am suddenly caught unawares by emotion. How could I have doubted this plan? In three short years here, our son, the shy, quiet one, has forged a large, generous community of friends and fans, people who have grown to care about him, who love to hear him play piano and feel invested in his future. No one is here because they have to be. They have come out on this cold November night because they know and love these two teenage boys, and because they trust them to deliver the goods.

And that is exactly what they do. Jeremy, elegant in his tuxedo, is by turns comical and impassioned, singing romantic arias, show tunes, and traditional European melodies. The strength and clarity of his voice is astonishing, and his disarming, easy way with the audience belies his age. Clearly he is in his element up on this stage, in full command, and no one cares in the least that not a single song is sung in English. Henry, the modest accompanist, cedes the spotlight to his friend with grace and plays impeccably.

But what surprises me most tonight is not the size of the crowd, or even the skill of the two young musicians, which I'd never doubted at all, but rather my own son's willingness to reveal a side of himself he's never shown before, not in all his years of piano recitals, not in any of his previous performances with various chamber music groups and jazz ensembles.

For the first time in front of an audience, he is at once fully exposed and completely relaxed, moving, swaying, playing with intense, passionate absorption, as if expressing the music through every fiber of his being.

Midway through the evening, he performs a Chopin piano solo from memory, not just flawlessly, but with such sensitivity and authority that I feel almost as if I'm hearing this familiar piece, and understanding what it means to him, for the first time. Music, I'm coming now to realize, is not just what my son does, it is who he is. If the piano was at first a refuge, his safe haven during all those lonely years of growing up without quite ever fitting in, it is now, paradoxically, the place where he is most fully in touch with his own power.

According to yoga teacher and writer Stephen Cope, every human being is born with a unique gift, a gift that, once discovered, is the doorway to a fulfilled life, to our particular path or calling. Not surprisingly, the gift requires practice, an enormous investment of time and energy and faith. But what is surprising, according to Cope, is that our gift is often paired with a wound. In other words, our strength seems to be born of our suffering, growing and flowering out of our limitations.

Henry learned early on that, for him, success depended on relentless, faithful practice and determination. Now, sitting here in the darkened auditorium, listening to my son imbue Chopin with his own deeply personal poetry, I suspect that this night is just the beginning of a journey beyond any of our imagining, a journey that will unfold as my son sets out not just to claim his gift, but to honor and share it with the world, transmuting some of the painful struggles of his childhood into a rich source of life and joy in his future.

"What does it feel like, to be able to do something that amazes people?" I ask him as we drive home afterward through the clear, cold dark. For there is little doubt that the audience was indeed amazed. The standing ovation had gone on for quite a while, even after an encore and even after the boys had finally shrugged, taken one last embarrassed bow, and run off the stage.

"Well, there are so many people in the world who really are amazing, and I have no idea what it must feel like to be one of them," Henry replies. "But, yeah, tonight was definitely fun."

And that is that. He is happy, and starving. The jittery nerves, the full house, the little mess-up on the second song, the perfect Chopin, Steve reaching for my hand as Henry finished his piece, the applause that went on and on . . . it is, all of it, already the past, a memory, and we are hurtling through the present beneath a star-strewn sky, traveling fast toward home, to mugs of tea in the kitchen and the pear-maple pie I made in the afternoon, knowing that later we would all be hungry, and glad to have it.

~ 13 ~

waiting

Do your work, then step back. The
only path to serenity.

—Tao Te Ching

My baby was due on December 24, but I was hoping that
an early labor would deliver us all from the complications of a
Christmas birthday. That year, my husband and I had our gifts
wrapped and mailed the week after Thanksgiving. The tree was
up weeks ahead of time, cookies baked and frozen, cards sent,
the nursery painted yellow, tiny diapers and undershirts stacked
in neat piles on a shelf. By the first of December, while everyone else rushed around on holiday missions, we were done,
finished with every Christmas errand and baby preparation.

There was nothing left to do but sit at home in our second-
floor Cambridge condo and wait. Evenings, we turned off all
the lights, plugged in our Christmas tree, and snuggled on the
couch, patting my huge belly, listening to Bing Crosby sing
"White Christmas" and "Silent Night" as we tried to imagine
the little person who was about to be delivered smack into
the middle of our lives. We had a girl's name and a boy's name
picked out, but somehow "Bing" was the name we'd settled
on for our baby in utero, and then, after a German friend's
autumn visit, "Der Bingle." It wasn't that we foresaw a

musical child (we didn't think about it), or that the name amused us (though it did); but somehow, without quite intending to, we'd made Bing Crosby the sound track of my final trimester of pregnancy. I craved his reassuring, mellifluous tones during my last months as intensely as I had plain baked chicken and potatoes throughout the first. And so it was that, for weeks, our unborn baby heard Christmas carols sung in perfect pitch.

When my water broke eight days early, in the midst of a record-breaking cold spell, I sent a prayer of thanks heavenward; no Christmas birthday after all. Just before dawn, Steve wrapped me up in my grandmother's pink-and-white crocheted afghan, and we sped through silent, frozen streets festooned with holiday lights and decorations. A Holiday Inn billboard proclaimed, "A child is born!" and I burst into tears. Twenty-three hours of labor later, I held my son in my arms.

For our first family photo, Steve and I posed in front of our Christmas tree, Henry cradled against my chest like a fragile treasure. We dressed him for the holiday in a tiny velveteen Santa suit and passed him around all Christmas Day for everyone to hold, a small sleeping bundle of slightly jaundiced contentment. He was the gift.

So it was not such a surprise to us that, as he grew, our first son held Christmas as his season. From earliest childhood, he led the campaign for Christmas trees in November, evening carol sings, and inviolable holiday customs. At four, he donned a Santa hat and recited "The Twelve Days of Christmas" from memory to my astonished family. By seven, he was picking his way through "The Little Drummer Boy" and "Up on the Rooftop" on the piano, and the next year, he began organizing the rest of the neighborhood kids into annual Christmas concerts that were rehearsed for days in our living room and then performed with much gusto and ado for all of us delighted parents.

When he arrived at High Mowing and discovered the annual Nativity pageant to be a highlight of the year, he signed on with joy, a hobbled freshman shepherd whose scraggly beard couldn't quite conceal the smile on his face. Since the school's beginnings over sixty years ago, custom has dictated that even the most self-consciously affected students put aside "coolness," not to mention religious differences, for the month of December to immerse themselves instead in this exquisite, time-honored pageant.

Created by the school's beloved founder, Beulah Hepburn Emmet, the production has been handed down intact from one generation to the next. The complex choral music is original, beautiful, never to be altered. The graceful movements of angels and shepherds, the kings' stately processional, Joseph and Mary's silent sojourn, all minutely choreographed decades ago, are devoutly repeated, unchanged and unchanging. Each year new students step into the old roles, reverently inhabit old gestures, carrying on the hallowed tradition with a commitment and grace that never fails to move those who witness it.

Costumes, props, the wooden barn and humble manger, the threadbare stuffed lamb, the hand-carved wooden boxes carried by the wise men, Mary's sky blue mantle—these simple artifacts are brought forth each holiday season, handled with care, then lovingly packed away again, having accumulated yet another layer of history. It is an immaculate production, sanctified by time, ensouled by generations of young people who for a few brief December moments give themselves over, year after year, to sacred rites.

We have had three years of the Nativity, the school's tradition becoming ours as well, and now, on this dark December

afternoon, I am mourning yet another "last." Perhaps we'll
come again, but forever after it will be as alumni parents, remembering how our son and his classmates embodied their
parts, as we watch a succession of new, unknown casts enact
the timeless story. This is the last time our own son will wrap
his feet in rags and don a burlap mantle. The last time we will
see these young women, all of whom we've watched grow up
over the last three years, their faces scrubbed bare of makeup,
shiny hair cascading over shoulders, as they rhythmically lift
and lower their arms, incarnating a host of heavenly angels.
The last time we will see this rowdy crew of teenage boys suddenly transformed by serious intention into solemn kings and
wise men.

We walk through the muffled quiet of early snow and enter
a room shadowed by dusk. Tradition calls for silence here.
Eyes meet, hands reach out toward friends, my parents slide in
beside us and nod hello, but no one speaks. We sit in stillness
as darkness settles like a blanket and breathing slows. It is, I
think, the holiday moment I've come to love most of all, this
interlude of shared reflection and meditation in the midst of
seasonal bustle. A sigh, a cough, a rustle of winter coats, quiet
expectation. Every seat fills, and still more and more people
arrive, standing now against the walls three and four deep.
Silently, we squeeze together, make room for more. No one
will be turned away.

At last two senior girls enter, barefoot, and light six tapers in
an ancient candelabra. They open a large leather-bound Bible
on top of the piano. Faces illuminated by the glow of candlelight, they begin to read aloud from the Gospel of Luke, their
voices pure and clear and strong: "In those days a decree went
out from Caesar Augustus . . ."

Tomorrow, we will discover that someone was smoking a

joint outside the costume room and that one of the heavenly angels has been suspended from school for three days. Reality is never far away, and teenagers invariably find a way to wriggle out of saintliness. But right now, here, we are a community bound by grace.

I haven't gone to church much these last three years, turning instead to woods and rivers and communion with the sky in my yearning search for spirit. Yet I know that the God I seek is also present in this hushed, crowded room, in the kindly faces of friends and teachers, parents and grandparents, in the warmth of bodies pressed close, flickering candles, solemn boys garbed in heavy robes, radiant girls, soaring harmonies.

There is one solo, for a senior boy, and this year it is Henry who's been entrusted with the part of the head shepherd. I have never heard my son sing alone before, not even once. In all his years of accompanying singers, he has never joined his own voice with theirs, let alone sung a note by himself. Now, to everyone's surprise, he has dared himself to stretch up and out of shyness, volunteering for the solo part, earning it. He stands at the middle of the stage, slight and unshaven, surrounded by a throng of lowly shepherds. Heart pounding, nervous for him, I clench my hands and hold my breath as he gazes out across the audience and takes a deep breath in.

His voice is deeper than I would have guessed, richer and more powerful. I sense the tie that has always bound us stretching, thinning, becoming thinner yet, until it is but a gossamer thread, shimmering into nothingness. And I feel something deep inside me releasing and softening as well. I have outgrown this old role, the nervous mother watching from the audience, willing a child's success. There is no need anymore for me to push or worry or fret. Nor is my son still a vulnerable child shrinking from the world, looking to me for protection and strength. He is testing his potential and claiming it; a young adult stepping bravely out of old, outgrown constraints and into his unique destiny, wherever it might lead. My heart stills. My fingers uncurl themselves, and I listen, really listen, to this beautiful young tenor voice, not a boy's voice at all, but the voice of a man. A voice that is new and strange to me and yet at the same time utterly, blessedly familiar.

Snow comes early this year. Two feet are due to fall on the long awaited Saturday, the early admission decision day. As the storm closes in and the snow deepens, we grow certain that no mailman will brave this blizzard. We have tickets for a Christmas performance in Boston, with our old best friends and next-door neighbors, a long-standing tradition. But the roads are impassable by noon, and snow is expected to continue through the night. We call our friends, take a pass at shoveling out the front walkway, light a fire, and hunker down. Sometime toward dusk, the back door opens a crack, and a neighbor's mittened hand reaches through to set a pile of wet mail on the mudroom seat—soggy circulars, junk, and one thin, damp envelope from Bowdoin. It is easy enough to guess the contents. But Steve and I stand there anyway, reading over our son's shoulder, "We are sorry to inform you . . ."

"Well," Henry says briskly, sliding the letter back into the envelope, "that's that."

"It's okay," I rush to assure him, blinking back a sudden, un-expected tear, "we all knew it was a long shot."

In the living room, the Christmas tree's jewel-colored lights shimmer blurred reflections in the dark windows. Evergreen boughs and pinecones adorn the mantel. The house is warm, solid, ready for holiday celebrations. But I am thinking of a day last spring, Henry skipping toward me, exuberant after his meeting with the music department chair. "They want me here!" And how when he went back to Bowdoin two months ago, to interview and attend classes, he found that it already felt familiar, almost as if he were a returning student rather than an aspiring one. The music professor, who went out of his way to get to know him, had been nothing but encouraging. On campus, he'd been met with such kindness and enthusiasm that he came away that day feeling almost certain of his future there.

Now the process that has been, at every step of the way, unstintingly friendly and reassuringly personal, ends with a form letter: "We wish you luck."

Henry is immediately pragmatic. "This is just the first really big disappointment I've had to deal with," he says, "but I'm sure it won't be the last." He doesn't want our sympathy. In fact, what he wants is for us not to care too much, certainly not to care more than he does. So I give him a quick squeeze, toss the whole soggy pile of junk mail into the recycling basket, and begin lifting hot, clean plates out of the dishwasher, stacking them on the counter. Henry wanders over to the piano and plays, of all things, "Put on a Happy Face." The snow turns to ice, pings against the windowpanes, and darkness claims the land.

"I almost cried," Steve confesses to me later in bed, our bodies pressed together under the down comforter.

"Me too," I whisper back.

But our son is made of sturdier stuff; he has learned nothing in his eighteen years if not how to bounce back. To him, being turned down by his first-choice school means that he'll be spending Christmas vacation completing all the applications he'd put on hold till now.

But I have a feeling that it means something else as

well—that he won't end up at a school that's a drive away from home after all. Call it mother's intuition, but all of a sudden I am certain that if his jazz CD earns him a live audition in Minnesota, and if he is then accepted at St. Olaf as a music major, we will be putting him on an airplane nine months from now.

"Henry will never go to college all the way out in Minnesota," Jack predicted with authority four weeks ago when his brother called home after his interview. But Jack hadn't heard the excitement in Henry's voice, and he'd never had the experience of feeling instantly at home in a strange new place he'd never been before.

"Everything here is exactly right for me," is what Henry told me that night, sounding a little astonished himself. "If it weren't so far from home, this would definitely be my top choice, even more than Bowdoin, or any other place I've seen."

I knew what my job was in that moment, and it wasn't to agree, "Yeah, you're right, Minnesota is too far away." My job was to say, "Well, go for it, Henry, and don't worry about the distance. We'll be fine, you know, and so will you. The important thing is that you end up in the right place, no matter where it is." I did get those words out, then made a silent wish for Maine and a son who might still be close enough that his dad and I could call him next year, spur of the moment, and say, "Hey, we're driving up, and we're planning to be there in time for dinner."

Now, with that door closed, all the rest stand open. Someday, in the not too distant future, he will take his leave of us and walk through one of them. Already, I feel life speeding up, spinning on, and I worry that this year is passing us by, tipping us all too quickly into a future I'm still not ready to inhabit. The more I wish to hold on to a fleeting moment, to this brief, lovely season, to snowstorms and Christmas carols and two sons at home, the more I feel time slipping through my fingers.

No one has touched the pile of Christmas books on the coffee table since I set them there weeks ago. Time was, each darkening Advent afternoon would bring a pause in the day's busyness, a ritual of plugging in the tree and then retreating to the couch as evening fell. With a small boy tucked in close on each side of me, a picture book in my lap, I would read our way into Christmas; we would learn the old stories by heart and then return to them year after year—*The Little Fir Tree, How the Grinch Stole Christmas, Harvey Slumfenburger's Christmas Present.*

I could not stop myself from unpacking the Christmas books this year, arranging them at last in our own living room, even as I anticipated the sorrow of January, the possibility that, after a long absence from our old tradition, the whole stack might well get returned to its box, unread. We are in new territory here, on the far side of childhood, yet I'm still not quite able to let go of the rituals with which we've always laced our lives, the ways we've always had of making Christmas Christmas.

No child has added a new homemade decoration to our tree for years now. I used to wish for a perfect Christmas tree, elegant with fragile, heirloom ornaments handed down through generations. What we've always ended up with instead is a hodgepodge of hardware store balls, bought cheap the year we married, intermingled with the occasional rare treasure and a swelling, motley collection of handmade creations, courtesy of two prolific little boys.

Yet a week ago, as I hung a drab, decade-old cardboard egg-cup gilded with glitter, and a faded Popsicle stick star, upon the branches of fragrant pine, I found myself yearning to re-weave, if only for an afternoon, the dense, sturdy tapestry of our old life, long since unraveled and already vanishing on the winds of memory. What I would give for one more hour at the beige Formica table in our old playroom, surrounded by glue sticks and scraps of paper, watching chubby, determined fingers gripping colored markers and blunt scissors, listening in as my sons plot small kindnesses: "I am making a snowman for Nana, because she loves them. . . ." "This Santa face will have the funniest nose. . . ." "Mom, can you help me . . ."

Now, we are trying to weave a new fabric, creating a home, a life that seems to shape-shift daily. And so, box by box, I unpacked our old decorations, only to find myself putting most of them away again. I used to decorate every room, every windowsill, of our old house with rows of tiny fir trees and snow-capped cottages. The wooden Advent calendar in the kitchen provided treats that appeared, as if by magic, each morning. Moss gardens revealed new additions daily, bright gems, smooth shells, tiny elves who would mysteriously take up residence in the dark of night. Steve and I strung lights in every doorway and around each tangled tree outside. We placed candles in the windows and then steamed up the kitchen late at night, baking dark, dense cakes studded with fruit and soaked with brandy. For years, we created Christmas and gave it to our children, delivered it in cookie tins filled to the brim for our neighbors and friends, packed it up and shipped it off in cartons to distant relatives and loved ones, wrote it into hundreds of Christmas cards and holiday letters that we stamped and addressed by hand, sitting at our old kitchen table, while Henry worked his way through *The Reader's Digest Book of Christmas Carols*. It was a way not only to make Christmas, but also to hold it in our hearts.

But I cannot bring myself to fill this new house with all the mementos of a life that's disappeared. So instead of tiny trees

and cottages, I head out into the woods one raw, gray afternoon, clippers in hand, in search of some other kind of beauty.
I cut branches of pine and hemlock and spruce and arrange
them in white pitchers. I set six small ivory reindeer in a row
on a windowsill, spread a red cloth over the dining table, and
realize that it's enough. Beyond our windows, the world is
frosted white. From every room we look out upon undulating
drifts, snow-laden maples, stone walls capped with poufs of
powder, gray green mountains against an ever changing sky.
Nature's decoration, winter's stark beauty, is everywhere I look.
Here in the house, there is no need to overdo. Our sons are
nearly men now, and we are in a different place. There are, I am
beginning to see, many kinds of letting go. Not just of children
and childhood rituals, but of old ideas about the way things
ought to look or be or feel. The wide arc of sky, the open fields,
our own light-filled rooms, all seem to suggest simplicity and
restraint. This year, I finally allow myself to give up the old
production, to stop thinking of Christmas as an event that must
be labored over, created, and presented. Christmas doesn't need
to be made anymore, at least not by me. Surely, one way or
another, it will come on its own.

The day after being turned down by Bowdoin, my son sits at the
piano and begins to work his way through the score of *Bye Bye
Birdie*. Come spring, he will be the musical director for his
school's production, and he knows that the practice time he puts
in now will save him stress later. Rough, repetitive, this is the
slow, painstaking work of sight-reading and first run-throughs.
Early this morning, I found him at my desk, reconsidering online a college he'd crossed off his list a couple of months ago.

Till yesterday afternoon, he'd dared hope that, just perhaps,
his near future might be all laid out for him, that he might be

donc with the job of applying to college and could move on, instead, to imagining himself there. Now, true to his nature, he is not wasting time gazing wistfully at a closed door; he's moving past it. Over and over, he resets the small black metronome and launches into the jazzy, upbeat overture, completely absorbed in the work at hand. Tomorrow, he will turn eighteen. He has a full-length score to learn, Christmas presents to buy and wrap, and six applications to complete by January. The house is filled with music. He's on it.

"I'll treat you to breakfast," I say to Henry on his birthday. It is a week until Christmas, Jack is sick in bed with a cold, and Steve is heading off to work. Other than a birthday dinner at home tonight, we have no plans. These last weeks have been intense at school, packed with finals, deadlines, holiday parties, and rehearsals. For people who live together, we've not seen much of one another.

Now, as we slide into a wooden booth at Nonies, it is as if we are on holiday in our own hometown, playing hooky from our normal, everyday lives. While the rest of the world is getting busy, we linger, spreading the *New York Times* across the table, our appetites quickened by the dense, comforting aromas of coffee, bacon, and eggs. The windows are steamed up against the cold, the day's Jumble puzzle is scrawled on a chalkboard, and the doughnuts in the case are decorated in merry seasonal icings, bright red and green. The breakfast regulars are in no hurry to eat and run; they joke with the waitresses, call for coffee refills, and leave extra-big holiday tips.

Henry orders chocolate-chip pancakes and hot cocoa with whipped cream, and then, as I've done every year since he was two, I tell him all over again about the glittering bright, freezing cold day eighteen years ago that he arrived on this earth. He has heard every detail before, knows them all by heart, but this is one story that he will always indulge and one that I embellish and enlarge upon with every telling. I watch my son polish off the last of his enormous breakfast, and I wonder where he will be next year on this day and whether the birthday story is yet another ritual that time and distance will soon steal away.

He's sitting right across the table from me, a chocolate mustache darkening his upper lip. But even as I reach toward him with my napkin, and he brushes my hand away, embarrassed, I succumb to unexpected longing. He is doing exactly what all eighteen-year-olds do, growing up. Separating. Looking forward, not back, as he prepares to embark on a life of his own. And even though he hasn't left yet, I am missing him already.

After breakfast, we wander through town, do Christmas shopping at the bookstore, and stop at the market for the makings of a birthday feast. At home, the day stretches out, a rare, quiet emptiness. The sky is gray, lead-colored, unwelcoming. And so, we stay in. Henry putters on the computer, collecting birthday greetings from friends on Facebook. Each time his cell phone rings, he heads for another room, and I hear him laughing, chatting, saying thanks.

Jack, feeling better, comes downstairs and offers to slice mushrooms and to cut beans while I make the cake. A classmate from up the road appears at the back door with a tin of homemade chocolate-chip cookies for Henry and a CD she's made him. We pour tea, and the kitchen fills with good smells, funky music, and teenage talk. All day, we are happy with one another, but it is Henry who sets the mood, his capacity for contentment an inspiration to me. While I tend to try to squeeze the most from every day and often come up short, he allows each day its own slow unfolding. And it is this, I realize, his innate ability to be glad for whatever is, without wishing for something more or something else, that makes this uneventful birthday day a good one.

Finally, in a burst of unexpected brilliance, a sinking sun breaks through clouds and turns the snow-white land to shades of rose and crimson. Henry and I pull on winter layers, grab our snowshoes, and tramp across the road and into the silent, waiting woods. After a day spent indoors, it is exhilarating to be out. It feels good to move, to feel the exertion of pushing forward, kicking along through deep snow, gulping cold, sharp air. With Gracie bounding ahead, tossing up sprays of powder, we take my favorite loop alongside icy streams and through deep pines, winding up at the edge of the pond, a vast, flat expanse of frozen white rimmed by evergreens.

We stop in our tracks and stare at the sky. The sun, sliding slowly behind the pines, is enormous, a giant orb blazing through shreds of low-hanging cloud, now dyed in hues of purple, pink, and red. We stand in silence for a long moment, still as statues, bathed in the golden, heavenly light.

And then suddenly the two of us, like fairy-tale characters breaking free of an enchantment, are both speaking at once, exclaiming at this magnificence. "Well, Happy Birthday!" I say, reaching out to put an arm around his shoulders, as if all this— the wide, frozen pond, the fringe of dark trees, the brilliant, painted sky—were meant for him. And surely, this moment of wild perfection is the real gift of today. All afternoon I've pushed back against a sense of restlessness, a vague longing for something more, something I couldn't even put a name to. Now, that hunger has been satisfied, out on a snowshoe walk with my son, in the unexpected splendor of a December sunset across a frozen pond. He feels it, too, I think, as if even the disappointment of this week's rejection is mitigated, once and for all, by an encounter with some greater, more compelling power.

How good it is to be here, side by side, feeling small, and full, and grateful. And how important it is, for me, but perhaps even more for my son, poised here on the brink of his adulthood, to be so powerfully reminded that the things that matter most—beauty, nature, love, companionship—are already ours, if we only reach out to claim them.

Trudging home, I watch Gracie's white-tipped tail waving in front of us like a flag as she bounds along, blazing her own trail. Already, the golden light of dusk is draining from the sky, and cold seeps through my jacket, through my fleece-lined gloves. Henry, pink-cheeked, turns back to say he's frozen and heading in for a bath. In a few minutes, I'll stamp the snow from my boots and slip back into the warmth and bustle of home. I will plug in the Christmas tree, change clothes, set the table for dinner, pile presents in the living room. Soon my parents, my brother, and his wife and baby will arrive. Steve will light the fire, pour wine, and our house will fill with noise and laughter and birthday wishes.

I stand outside for a few moments after Henry goes in, watching the first stars appear. A stillness, a healing quiet, settles over the landscape, the mountains black and solid against a lighter sky.

"We are born not all at once, but by bits," wrote Mary Antin after immigrating to America nearly a hundred years ago. "The body first, and the spirit later; and the birth and growth of the spirit, in those who are attentive to their own inner life, are slow and exceedingly painful. Our mothers are racked with the pains of our physical birth; we ourselves suffer the longer pains of spiritual growth."

How little I knew of such things on that day eighteen years ago when I gave birth to my first child and, at the same moment, to myself as a mother. How surprised I would have been then, to think that the birthing would continue for both of us, that the journey of the spirit was only just beginning, and that the long, hard labor I'd just endured was not an ending, but an initiation into much greater tests to come. Having brought a child into the world, I was suddenly overcome by awareness: of how precious and fragile life is, and how great my new responsibility, to keep this small, dependent being alive and safe through his long passage into adulthood. Now the time that always was the future has become the present. That tiny infant, my first great spiritual teacher, is eighteen and ready to take on the task of figuring out his own life. And I am called upon not only to let him go, but to relinquish as well any illusion I might have had about my ability to protect him. The truth is, we can't keep our children safe, all we can do is love them, teach them as best we can, and then trust in their destinies as they embark on their own necessary journeys, out beyond the sheltered shores of childhood.

I allow myself a few more minutes outside in the dark, on the crest of our hill. I try to imagine what it would feel like to be truly alone, with no one to love or laugh with, no one with whom to share the beauty of the stars or the splendor of a winter sunset. And I realize that even in solitude, it is my sense of connection with friends and family, both near and far, that makes me feel alive and a part of things. My children will take their leave, come home, and leave again. Already, their lives are changing, each gesture toward independence hinting at the far greater changes in store for us all. Yet the joy of loving them, knowing them, watching them grow and risk and learn, will endure.

Behind me, our house contains the outward manifestations of that love, each cherished book and polished candlestick and framed photograph a testament to family life and domesticity.

Out here, beneath a sky slowly filling with stars, I stand on the threshold of some other world, a vast realm beyond my reach and understanding. And yet, what I feel is the opposite of loneliness, but rather a kind of deep acceptance, a sense of the intimacy and interconnectedness of all creation. Letting go, I am beginning to understand, is not just an idea or a gesture, but a kind of spiritual maturation, a movement away from the physical realm and into a place of greater faith and mystery.

Our house is beautiful at night, a glowing, welcoming sanctuary amid the empty enormity of snow-covered fields. The Christmas tree glimmers like a beacon in the living room. Golden rectangles of light pierce the darkness. Looking in, I see that my husband has come home, that he is washing his hands at the kitchen sink. Upstairs, Henry's head moves past a bedroom window. My family is waiting for me. I turn my back on the mountains, on the stars, the silence, and step inside.

The applications are in. The deadlines have come and gone. After months of lists and forms and soul-searching essay writing, my son has finished the job, sent the last online application orbiting through the ether. One final package sits by the door, a CD he's made for a conservatory added late to the list. Three music auditions are as yet on the calendar, the final pieces in this still-evolving picture. And then my son's future will rest in other hands. There's a funny kind of relief in that. His efforts, for the moment, have come to an end. It is January. Now begins the season of waiting.

Yesterday, Steve dragged the Christmas tree into the backyard, and I swept the brittle needles from the floor. In one gray day of thaw and melt, I emptied every room of Christmas, packed the decorations back into their boxes, and stacked them in the basement.

Now the house is quiet, empty, stripped bare of holiday magic. Both boys have returned to school, and Steve left this morning for a three-day business trip. I sit on the couch and look out the windows, to a world obscured by thick, damp fog. I try to reacquaint myself with the pleasure of silence, unfamiliar as that feels after weeks of togetherness. We have had a month of celebrations—friends and family coming and going; first-time visitors from our old life, eager for house tours and to know whether this move, in the end, was "worth it"; holiday meals conceived, prepared, and cleaned up after; the refrigerator filled and emptied countless times.

One night, a writer friend came for dinner. Edie's husband died too young, before, as she once said, "we even had a chance to get sick of each other." Widowed now for fifteen years, childless, she stays too busy to allow for much loneliness. At our house, she is a favorite guest, having developed to a fine art the gift of being with other people's families, taking the time to get to know small children, teenagers, and dogs. We sat squeezed in around the kitchen island, cozy and content, glad for one another's company and good conversation. Afterward, we lit candles in the living room and gathered around the fireplace.

When I suggested that it would be a good night to read Truman Capote's "A Christmas Memory," neither son protested or drifted away muttering excuses. In fact, we threw another log on the fire and took turns reading aloud to one another, pausing, as we always do, to savor and repeat our favorite line—"a hateful heap of bitter-odored pennies"—and to marvel at a time when kites were made by hand and a sack of tangerines would be anybody's favorite present. Each year, if nothing else, we read this most perfect book, and each year we are surprised by its capacity to surprise us all over again.

This night, it was Jack who read the final pages, taking over

when my own voice suddenly caught in my throat. "Life separates us," he read, his voice newly deep and matter-of-fact.
Knowing that, anticipating the bittersweet truth of these words,
I looked around at my husband and sons, at our dear friend, at
a room transformed for Christmas, and tried to memorize the
moment, to burnish it by my own attention into a keepsake
that I might store away now and retrieve later, on a day when
the sparkle and intimacy of the holiday had long since vanished
from the house.

The irony, of course, is that every moment of our togetherness contains the seed of a farewell, that life is always a dance of
coming together and moving away again. Somehow we must
learn to be nimble in our steps, to welcome both togetherness
and solitude, to move boldly, easily, out into the world, and to
honor as well the soul's requirements for rest, replenishment,
and reflection.

What has amazed me most in the last month or so, as my
older son has expanded his horizons outward, carefully and
deliberately doing the hard work of applying to five more colleges, is the way he has grown, with each completed task and
each finished application, more comfortable with the reality of
our own impending separation. It is as if the job of applying has
strengthened and readied him for what comes next, the even
greater job of leaving. For now, though, he has no choice but
to embrace uncertainty, to live for a few more months with the
great unanswered question—leaving for where?

For months, I've watched Henry compose honest answers to
questions on admissions forms. He has shared his innermost
hopes and dreams, sight-read strange music on unfamiliar pianos,
conversed with interviewers and admissions officers, willingly
opened himself up to perfect strangers. In good faith, he has

forged human connections at each step of the way. More than anything now, he needs to retain some faith in the process itself, to believe that his own best efforts will at least be considered objectively and fairly by professionals who bring integrity to the job. But it also seems important, at this vulnerable moment, that he be reminded that what will matter in the long run is not where he goes to college, but what he does when he gets there, that the quality of the education he receives will be determined by him and not by the exclusivity or competitiveness of the school he attends.

Looking back, I see how much he has matured since he began this consuming process six months ago. He took something valuable even from the sting of having his early admission application bureaucratically rejected by a school he loved so much that he was sure it already loved him in return: Don't take it personally; life does go on.

Two days ago, an e-mail arrived from a jazz piano teacher at another school in Maine. This professor had squeezed a half-hour piano lesson into his schedule when Henry visited; now he's written to say he has put in a good word for his application. Whether the recommendation helps or not, I'm thankful that this kind man let my son know that he had been seen and valued for who he is. He reminded him that this is, still, a human process and that a college education is not a prize to be won, but a shared enterprise.

It is more than a little strange to realize that while my son is fixing himself an English muffin after school this afternoon or playing music with his kid brother in the living room, strangers across the country are debating his desirability as a member of the class of 2012. Somewhere, perhaps today, an overworked committee will spend about four and a half minutes sizing him up against however many thousands of other applicants they have in their pile. If the enormity of that makes him feel power-less, or worried, he's not saying. But I know he's thinking about it, trying to make his peace with this season of uncertainty.

What I most want my son to understand at this odd and vulnerable moment, when it feels as if the future is beyond his control, is that we're *already* proud of him, that we don't need to wait for an acceptance letter to land in the mailbox before we celebrate. How much better, in fact, to honor him right now, in darkest January, for the job he's just completed with such competence and for the huge steps he's already taken in the lifelong work of becoming more fully himself.

And then, perhaps we can all embrace these waiting months and appreciate them simply as a time of release after all the stresses of fall and application deadlines. Here, in the quiet of midwinter, is breathing room. The future is never ours to call anyway. No matter how carefully we may try to orchestrate or foretell outcomes, there are forces at work in this universe that are far more powerful than any of our human machinations. So be it. We all learn by going where we need to go. Let us welcome the mystery, then, and trust that what is meant to be, will be.

～14～

settling

*To stay in one place and watch the
seasons come and go is tantamount to
constant travel: one is traveling the earth.*
—MARGUERITE YOURCENAR

*I*t has been a relentless winter, storm followed by storm, ever since the first drifting flakes surprised us in November. We haven't seen bare earth since. This morning, the phone rang in darkness and a just-waking voice on the other end of the line murmured, "No school today." A look outside explained why: It had snowed all night, it was snowing still. Now, hours later, icy rain pounds the roof, the car is stuck fast at the bottom of the driveway, the doors of the house, all but one, are banked with snow and frozen shut. The power went out a while ago.

There's nothing more delicious than this—a deep settlement of snow, a quiet house. Without heat, lights, Internet, we're marooned for a time with just one another for company, one charged cell phone our only link to the outside world. The snow has delivered its gifts of silence, time, peace. And with this sudden absence of choice and activity comes abrupt, improbable relief. There is no place to go, nothing to do but read near a window, perhaps, pick up pen and paper, find the old deck of cards. We build a fire, pull on fleeces, and settle in. Time slows.

Someone gave us a board game for Christmas. For the first time, we take it out. It is almost impossible to lure Jack away from the computer these days, and I'm tired of trying to enforce limits, of begging him to join us. But today events are on my side. He pulls up a chair, opens the game, and begins to read the directions.

Outside, the landscape hardens by degrees, the falling temperatures turning rain to sleet and then to ice that encrusts every branch and bough. The trees bend low, shouldering their heavy burdens. Inside, our own moods lighten. Instead of productivity today, we have been released into freedom.

When my sons were little, snow days meant a race to get outside before the neighbor kids, hats and boots and mittens and sleds, shouts of joy and hours of hard, wet play. Snow days are different now, but they are magical still, releasing us from the demands of the world beyond our door, delivering us from scheduled busyness into the unexpected ease of empty hours. What a pleasure it is to realize that everything on the calendar must be canceled or postponed until some clear moment in the future. The empty day stretches before us.

Much as I aspire to simple living, to close daily connections with my husband and sons, the truth is, much of the time life feels anything but simple. We are moving fast these days, usually in four different directions. Lately, I've noticed that when someone asks me how I'm doing, I reply by telling them how busy I've been. When someone inquires after my sons, I talk about what they're *doing*—playing basketball, working on a senior research paper, rehearsing for a show—instead of how they are.

It is so easy, living with teenagers, to confuse life with performance, and busyness with meaning. I see how my own responsibilities expand to fill every moment of the day and that my sons have grown accustomed to having something going on during every waking hour. Even when they are home, they often seem only half-present, here in body but connected elsewhere. If they're studying or doing homework, chances are they are also texting and listening to music, distracted and occupied at the same time. Yet I keep hoping, for all our sakes, that we might strike more of a balance between being and doing, between meeting the demands of life and pausing long enough to appreciate its sweet rewards.

This morning, a downed power line and an unplowed driveway have changed our routine. Lights, running water, flushing toilets, and all the other comforts that we normally take for granted suddenly seem like precious gifts, if only because today we must do without them. Stillness has been thrust upon us. The house, unplugged, is eerily quiet, the only sound the spattering staccato of icy rain against the windows and onto the frozen landscape beyond. Even our voices grow quiet. A soft shuffle of cards. The scrape of a chair. In the fireplace, a log falls, sending a spray of embers twirling up the flue. The sky darkens and closes in.

I've spent quite a lot of time over these winter weeks thinking about just what a well-lived life might look and feel like to me now. A balanced life has a rhythm. But we live in a time, and in a culture, that encourages everyone to just move faster. I'm learning that if I don't take the time to tune in to my own more deliberate pace, I end up moving to someone else's, the speed of events around me setting a tempo that leaves me feeling scattered and out of touch with myself. I know now that I can't write fast; that words, my own thoughts and ideas, come to the surface slowly and in silence. A close relationship with myself requires slowness. Intimacy with my husband and guarded teenage sons requires slowness. A good conversation can't be hurried, it needs time in which to meander its way to revelation and insight. Even cooking dinner with care and attention is slow work. A thoughtful life is not rushed.

The days are long gone when I could lead my children by the hand into pools of quiet, knowing each gift of downtime would be gratefully accepted—snuggling on the couch, reading stories, talking softly in a darkened bedroom. I cannot force them to do as I would have them do or to be as I would have them be. All I can really do now is hope that as I put more thought into the rhythm of my own life in this place, my sons, in time, will come to appreciate something of its sustaining beauty and the impulses that led us to settle here in the first place. Perhaps, growing up and out, they will carry with them something of what they've had—quiet nights and full moons, sunrises that are worth waking up for, the light-filled peace of these rooms, the time and space to seek out their own nurturing rhythms. Gratifying as it is to watch my sons grow and change and become more fully themselves, I still tend to forget that they are individuals, and one speed doesn't fit all. They are old enough now to find their own rhythms, to figure out for themselves that even a highly scheduled day is well punctuated by a pause for stillness. Yet I can't help but be nostalgic for the rituals and routines that once defined us as a family, holding us secure and in place in a fast-paced world. The art of living, as I once read, "lies in the fine mingling of letting go and holding on." That's a pretty good way to define the art of parenting teenagers as well. The great challenge of my own middle age, it seems, is to mellow into that fine mingling and to grow comfortable there.

The changes I long for now are not changes of address or circumstance, but changes within myself. If I am going to master the knack of holding on and letting go all at once, I need to figure out what's still worth reaching for, even as I begin to give up some of my old props—the demands of family life, ambition, the need to be right, material things.

After three years of having most of our possessions in storage, living in close company and borrowed rooms, struggling to make new connections and to fashion new lives in new places, we have finally unpacked our boxes, filled closets and drawers and shelves, and settled in. The house we envisioned for so long exists at last.

For months I've been checking items off punch lists, running errands, organizing, cleaning. Now, those jobs are finished as well. Even our old friend the finish carpenter has finally wrapped it up, having installed the last drawer pull and bookcase molding. There are still some boxes in the basement, family pictures to hang in the upstairs hall, a garage to close in when our bank account allows. But for the most part, the house is built, the work of moving in is done, and the novelty of all this newness has faded some. We've celebrated birthdays, holidays, the dawn of a new year. We've had a taste of the life that will go on here.

Today, in the blessed quiet of snow, I take stock. It feels as if we have been on a kind of self-imposed pilgrimage, my husband, two sons, and I, one that we set forth on without knowing where we were headed or even quite why. Compared with the enormous life challenges so many families face, ours wasn't much—we left a comfortable life, we shared a house with my parents for a while, we moved five times in three years, and we ended up here, in a quiet house on a quiet road in a quiet town. Yet even this modest journey has tempered us. Living through the twists and turns of these years, we have learned to make some kind of peace with ambiguity.

Sometimes the boys' recollections of their early childhoods amaze me. They have just enough distance now to reminisce about what was without mourning all that is no more. Their memories are keen. What they remember is not the big picture at all, but the details, the tiny minutiae of life as experienced from a child's point of view: peeking from the bathroom window as their dad hid colored eggs on a chilly Easter morning, the peculiar odor in our laundry room on a humid day, the tiny plastic pirate who disappeared down the drain with the bathwater, never to be seen again, the time I fell sound asleep while reading *The Hobbit* out loud and kept right on talking anyway, making no sense whatever.

My sons' memories of their first home are full of such particulars, the sound and feel and smell of things. "I remember," says Jack, "how I used to run down the hall to my bedroom, and I would always jump up to try to touch the chain hanging from the light on the ceiling. For years and years, I never even got close. And then one day, I finally did it, I touched the chain, and I suddenly realized that I had grown."

Even now, I regret the loss of a container for such memories. I wish that Jack could stride through the very same hallway today, know what it feels like to have that chain brush the top of his head, and feel secure in a life that never changed. Yet I also know that change is the essence of life. For everything we left behind, we have gained something new; for everything we have found along the way, we have had to let go of something else. And so it is that we ourselves have changed, and grown, and come to a deeper appreciation of the transience of all things.

I used to think that someday I would have a revelation that would suddenly illuminate the path we've traveled. And then, in a flash of understanding, I would know exactly what it was that compelled us to leave one home, one life, for another. I liked the idea of a cosmic message, one that would instantly explain everything, making all our decisions clear to us in retrospect. But now I suspect few of us ever really get that "Aha!" moment, the spark of insight that finally makes perfect sense of our muddled, complicated lives. It may be that some kind of divine wisdom did lead us here, to this town, this place, this house. But I think the truth is simpler and plainer than that. The small choices we make each day, the doors we open and close, determine the lives that we live.

Attempting to explain his intentions for Stuart Little, the tiny mouse born of human parents, E. B. White once wrote to a friend, "Stuart's journey symbolizes the continuing journey that everybody takes—in search of what is perfect and unattainable." Perhaps that search for something perfect and unattainable is what propelled us on our way as well. We ventured out beyond what was familiar in our lives, in the hope of finding a kind of perfection. Yet surely, at some level, I also knew the truth—perfection is nowhere, and everywhere. Which is really the same as acknowledging that whatever it is we seek, if it exists at all, is already within us.

At midlife, I managed to convince myself that physical movement was a prerequisite for change, that a different geographic location would satisfy a restlessness of spirit. Now, I think I recognize that restlessness for what it was—the first stirrings of fear that my own life would be over when my children left home. Afraid to ask the question "Who am I now?" I asked another one instead: "Where should we live?" And then I set out with such urgency to find an answer that in the end the question itself sent us all into motion.

For a long time, the work of house selling, house buying, house razing, house building, and caring for two adolescent boys has kept us really, really busy. We found ourselves overextended and overcommitted, in flux, and increasingly adept in temporary situations. Now our task is to put down roots once more, to settle here and fashion a life once again that is built around a place.

At a certain point in every journey, the traveler stops turning around to look back at what's been left behind and faces only forward, toward a new horizon. It has been a long time now since we moved away from our old green house. Our children grew up while we were in transit, which means that the young men they are today bear little resemblance to the boys who so carefully packed up their prize possessions four years ago. Our own needs changed as well, and when it came time for me and my husband to sort through our past and choose whatever we wished to carry forward into the future, we found ourselves sloughing off layers, casting aside decades' worth of accumulation. Having lived without our things for so long, we found it easier to get rid of stuff than to shoulder the weight of it again.

So it is that the back wall of Steve's office is stacked high with moving boxes we opened last fall and then taped shut again and marked with the words *Yard Sale.* He will turn sixty next year, and I am staring fifty in the eye. After all those years of gathering in, acquiring and owning and caring for things, we are ready to travel more lightly.

Still, even this voluntary letting go is not without its sorrow. Just as our sons' readiness to dispose of hand puppets and Halloween costumes and Legos was a testament to the end of an era, so has my own slow sorting process evolved into a reminder of all that has imperceptibly slipped away. Camping gear, boxes of fabric and quilting supplies, even an almost new pair of Rollerblades—discarding all these things has meant admitting to myself how much life changed while we were busy doing other things. Paring down has meant coming face-to-face with lost hopes and dreams and with the fact that who I was is no longer who I am. It has been years since I flipped pancakes outdoors on a Coleman stove, stitched a quilt by hand, or, Lord knows, skated up and down the driveway while my sons cheered me on.

We have so little past in these rooms, so few shared memories upon which to layer the present. The time that we will spend here all together is short. Today, the simple blessing of snow has given us the company of one another. Late in the afternoon, the sleety rain ends, and the sun makes a brief appearance. Steve and I insist that our reluctant sons get out of their sweatshirts and flannel pants and into outdoor clothes. It is time to clear paths, scrape cars, free ourselves. The two of us are already hard at it when they finally emerge, grumpy and squinting like bears crawling out of the den. The fresh, cold air works its magic, though. Before long, the silent, grudging work is broken by chatter, then laughter. The shovelers grow lively, Gracie leaps into the air trying to catch every flying shard of ice, and the job devolves into a wild slipping and sliding contest down the driveway.

By the time the job is finally done, the doors shoveled clear and the stuck car returned safely to the garage, it is almost dark. We stand outside in the stillness, leaning on our shovels, contemplating the icebound solidity of things, the last gleams of light reflected back from solid expanses of white, lifeless fields. It feels as if the earth itself has ceased to turn, as if the flux and flow and forward motion of life has stopped, once and for all. The world spread before us seems impermeable, unchangeable, fixed in place, as if who we are in this moment—four cold people, breathing plumes of vapor into frigid air—is who we will always be. And as if what we see—a dark, silent house; a frozen landscape beneath a purplish, wintry sky—is all that we will ever see.

Suddenly, inside, the power returns and the house bursts into brilliant, electric life, every upstairs and downstairs light popping on at once. The boys let out whoops of relief and dash for the door. A wan sun slips away behind the trees. Time reasserts itself. And this day, too, ends.

The early action news from Berklee comes a week later than expected. Too many applicants, too little staff; the whole process is slowed. Finally, though, the moment is at hand. Henry's been notified that acceptances will be e-mailed at six p.m. At six-thirty, dinner is getting cold on the stove, and he is still waiting, pacing, pausing on his route through the kitchen to sit at my computer and anxiously refresh the page, again and again. He holds his cell phone in one hand, checking the time, texting incessantly. His friends are all phoning in; everyone wants to be the first to know. Finally, at seven, I serve up the lukewarm chicken and rice and we sit down at the table. Henry's phone buzzes and spins next to his plate. He leaps up, heads into my office, and closes the door. A moment later, he's back. "I'm in!"

On a cold night in February, it all becomes real. There is a school out there that wants my son, a school where he applied, auditioned, and made it. It's the best possible news, yet even as the four of us clink glasses and grin ourselves silly congratulating Henry, there is a touch of wistfulness in the air as well. What no one says out loud, but what we know full well, is that this moment of happiness and relief is already connected to a future one, a parting.

Life moves on not randomly, but as a continuing chain of events, cause and effect, each small step we take leading on to the next. For weeks we have been waiting for news, eager to find out how our son's life would unfurl before him. Tonight a cheerful e-mail from the Berklee admissions office suggests that he will have some choices after all. In the meantime, though, we are here, eating dinner together as we have on a thousand other nights, all jumbled together now in memory. Next year at this time, life will be different in ways we can only begin to imagine. But one thing I know for sure is that the present moment goes by so fast that there's barely time to catch it, let alone savor it or live it fully, before it's lost forever.

And maybe that's why we find ourselves this winter with an otherwise inexplicable passion for the seventh season of *American Idol*. Our family has never had much of a TV habit, but my mother has her favorite shows, and *Idol* is one of them. Living with her for three years, we couldn't help but be pulled in, too. Henry was the first to get hooked, but pretty soon even Jack, initially the most disdainful critic, and Steve, way too busy for reality TV, succumbed to the steady process of trial and elimination by which amateur kids with good singing voices are transformed into seasoned performers. It's cheesy, it's over-the-top, and it's a ridiculous time suck—two nights a week for months on end, from the excruciating auditions on through the live performances. Yet come January, there we were, four merciless, fanatically devoted viewers.

We may laugh at ourselves for watching it, but now, midway through the season, I am unreasonably proud to say that we haven't missed an episode. That may qualify us as true fans, but I'm pretty certain that some other, equally compelling impulse is at work here as well. It is not just a singing competition that brings us together in front of the television night after night, but our own unspoken longing for connection.

Through the long, dark months of winter, we set up the

TiVo on Tuesdays and Wednesdays, and then once everyone is finally home and all schoolwork and tasks are done, the four of us head downstairs, mugs of tea in hand. We reach for the afghans my grandmother crocheted years ago, and we squeeze in side by side on the broad, soft sofa in the basement, drawn to the comforting repetition of routine, the talents of a bunch of aspiring young singers, and our own easy ritual of togetherness.

Nestled in between my husband and sons, who are unfailingly funny and vocal in their opinions, I'm reminded yet again that the things we do together don't have to be particularly meaningful or exalted to be special. In fact, the times I treasure most these days are the unremarkable moments when we simply happen to find ourselves within arm's reach of one another. They are the very moments it's so easy to take for granted, or to miss altogether, so focused are we on the "important" demands of this week's project, the big test tomorrow, Friday's social plan, the text message that just came in this very minute. My sons seem to move from one drama to another. Sharing a home with them, I am constantly reminded of just how high adolescent highs can be on any given day and just how low the lows. What I love most, though, are the rare and deliciously peaceful plateaus in between.

And so I gather up the monotonous winter days, the snow days, the mundane weeknights, the hours we spend together watching a silly TV show, and I string them together in my mind like matched pearls on a thread, finding satisfaction in their very sameness. Ordinary days. The days in which nothing momentous happens, no great victories are won, no huge disappointments suffered, no milestones achieved. Most of our lives are made up of days just like this—if we're lucky, that is, and the seas of fate are calm. Days that are not particularly memorable, but that are nonetheless the only days we have. Days in which we simply attend to the humble business of life—making meals and eating them, cleaning up afterward, doing algebra problems, practicing for next week's piano recital, paying bills, coming and going, until finally, at day's end, we are reunited for a little while, to share a laugh, a foot rub or a back scratch, a game of Cribbage, the satisfaction of our togetherness. If I'm paying attention, then I do experience these days, and all these plain, unadorned moments, as gifts. And I remember that grace, like any other gift, can easily be mine, if I open my hand to accept it.

"Grace is available for each of us every day—our spiritual daily bread," writes *Simple Abundance* author Sarah Ban Breathnach, "but we've got to remember to ask for it with a grateful heart and not worry about whether there will be enough for tomorrow."

This is the message I take from our first winter here, this winter of steady snows and poignant family transitions, college admissions and freshman struggles, and my own renewed intention to slow down at last, to settle fully and wholeheartedly into this house, this place, so that my everyday life really does fit the person I am, the person I am still in the process of becoming. Grace, I remind myself, is right at my fingertips. I need only open my hand to accept it.

And grace is what I need these days, as I endeavor to stop viewing the world through the needs of my children and to attend more conscientiously to my own. I guess I never quite anticipated that after all these years of family life, I'd still be on the learning curve, would still be trying to figure out how to be a mother, even as I come to the end of one of the great cycles of human existence, raising young children to become compassionate, self-sufficient adults.

Once upon a time, I took pride in the predictable patterns of our days, nap times and bath times and bed times, finger paints and made-up stories and whole-wheat bread, baked seven loaves at a time. Spread out to cool on the kitchen counter, those brown, fragrant loaves were tangible proof of the depth of my caring. Later, I taught my sons to cook for themselves. I proofread book reports, vetted movies, played chauffeur to carloads of boys, did my best to impart such homely skills as bed making and trash emptying, teeth flossing and face washing.

Now, we're in a different place and a different time, and I need to become a different kind of mother. A mother who knows how to back off. A mother whose gaze is not quite so intently focused on her own two endlessly absorbing children, but who is engaged instead in a rich, full life of her own. A mother who cares a good deal less than she used to about what time people in her household go to bed, what they eat for breakfast, whether they wear coats or not, and what they choose to do, or not to do, with their own time. A mother who, though her protective, maternal instincts run as fierce and deep as ever, manages, in all but extreme moments, to keep those instincts in check. A mother who trusts in who her children are, even if they aren't exactly who she thinks they ought to be. Who keeps faith in their futures, even when the things they do, and the words they say, give her pause in the present. A mother who remembers, above all else, that the greatest gift she can give to her own two wildly different, nearly grown sons is the knowledge that, no matter what, she loves them both absolutely, just exactly as they are.

Writing these words, I'm reminded that what confirmed me once and for all as a mother, at the moment my firstborn son was laid upon my chest, is the very same thing that makes me feel so unsettled and proud now, as that boy prepares to leave home, with his kid brother following right behind in his footsteps. A heart full of love. That is the constant, the only thing that's never changed, the only thing that never will. Love is the infinite, durable strand that's woven itself through all the days and nights of our shared past and that will wind its way, uninterrupted, through our unknowable futures, no matter how much life separates us, no matter where my sons' journeys may ultimately lead them.

Even now, our relationships with one another are transforming. I sense my sons, each in his own way, pulling away, creating new kinds of distance between us, and then testing to see what that distance feels like. And there are moments when I think my heart just might break with the loss of what was, what's almost over. But then I realize: It's not breaking, it's overflowing. It's not grief, I feel, just love taking a new form. Love, stitching its own sturdy seam through all our souls. Love, binding together all that has been most important to me and attaching it here, in this new life, in this new place, to some new sense of purpose. Love, I'm beginning to understand, is the only thing I really need to hold on to after all. On everything else: Ease up.

And maybe this is how I can become a new kind of mother, by practicing the simplicity of not having to judge and control and worry quite so much. And by not expecting the three men I live with to be anything other than who they are. Shifting focus a bit, allowing life to offer itself to me in new ways, I ease my way into this challenge of letting go and holding on. Yet I can't help but wonder as we enter this new family chapter, in which our sons move steadily outward, into ever wider orbits, needing me less, and in different ways: What exactly does it mean now for me to be at home? The answer, not surprisingly, is revealed slowly, in glimpses and by degrees. It still has much to do, of course, with caring for our house and the people in it. But I suspect that, more and more, being home will have to do with a gradual, deepening sense of place.

"If you don't know where you are," as Wendell Berry claims, "you don't know who you are." For me, for any of us, to truly inhabit this house, this land, this particular corner of the earth, will involve a new kind of knowing, a knowing that will be born of time and will come only with the passing of many mornings and evenings, a thousand rainstorms, snowstorms, and star-strewn nights, countless sunrises, sunsets, and clear, hot afternoons. This is a knowing that I hunger for.

One morning, early, I am standing at the kitchen door peering out into a gray, misty dawn. Suddenly, right at eye level and only a few feet beyond the glass, a great horned owl glides silently by, wings outstretched, tipped toward me in the shadowy first light. It is unbelievable, more like a scene from a Harry Potter movie than real life. Yet there is no mistaking the tufted horns, the heavy, solid body, or the thrill of this silent visitation. The hairs on my arms stand straight up, as if the very air is charged by the presence of the huge, stealthy creature, a powerful reminder that a whole wild community exists right beyond our doorstep. It is a community I am just beginning to discover but that is inextricably bound to our human lives here.

Weekday afternoons, I buckle on my showshoes in the driveway, tramp across the road with Gracie at my side, and then pause for a moment between two realms. Behind me, the domesticity of our snug, silent house; before me, the dark cathedral of trees. I duck low to enter, shaking sheets of snow from the branches. They shimmer in the dwindling sunlight, shatter, and slowly fall. And then I'm inside, kicking through powder, the path opening up before me. And with that, it seems, the physical world gives way to spiritual territory. What a gratifying discovery it is, too, to find that I can align myself with nature, can partake of this universal, untamed energy simply by stepping into it. There is no chance of getting lost, with my own showshoe tracks to follow home, so I'm free to lose myself in a kind of walking meditation, drinking in silence, slowness, and solitude.

Perhaps what I'm coming to appreciate most of all about living here is not the indoors but the outdoors, the way the world beyond my own back door invites me to experience firsthand my connection with all of life—the winter jays, complaining loudly as they hop along a pine bough overhead; the rabbits and moose and deer, whose intermingled tracks I follow along the old logging roads; the bold turkeys who startle me every time I come upon them marching across the path; the pure white weasel I spot just once, scurrying along the top of an old stone wall deep in the woods. Listening more intently, looking more closely, I sense my own soul settling, as if this deepening attachment to a physical place allows for easier access to an inner one.

Learning to be comfortable in this solitude, to turn inward for answers, to live right into these empty days and accept them, rather than trying to fill them up, appears to be a kind of spiritual assignment, the entrance requirement for contentment in this new, letting-go phase of life. So I find myself seeking out tranquil places that can support such private investigations—a snow-covered hilltop, a deserted trail in the woods, or even a comfortable chair pulled close beside a window and hallowed by my own quiet presence there.

 Wherever You Go, There You Are is the title of one of my favorite meditation books. It is also a bit of profound wisdom that I'm only now beginning to fully understand. We may think we move from one place to another, or set forth on great journeys, in the hope of learning the truth about our lives or to improve them somehow. But no matter how far we roam in that search for "what is perfect and unattainable," or how much we shake things up, there is no escaping our own humanness; our fears and shadows always come along for the ride, as much a part of who we are as our blithe, adventurous spirits.

After all these years of searching, without even quite knowing what I was looking for, I am beginning to wonder now if what I needed has in fact been available to me all along, if I'd only known how to claim it. Oddly enough, I realize, it probably has less to do with *where* I live than with *how* I choose to live. How I recognize the things in life that really matter and how well I manage to push aside the great swirling mass of fears and desires and aspirations that sometimes obscures my view of the beauty that's right in front of me. What I was seeking, perhaps, had always been within my reach, but I hadn't been quiet, or patient, enough to see.

The secret of contentment, as I've come at last to know, is not in getting what I want. It's not about being in the perfect place or having just the right sort of life. Contentment and grace may just be two sides of the same coin. And they are both mine whenever I remember to stop, look around, and appreciate where I already am and what I already have.

In time, I might well have arrived at this simple wisdom even if we hadn't moved from suburbia to a small town in New Hampshire, hadn't left a comfortable life for one that has turned out to be, in some ways, much more challenging. But our long journey from one home to another certainly speeded up my education. And one reason I am happy here is because I have decided to be.

It may be that choosing contentment is just another aspect of growing and maturing, a way to begin reorienting life away from effort and desire toward noticing and appreciating instead. After three years in transit, I realize now that getting to know one place well also means letting go of the notion that there is an even better, more worthwhile place somewhere else. Living here, learning to pause, observe, and enter into a more intimate rapport with the world as it is, I do slow down. Beauty, serenity, mystery, solace—it is all at hand. Perhaps it always was. But now, with a little effort, I begin to tune in to a different rhythm, to view the world through fresh eyes. If being home now means learning to be alone, and to be still within myself, I see that it also means opening and softening into a new, more attentive relationship with the visible world.

I sit on the love seat in our kitchen, laptop balanced on my knees, writing. Everyone is gone until dinnertime—to school, work, basketball practice, play rehearsal. The house is empty. Gray mist drifts across the mountains, softening every edge. On this winter afternoon, I can't tell where the hills stop and the sky begins. Every time I lift my eyes from the words on the screen and look out, the landscape is different. Finally, I give in, turn off the computer, and watch the clouds float by. I listen to the silence. The day expands. The art of stretching time, it seems, is about moving even more deeply into the present.

Certainly the journey I'm called to now is not just physical but spiritual in nature. And if what I most need to do at this stage of life is reconnect with some quiet part of myself, then I am ready at last for such work. Where once my days seemed to comprise many sensations and experiences, I'm finding, during this first long winter in our new home, that I can be filled and satisfied by just a few, deeper ones.

Yet keeping an open heart and an open mind still requires self-discipline. Writing each morning, snowshoeing at noon, savoring each day that the four of us wake up in this house, each night that we all go to sleep tucked safely under its slanted eaves, I am learning to be grateful. But even this—taking pleasure in the simple tasks that bring order to my days and sustenance to my soul—requires practice.

A few miles down the road, our small town bustles with life. The newsstand, the market, the café, the health food store, the airy yoga studio above the bookstore—these are all familiar places now, the commercial faces of a close-knit community where people know one another's names and stories, accept one another's failings, and make an effort to bend toward kindness as they conduct the everyday business of living. There is nothing remarkable about this community; there are plenty of others like it in New England—picturesque, imperfect, trying always to be better than they are. Here, as everywhere, the intricacies and demands of human existence have no end. They are the very framework upon which the fabric of our days is woven, each strand contributing to the quality of life in this small rural town that's feeling more and more, as time goes by, like a place where we belong. Someday, perhaps, the threads of our own lives will be caught up here as well, and woven into this larger communal tapestry, and we will know that we're held fast once again by friendship, loyalty, and the resilient bonds of shared history and affection.

For now, though, like everything else in life, this befriending of a place is in itself a process, a gradual movement into intimacy. So I read the town newspaper front to back and make a point of chatting with the high school boy who carries my grocery bags to the car. I buy novels from the shy bookseller whose well-stocked store is the beating heart of town, coffee from the village roaster, shoes from the kindly man who carries his discounted wares out onto the sidewalk every morning. I begin to learn the names of the women who appear at yoga class on Wednesdays at eight. I meet a new friend for tea.

Evenings, I step outside after dark and watch the stars prick out above our roof, memorize the scattered pattern of lights across the valley, note the scrunch of snow beneath my boots, the vastness of the sky. We've been calling this place home for quite a while now. Finally, the word feels true again.

In March, Steve and Henry and I fly to Minnesota for the final round of auditions in the music department at St. Olaf. This is the school Henry first visited to please a guidance counselor who had advised him to consider at least one college far from home. What he found, in this Lutheran school of three thousand students, was a strong liberal arts program that placed music, and a conservatory-style department, at the front and center of campus life. It was precisely the combination he'd dreamed of. Now, having been selected from a thousand first-round applicants, he's been invited back for Music Scholars weekend, two days of auditions, luncheons, interviews, and theory tests. He must be accepted twice here, first to the college itself and then into the department as a major. For Henry, who's been pretty sanguine about the whole application process, this truly is the big moment. He's certain he belongs here; now is his chance to show the music faculty why.

The music building is a hive of activity—registration tables, information tables, CD tables, food tables, all set up to orient the newcomers quickly, get them fed and moving along to auditions, tests, and parent seminars. Henry has been in touch so often with the administrator that she greets him as an old friend as she hands him his name tag. Somehow the impressive setup here, unlike those at some of the other auditions he's done, manages to be at once welcoming and professional. It's clear that these people know exactly what they're doing. And now that I'm on campus for the first time, I see why my son clicked right away with this particular school, a place where music is taken seriously but is taught and played in service to beauty, and spirit, and one another. What's immediately evident is not just a high standard of excellence, but also a sense of caring within a strong, congenial community. What's missing is the sharp edge of competition.

Nevertheless, and welcoming as the many student mentors and volunteers are, there's no escaping the fact that our son is here this weekend, along with hundreds of other nervous young musicians, to compete. It is five below zero, and Henry has a horrific cold. He snuffles loudly, blows his chapped, red nose for the hundredth time, and heads down the hall with the head of the jazz department.

Later, when Steve and I leave in our rental car, he waves us off, then stays behind to spend the night with an assigned sophomore host. We drive into town and walk around, not saying much, trying to imagine our son spending the next four years on this windswept, frozen prairie so far from home. The air feels harsher here, drier than the damp New England cold. And the wind is cruel, slicing right through my heavy winter coat. It is so cold that my eyelids freeze and stick to my eyeballs, and the tips of my ears throb as if pinched. But I pull my hat down lower, glance over at my husband, and force a smile. For we both already know this: If they'll take him here, he'll want to come.

The two of us sit at dinner feeling as if we've had a couple of limbs lopped off, so strange is it to be alone in a restaurant in the Midwest, both of our children elsewhere. Jack, back home with friends, hasn't called since we left. Henry will sleep tonight, sneezing and sniffling, on the floor of some dorm room. We talk about our sons, try to imagine what they're doing, and then end up laughing at our own awkwardness without them.

After a restless night, we're up early and headed back to campus, each trying, and failing, to resist the urge to call our son before he calls us. We leave messages. "No hurry," we say, "take your time." It is a clear, cold Sunday morning and way too early for any self-respecting college student to be out and about. So we find ourselves the only diners in the empty, light-filled cafeteria, drinking cup after cup of strong coffee, feeling a little silly, and old, and alone. Already a page is turning. If we want to peek ahead in the story to see what's coming up, I suspect we need look no further than this room, with its scattered chairs and tables, its tall arched windows, and its views of the austere limestone buildings of St. Olaf.

At last our son appears, hair mussed, stubbly-faced, wearing a black hooded sweatshirt beneath his leather jacket. He carries a Styrofoam coffee cup and is laughing at something his tall, affable-looking companion has just said. I watch him walk across the room, not seeing us, absorbed in conversation. And I think that this rite of passage, releasing our children into their grown-up lives, is piercing in a way I could never have imagined when my sons were small. Back then, I couldn't believe that the day would ever come when I'd actually have to let them go. Now, watching my older son embrace his future, I see not only the bittersweet end of one chapter, but also the first exciting glimpse of a whole new life—his.

There is indeed an art to it, this fine mingling of letting go and holding on. And what this particular moment is offering me is a trial run. In a small plastic bag at my feet, there is a gray St. Olaf T-shirt, an impulse buy from the college bookstore.

My guess is that some spring day two months or so from now, it will make a fine present. I imagine the end of winter, and the end of waiting. I imagine green buds on trees, a bursting forth of new life, and a fat package stuffed into the mailbox at home. A package that contains good news, words of welcome into a future that, in that very instant, will begin to feel preordained. I imagine that Henry, being Henry, will not say much at all until then, until he knows for sure that they want him here. And I imagine that once he does know that, there will be no question left in his own mind whatsoever. I'll be ready then. I'll present him with a gray T-shirt that says "St. Olaf," in celebration of who he's becoming and in honor of what's next. And as a reminder, to both of us, that letting go is also a way of saying, "I love you."

~ 15 ~

pansies

To sit and wait is as important as to
move. Patience is as valuable as industry.
What is to be known is always there. When
it reveals itself to you, or when you come
upon it, it is by chance. The only condition
is you being there and being watchful.
—WENDELL BERRY

I make a list one day of things I'm grateful for. Amid the comings and goings of teenagers, I can still get so enmeshed in the necessities and logistics of life that I miss the beauty. "We do not remember days, we remember moments," the saying goes, and surely it is the moments, the small, fleeting details of us as we are right now, that I want to seize and capture. If memory is the art of attention, then pausing to be grateful is a way of remembering. And remembering is a way, perhaps the only way, of holding on to the way we are now, the things I love, the moments I wish never to lose.

Maybe it is a form of prayer, this list making in the name of gratitude and remembrance. If so, I pray for ordinary things. The golden wonder of sunrise and the deliciousness of coffee. The sight of sons, sleep-softened, side by side in T-shirts and flannel pants, bent over cereal bowls, dissecting the morning's sports news. The clutter of breakfast dishes, the plans discussed, the ticking clock. Jack, astonishingly tall, just showered and dressed for game day in a blue-and-white-striped shirt and his father's twenty-year-old green necktie.

Backpacks that weigh a ton, jackets that are never zipped, shoes with broken heels that no one ever bothers to untie. My husband calling, as he has every school day morning for fourteen years, "Train's pulling out." (Always, there is something forgotten upstairs.) The hasty good-byes as they rush out the door, cutting it close. The scent of Old Spice lingering in the upstairs hall. Wet towels. Solitude. The prickling silence of a suddenly empty house. The vastness of sky beyond the kitchen window and the blue quietude of morning.

In the right mood, I am thankful for laundry, the gray T-shirts, worn jeans, and plaid boxers that I wash and fold and wash again each week. Even this will end. I am glad for wide pine floorboards, smooth as satin beneath my feet. The sponge in my hand, the bare countertop. Empty rooms that will soon be filled again. Thyme and rosemary and jasmine plants, sprawling green in a sunny window. Books on the shelves, tangerines in a bowl, the flickering flame in the stove. Warmth.

The sofa in the kitchen that invites contemplation. A stack of pages, slowly growing. Voluminous hours. Surprise at what rises to the surface. Silence. The interplay of words, the exchange of light and shadow on the wall, the sun climbing slowly across the sky. Ginger cookies and ginger tea.

Silk long underwear, wool socks, and winter boots. Gracie's impatient scratch to go out, the squirrel in the tree, the leash on a hook by the door. The barrenness of snowy fields, the first soggy patches of bare earth. Chilled air that breathes a promise of spring. The old man with the basset hound I meet on the bike path every afternoon. And the wild-haired man in the

battered blue station wagon, who drives from the passenger
seat, left hand on the wheel, and shoves the mail into our black
metal box by the road. The package addressed to Henry that I
have promised not to open. The dissolving splendor of late
afternoon.

A chopping board, a sharp knife, sweet carrots. The scent of
garlic and onions softening in hot oil. Fresh bread. A glass of
wine. The whoosh of cold as the back door opens, three times.
The dog's frenzied greetings. Four seats filled at the kitchen
table. The college in Maine that has said yes. Deep, unguarded
boy laughter. A son's hand in each of mine, my husband across
the table, our voices in unison. Grace.

Piano music after dinner, jazz floating down from an upstairs
bedroom, Guitar Hero thwanging up from the basement TV
room. Jack inscribing cities and capitals and rivers onto a map
of Asia, shading with colored pencils as his dad reads aloud
from the atlas. Henry passing through the room. "Hey, Mom."
The way he says it. The way life allows us, still, to take one another utterly and completely for granted.

A rising crescent of moon, cold and sharp as a scythe, in a
black night sky. The thwack of a textbook closing. The crackle
of my husband's newspaper, my feet in his lap, my heel in the
cup of his palm. Love.

House lights going out, one by one. The click of the latch.
The low, distant bark of a dog. Knowing my way down the
hallway in the dark. A shadow dancing across the ceiling. The
ritual chorus of good-nights. A full house. Peppermint tooth-
paste. Worn flannel sheets that smell of us. Spooning. Drifting.
Falling asleep looking at stars. The stars themselves, framed by
my own bedroom window, shining across the millennia, eter-
nity's cold, bright torches. Life as it is.

•   •   •

Spring comes slowly. Deep snow turns to crusty ice. The roads are rutted, pocked, rimed with salt. But the warming air is irresistible. Maude and I discover a seven-and-a-half-mile loop that takes us from my back door, up the road, and through woods to a narrow bike path by the river, across bridges, down country lanes, up a long, steep hill, and back out to my road again. The first time we try to walk it, we pick our way alongside the frozen path and over rancid snowbanks, but we can see the route has promise—someday the dormant farm fields will be green, the dogs will swim in the river, berries will ripen along the roadside. Even on this chilly, slippery April day, when the trek takes us almost three hours, we are struck by the varied beauty of the landscape, the companionable pleasure of walking together, and the luxury of time, time enough to talk of books, children, past and present lives.

Maude has one daughter, full-grown, working in the film industry and living far away. I know there is no escaping that trajectory, that soon enough my own sons, too, will live elsewhere. But I still can't imagine all the days and nights and Saturday morning breakfasts of our separate futures. Can't conceive of a life in which my sons aren't front and center, their needs and desires dictating and sculpting mine.

"If you want to be reborn," it is written in the Tao Te Ching, "let yourself die." This is what I've been having trouble with, the fact that letting go can feel, at times, like a death. Someday, I know, I will lose everything. All the small deaths along the way are practice runs for the big ones, asking us to learn to be present, to grow in faith, to be grateful for what is. Life is finite and short. But this new task, figuring out how to let go of so much that has been precious—my children, my youth, my life as I know it—can feel like a bitter foretaste of other losses yet to come.

Grown children do come home again, of course, but never again do they live with us under quite the same circumstances or allow themselves to be parented on quite the same terms. Come spring a year from now, my son will walk back through our door as a visitor, having traveled from elsewhere and carrying bags that will soon be packed again. And we'll grow used to a new kind of family life, our time together marked by boisterous arrivals, poignant departures, and the ongoing work of accepting that I don't always know anymore where he is, or what he's doing, or what kind of day he's had. Nothing will ever again be as it was, as it still is for a little while longer. And already I feel unsettled by that, awash in feelings of pride, joy, anticipation, and hardest of all, regret—for what could have been, for what will never be, for what was.

It is Maude, only three years older than me yet already so far along on this path I'm just about to set foot upon, who reminds me that there is growth and new life on the other side of this death. Maude, whose luminous writing and meticulously crafted books are an inspiration and whose devotion to other people's gardens, to plants, animals, dear friends, and any soul in need, shines a light for me as well. She and her husband live alone, artful, generous lives in a house without children. In her presence, I begin to see that the process of releasing my hold on this stage of motherhood might actually yield profound new freedom in the next.

One day, I walk along the river with another friend who has rounded the corner into her fifties. Joan's only son, away at college now, will leave for Europe when school gets out, return just in time to live and work in Boston for the summer, then head to Denmark for a junior semester abroad studying architecture. Quite a life, we marvel, amazed to realize that this boy who was so recently a child is suddenly grown up enough to hit the road, to plan for and embark on these travels on his own. A little sad, too, for she realizes that she won't be seeing much of her beloved son this year.

Somehow, my friend is managing to accept this new, long-distance approach to mothering, which demands that she share her son's delight in his adventures while at the same time facing the fact that he really has moved up and out of their family life, into a grown-up life of his own creation.

"They don't belong to us," Joan says, a touch of wonder in her voice, as if trying to balance this sense of loss and blessing. "We are so lucky, really, to get to have our children with us for as long as we do. But we certainly don't get to choose their destinies, and we can't be holding on when all their life force is urging them to go."

The river is high today, rushing and full with snowmelt and icemelt. We are stuck in the gray, boggy season that follows winter in New Hampshire but is, in anyone's book, a far cry from spring. It is a season that demands forbearance, for beauty is hard to find. The frozen purity of winter is a memory, spring is a dream. There is no one else on the path but us, two middle-aged women, bundled up and walking fast, two joyful dogs bounding ahead.

A serious painter and a lifelong yoga teacher, Joan tells me that she is preparing to deepen her practice and her commitment to her spiritual path by being initiated as a Sikh, thereby formalizing her dedication to a modest life of prayer, teaching, meditation, and service. Already, in addition to running a busy yoga and art studio, she is volunteering, teaching yoga at a local shelter for teenage girls. Now she is about to respond to an even deeper calling. In a few weeks, after the day-long initiation ceremony, she will no longer be Joan, but will be known as Hari Kirin; she will cover her head in public, eat no more meat, never shave again or cut her hair.

"It's something I've been moving toward for years," she explains simply, "but I had to wait until the time was right, until the space cleared at home so that my choices wouldn't negatively impact the rest of the family. These days, no one is asking me to come paint scenery at the kids' school. My daughter is seventeen, and fully engaged with her own friends. No one needs homework help at ten or eleven at night anymore. So, I can finally go to bed early and get up to meditate an hour and a half before dawn."

I tighten my wool scarf and ponder this, a bit in awe of her clarity and sense of purpose. Every single morning, in a house just a mile down the road from mine, my friend awakens beside her sleeping husband, slips from their bed, wraps her head in a long white cloth, and then sits in darkness before a lighted candle, praying for the well-being of all mankind. I put my arm around her slender shoulders and give a little squeeze, not sure what to say, other than how honored I am to know her, how good it is to learn that such love is at work in the world.

Kicking along through the slushy remnants of snow, I am suddenly glad for life's mysteries. Marriage and family life, love and loss, friendship, vocation, life and death, and every kind of rebirth—we spend our lives looking for answers and explanations for the great forces that move through us, only to discover instead how little of it all we can ever really understand. And yet, how varied are the paths that call out to us, how strange and compelling the passions that shape our lives and inform our destinies. And how lucky we are to participate in these mysteries, which bring such depth and wonder to our everyday experiences. It occurs to me that the courage I need to summon now, at midlife, isn't the kind that would impel me to scramble up mountains, to return full-time to the career I abandoned for motherhood nearly twenty years ago, or to reinvent myself from whole cloth—much as I admire friends who are doing all of these things as their children grow up and out.

There is another kind of daring that I aspire to, more an expansion of heart and spirit than an ambition to accomplish any particular thing. After years of defining myself as a mother of boys, I've been afraid that what's mattered most in my life will be over when my sons leave home. Even now, when Jack turns on me in anger if I suggest a bedtime or enforce a rule, or when Henry makes a plan without consulting me, I feel like someone who's had the rug pulled out and is still trying to catch her balance. What worked eight or nine years ago, or even last month, doesn't work anymore. Not only have the everyday facts of our lives changed, but we have changed as well.

Losing this part of my life, this time of being a mother to growing children, is indeed an ending. For months, I've carried that quiet sorrow, getting used to its heaviness, the way one learns to live with the chronic soreness of a joint, a tenderness in wrist or knee. What I long to do now is to let the sadness go as well, to have faith that even as my sons graduate from high school and leave home, and this phase of our family life draws to a close, there will be new beginnings not just for them, but for all of us.

Seeing the handmade books Maude creates with such pains-taking care in her studio and the glorious gardens she designs for clients; practicing Kundalini yoga with Joan or gazing upon the lovely Buddha images she fashions from the junk mail that arrives on her doorstep, somehow eases the heartache of my own letting go. The work my friends do now that their chil-dren are grown is indisputably the work of mothers, of women whose passionate maternal energies, no longer required at home, are lovingly offered up to the world instead. Their lives have not contracted, their hearts have not narrowed, they've expanded.

The message is not lost on me: The world is filled with need. If I am to be of some use, I must first rise to the challenge of my own rebirth and growth, must engage in the gradual, demanding process of discovering the person I am meant to be now and taking up the work I am called to do.

"Go into yourself, and see how deep the place is from which your life flows," the poet Rainer Maria Rilke once instructed an aspiring young writer. The advice might as easily have been written for a middle-aged woman contemplating her emptying nest. The work my friends seem compelled to undertake in their forties and fifties is no longer what they think they *should* do. It is what they feel, in their deepest souls, that they are *meant* to do. What the example of their lives suggests, what I desperately want to believe, is that once we have weathered these changes, honored our sorrows and released them, there is also great joy in moving on.

Today, Joan's curly red hair is tucked up inside her hat. Her face, without makeup, looks fresh and youthful, and the thyroid troubles that have plagued her for years are in retreat. "I spend a lot of time these days standing on my head," she explains with a laugh, "and doing some very intense yoga. It definitely seems to be working!" If ever there was a model for exhaling old energies and inhaling new life, Joan embodies it. It is not every middle-aged mother of two who fulfills her life purpose by taking religious vows, but there is no mistaking the power of this particular rebirth. She is transcendent.

Finally, we reach the spot where the river bends and the view opens up to marshes and mountains. One golden day last fall, I came into this clearing in time to see two moose lumbering up out of the water after a swim. Today, the roiling water is dark and uninviting; the soaked landscape, empty, devoid of color and life. We are suspended between seasons, like becalmed sailors waiting for wind. It used to be that these cold, patchy-snow weeks of in-between time would fill me with discontent, so eager was I for spring, for the warmth of the sun and the turn of the season, for good footing and new, green life. For whatever might be next. But on this damp, wind-tossed afternoon, what I feel is not my old restless yearning for something else, but a new, unfamiliar patience. Why rush the passing of time? Why long for a future that can't be foretold, only to miss the muddy magnificence of now?

Perhaps it takes a lifetime to really learn to live fully in the moment, but there is no better classroom than the raw, damp month of April in New Hampshire. As soon as I stop wishing for things to be different, I am met by the beauty of what is—a family on the brink of change, a friend at my side, a narrow country road slick with rain, the first tiny coils of sweet fern, tender and delicate as question marks, poking up through the hummusy leaf rot on the forest floor.

The school year is winding down. It feels like both a culmination and a marathon. Now, though, the finish line is in view at last. Henry will be a music major at St. Olaf, with a much appreciated scholarship and all his piano lessons paid for. He will take his lovely friend Serena to the prom, organize a chamber music concert for the end of May, work on the yearbook, graduate on a Saturday in June, perform a solo jazz concert at the New England Conservatory a day later.

His life these days is a series of accomplishments and happy events. Finally, he is seeing the fruits of his labors. Finally, too, the shy, small boy who once disappeared in every crowd is stepping boldly into his life, and the world is starting to pay attention. He had his pick of colleges; after Bowdoin, every other school he applied to said yes. The musical revue he conceived last August in a lawn chair in Maine, this enormous project that has occupied so many of his waking hours since and has taken up so many February and March evenings, is performed at last, on two triumphant nights, to standing-room-only crowds of students and parents and friends. No sooner is it over than he's back to work, as the musical director for the spring play, eating dinner at school, attending practice every night, getting home at nine-thirty or ten in time to do some homework and fall exhausted into bed. He is growing in confidence by the day, relishing every moment of these last months of senior year, even as he casts an eager eye toward the future.

Late one night, he writes a very last college essay, this one to apply to an intensive two-year program at St. Olaf called The Great Conversation, a curriculum that immerses students in the major works and epochs of the Western tradition. Determination—to make his own decisions, to take charge of his own life, to be all that he can be—rises from him like heat.

Meanwhile, spring sports begin, weeks before there's much sign of spring. When Jack hears that the tennis team practices before school, at five-thirty in the morning, he nixes tennis. "No way am I getting up that early!" he insists. Until the night before practice begins, when, to my surprise, he says, "Will you wake me up at four-thirty tomorrow?"

There is still snow on the ground, and the only practice time available, on the only indoor courts in town, is early in the morning. Two nights a week, Jack plays basketball in an AAU league two towns away. Weekends, his team travels to tournaments all over New England. With the addition of a second sport, he's even busier, uncharacteristically motivated, rarely home. He has grown so much this year, many inches in height, but in unsettling, unseen ways as well, as if he's gotten too big for the enclosure of our house, too restless for our mundane family life, too intense for the confining rhythms and routines of school, homework, three square meals a day, and eight hours of sleep a night.

I feel him bursting at the seams, sucking the air out of any room he enters, willing to push against old boundaries, then daring his father and me to call him on it. Sports save him, offering an outlet for all that explosive adolescent energy. If that means setting my alarm for four-thirty, making a protein smoothie in the dark, and driving him to a tennis court to whack balls for an hour before school, I am delighted to do it. Our best moments are before sunrise, alone in the car.

"Isn't it funny how friendships begin," he muses one morning. "It's something I hardly even think about, but now I'm friends with people I never would have expected to be friends with when I first saw them. I don't even know how it happened. It's like I want to say, 'Hey, dude, how'd we get to be so close?'"

Most of the time, the inner workings of that fifteen-year-old brain are off-limits to me. Whenever the door does crack open, even if it's at five a.m., I'm grateful for a glimpse of what's going on inside. Especially since, so much of the time these days, we are at odds with each other.

He is so certain he is right—about the effort, or lack of it, required for homework, the unimportance of grades, the Doritos before dinner, the video game marathons at midnight. And I am so certain I know what he needs. "You don't understand!" he shouts. "You think you're so much better than me!"

"I'm the parent," I insist, my mouth dry and tasting of metal. Even I realize how lame that sounds, as if being the parent of this fierce boy-man carries any weight anymore, as if I can still hold the old line. I represent everything he resents at the moment, the boring values he's so eager to overturn, the container he is determined to shatter, the weakness he needs to defeat.

Evenings, it is often just the two of us in the house, without much to say to each other. Steve and Henry share a car, so Henry's late nights at school mean late nights for Steve as well. There is no point in either of them adding an extra hour-long round trip to the end of the day, so Steve stays at work, sometimes meeting a friend for dinner or a movie while he waits for Henry to be done. It is an odd, unsatisfying schedule, everyone off in different places and absorbed in different things, a preview of the life to come. Already I miss our old ways—the regular family dinners, the easier relationships, the laughter and togetherness.

I buy a bouquet of flowers and realize that I'm the only one who's even noticed them. The piano top is covered with dust. I make soup and then eat it alone for too many nights. Jack reminds me that it's hardly worth it to cook dinner; no one else is ever home, and he'd rather eat eggs and toast at four, before basketball practice.

We are wary of being too close. He chooses not to be in a room with me if he can help it. He does his homework in my office with the door closed, watching YouTube instead of writing an English paper, and then slips into the basement to play Halo when my back is turned. I ask him if he's practiced his guitar, and he tells me yes. I know he hasn't, and he knows I know; it is his way of showing me he doesn't care that much anymore, that he thinks guitar lessons are a waste of time and money, that he's got more important things to do.

The days grow longer, brighter. At sunset, the trees are bathed in rosy light, the sky the color of stained glass. I stand in the silent kitchen, eating a sandwich at the sink, waiting for no one,

watching the evening come. For the first time ever, I find myself feeling lonely in my own family, as if everyone else has
moved on and left me behind. I realize that the life I've loved,
the life I still yearn for, has already slipped away.

The pansies are yellow and purple, crowded into a plastic pot. I
don't know how they come to be at my back door, until my
neighbor Debbie finally confesses two days later. "An early
Mother's Day present from me and Gracie," she calls from the
driveway, stooping to pat my gift-giving dog.

I crank open my office window, surprised to discover that
the air outdoors is suddenly warmer than the indoors. "But
Mother's Day isn't for weeks," I protest.

Debbie throws up her hands, then snaps a leash onto Gracie,
and the two of them make their way slowly out to the road,
Gracie seeming to know intuitively that for this walk, she must
resist the urge to pull.

Turning back to my desk, I reread the lines by Clarissa
Pinkola Estés that I've just copied into my spiral-bound notebook. "Anything you do from the soulful self will help lighten
the burdens of the world. Anything. You have no idea what the
smallest word, the tiniest generosity, can cause to be set in
motion. . . . Mend the part of the world that is within your
reach."

On this mild spring morning, the simple words strike me as
a kind of touchstone, the very guidance I've been looking for.
Here is an instruction I can take to heart.

I've known for months now that the hardest part of letting
go, at least for me, is not just about my grown children leaving
home, emotional and momentous as that milestone will be.
The real challenge is how to relinquish with serenity the role
I've cherished for so long, to stop identifying myself so com-

pletely with motherhood and allow for a new, more mature
self to be born.

The other day, Jack and I were out in the woods, throwing
sticks for Gracie and marveling at her tireless capacity for
chasing them down. "It's her instinct," I said. "She's programmed
to fetch."

"What are you programmed for, Mom?" Jack asked, joking
with me.

"Nurturing," I said without missing a beat.

"Well, you can nurture me for a little while longer," he said
lightly. "But then, you know, I'll be gone."

"Yeah," I replied. "I'm trying to prepare myself for that."

And so I am.

After years of striving, caring, trying so diligently to create
a family life, to make a home, to tend our hearth, the end of
all that labor is in plain sight. It's funny now, to realize how I
lived my life for so long, and poured myself into the work of
raising children, without ever thinking much about where
we were headed, even as my sons were growing up and
changing before my eyes. But now here we are, in the homestretch of high school, with one son about to graduate and
the other pushing hard against me, harder than I ever could
have imagined.

I must remind myself these days that life is what it is, wonderful and heartrending all at once, and that my two children
are doing exactly what they should be doing—rebelling and
leaving.

Yet acceptance has come hard for me. What I aspire to
doesn't seem like much—a peaceful heart, simple happiness.
But lately I've felt unmoored, not sure if, or how much, I'm still
needed.

"Mend the part of the world that is within your reach," Dr.

Estés writes. I think about what this might mean. I am so often tempted to cast a wide net, to get overly invested—in my children's lives, in the way things ought to be, in my goals and their outcomes—that I end up not doing the small tasks right in front of me really beautifully, joyfully, or well.

Now, life is shifting. And all I really need to do is welcome the change and shift along with it. How glad I would be to move through all these transitions and challenges with a lighter heart. Perhaps it really is as simple as those words: "Mend the part of the world that's within your reach." It's all I can hope to do anyway. It may just turn out to be enough.

An hour later, I look up from my desk to see Debbie and Gracie returning from their outing. I watch from the window as Debbie fills a water bowl for Gracie from the outdoor faucet. Then she bends on one knee by the pansies and plucks off a couple of limp blossoms. And that is when I understand that another partner has appeared in my life, a friend who seems to be pointing the way toward what's next.

In the hectic, busy months before we moved in last fall, I often noticed the old woman who seemed to spend her days alone, trudging back and forth, up and down our road. She moved slowly, leaning on a cane, stopping often to rest. She usually carried a shopping bag and wore layers of clothes, dark sunglasses, a hat pulled low, and an orange reflective vest. I wondered about her, but not much; instead, I wrote her off in my mind as a bit of local color, a character, harmless, but none of my business.

One day, I looked out and saw that she had stepped into our yard and was deep in conversation with Gracie. After that, she always stopped, and Gracie began to wait for her. Our dog figured out right away that this kind visitor had time for her, and treats in her pockets, and that she was always happy to play a game of fetch or two.

Once we were finally living in our house, a visit and a dog biscuit for Gracie became part of the solitary walker's daily route. Pretty soon she was leaving treats for me, too—a cheerful card, a bundle of pens in a rubber band, a magazine. We began to talk. And before long, I learned that everything I'd assumed about my unusual neighbor was wrong. She is not old, for one. She is just fifty-three. Nor was she wandering aimlessly up and down the road. She was walking to save her life. She is not a nut. In fact, I've begun to think that she just might be an angel.

Eight years ago, Debbie contracted E.coli from a cup of chili at a fast-food restaurant. Misdiagnosed at the hospital, mistreated with the wrong drugs, she suffered excruciating pain for months and nearly died. In the last eight years, fourteen surgeries have removed much of her digestive system and lots of other anatomy that the rest of us consider essential to life. Midway through this ordeal, she also lost a beloved younger sister, who had flown in from California to be at her bedside, caught a mysterious infection at the hospital, and died in great pain ten days later.

Debbie wears an ostomy bag, goes into the hospital for IV iron once a week, deals constantly with internal and external bleeding, cauterizations, blockages, and episodes of twisted bowel. Her wound will always be open, raw, and vulnerable, and she will always hurt. She doesn't dwell upon what's wrong with her, however. Instead, she spends her days taking care of her neighbors.

Debbie told me once that she realized sometime during the fourth or fifth month she spent in the hospital that she had no control over the illness wreaking havoc in her body. The only

thing she could control was her attitude about it. She could lie
in her bed and feel sad and angry about what was happening to
her, or she could start to joke with the nurses and try to charm
smiles out of the surgeons who kept coming to take away more
of her insides. After removing a piece of her small bowel a
couple of years ago, her doctor warned her that if she wanted
to survive, she would have to walk. So that is what she does.

Debbie's health has improved dramatically in the months
that I've known her. When we first met, she was recovering
from her most recent surgery. As always after an operation, she
had forced herself to get out of bed, to fill a bag with carrots
for the horses, and set out on her rounds. Sometimes, she told
me later, she couldn't even make it beyond the end of her own
driveway. The days when she actually managed to deliver the
carrots, half a mile down the road, were the good days.

A couple of months ago, Debbie gathered her courage and
asked me a favor: Could she come by and get Gracie to join
her on her walks? At first I couldn't quite believe what I was
hearing. I could do this woman a kindness by allowing her to
walk my dog? It seemed too good to be true. Dog guilt vanishing overnight, more exercise for my boundlessly enthusiastic
border collie, and more freedom for me? I accepted.

So began a friendship that soon expanded to include us all,
human and canine family members alike. Debbie and I began
by exchanging dog news, but as I've gotten to know her better,
I've come to see her as a kind of spiritual mentor. Her daily
presence in my life is a reminder that the heart's transformation
is arrived at not through the will, but through surrender.

"To live is to die to how we wanted it to be," writes Jack
Kornfield in *A Path with Heart*, "and to open more to truth. To
love is to accept. It is the most extraordinary power."

And love is what Debbie is all about. For what she did with

that life-or-death instruction from her doctor was not just walk, but begin to mend the part of the world that is within her reach, the little stretch of country road where we both live. She made friends with every creature along her route, the horses, dogs and cats, sheep and goats and chickens. She carries, always, treats for all, apples and carrots and dog biscuits and kitchen scraps. She spends time every day with each of these animals, scratching bellies, talking softly into cocked ears, feeling for ticks, and checking water bowls. Along the way, she's come to know and love the children on our road as well. She bestows gifts for every birthday and remembers everyone's favorite kind of candy. It turns out that Jack and Debbie share a penchant for Good & Plenty, which she knows I will never buy. Sometimes they appear, though, inside our back door, in a bag that's stapled shut.

When any of us goes away, for a night or a week, Debbie is the one who comes to water plants, feed animals, collect eggs, do whatever needs doing. She won't take any money. She insists—and it is the only thing that she's really adamant about—that she does what she does out of love.

Now, I'm beginning to understand. Debbie had no choice but to die to how she wanted her life to be. But she could choose love as a response to all that she had lost. Reborn, she embodies the idea of acting from the soulful self. Small gestures, simple acts, set larger things in motion; they release more goodness into the world.

Before she got sick, Debbie and her husband owned a nursery and a miniature golf course. She swam and hiked and kayaked and biked. She tended ambitious gardens, ran a business, traveled. Now, her world is a mile-long stretch of country road in New Hampshire, and along that road there is not an animal or a potted plant or a human being that she doesn't love and care for on a daily basis.

So I am not too surprised that the pansies turn out to be Debbie's doing. I am touched, and grateful for the first spot of bright spring color on my doorstep. But what I don't realize until a few weeks have passed is that the real gift is not the pansies themselves, but what comes after. Every single day, Debbie stops by to pick up Gracie. When she does, she takes a few minutes to water my pansies. She fertilizes. She deadheads. She moves the pot into a sunny spot, then later moves it back again.

I have bought pots of pansies to herald spring's arrival every year of my adult life. But I have never once had them looking as lush and beautiful in June or August as they do in April. I have never cared for any plant the way Debbie cares for the one she gave to me. By the time Mother's Day actually arrives, though, I understand the full measure of her gift. It is not just flowers she's given me, but her own sustained devotion as well, the spaciousness of love not burdened by expectation.

Sometimes I can't help but think about what Debbie has been forced to give up in the last eight years—her health and strength, her youthful looks and sexuality, her ability to enjoy normal food, sit on a bike seat, or sleep through the night. She has lost almost every pleasure in life that I take for granted. Yet she told me once that she gives thanks every day that she lives where she does, on this beautiful, quiet road, surrounded by so many good friends.

I remember what Jack said not long ago about his friends, how surprised he is to realize that he's grown close to people he might just as easily have written off or passed over. Surely I would once have considered Debbie an unlikely soul mate. Now, I wonder what I've done to deserve her friendship, what stroke of luck brought me into her magical circle of concern.

Illness meant the death of Debbie's old life, and just to make sure that she died completely, fourteen surgeries completed the transformation. Only when she had surrendered everything did grace allow her to be born again, to move again, though slowly and with great care. And somewhere along the way, as she walked up and down the road in order to save her own life, she figured out what she was being called to do. She realized that even here, even now, she could do her part to lighten the burdens of the world.

Now, among other things, she is teaching me what it really means to be grateful, and about giving and receiving kindness. Most of all, though, she reminds me of the unlimited possibilities that exist just beyond surrender, if we can die to what was and then open ourselves to what is.

I have been a reluctant student. But in just a couple of weeks, my older son will graduate from high school. Yesterday, I handed my younger one the car keys and allowed him to drive me around an empty parking lot. I didn't have to tell him much. There is no doubt that both my sons are on their way. The only question now is, How gracefully will I be able to step aside and allow them to become the adults they are meant to be.

For the first time, I'm beginning to think I can do it. For it seems that there is a road map to guide me on this part of life's journey after all. The landscape is drawn in bold, beautiful colors by all the valiant, loving women who have preceded me into this unfamiliar country called surrender. If I listen carefully, I can hear them calling back to me. "Let go," they say. "Let go, let go, let go. And then, trust."

postscript

*T*here is a hushed, expectant air in the vast gymnasium, transformed now into a holiday concert hall. Magnificent Christmas trees grace both sides of the stage, beneath twinkling lights and a banner proclaiming, "My Spirit Sings of Wondrous Things." Students hand us programs, and my mother and I climb into the bleachers to find our seats.

The plane fare for this trip to Minnesota was my fiftieth-birthday gift from her, presented after I'd wistfully mentioned how much I would love to hear Henry sing in the annual Christmas festival at St. Olaf. Yesterday, the two of us flew into Minneapolis, rented a car with all-wheel drive, and drove icy roads through swirling snow to Northfield. I called my son from a campus parking lot, and three minutes later, I had my arms wrapped around him.

It seems a lifetime ago, the hot, sticky August afternoon that Steve and I bade Henry good-bye in the lobby of this very gym, surrounded by a sea of other parents and sons and daughters, all snapping last pictures and trying not to cry. There was no escaping the emotion of that day, the realization that this

really was it, the moment when our life paths would diverge
for the first time.

We tried, the three of us, to be nonchalant all through the
maze of orientation details and errands—picking up a campus
map and room keys, getting an ID photo taken, finding Henry's
mailbox, setting up his side of the tiny dorm room.

My son, it soon became apparent, had packed every single
article of clothing he possessed, both clean and dirty. Incredulous, I watched him open his duffel and pull out every frayed
and faded concert shirt he'd ever owned; all his pants, half of
them in need of a wash; piles of pairs of socks and boxer shorts.
It was as if he thought he was never coming home again, or
else planned to make doing laundry an annual event. I stood by
as he began to shove his things, willy-nilly, into the minuscule
built-in drawers. And then, despite my best intentions, I seized
control one last time.

"Why don't you and Dad go see if the books you shipped
have arrived," I suggested, "and I'll work on your room."

I packed up half the T-shirts to take home again, half a dozen
pairs of soiled jeans, a large heap of socks and underwear. I put
the brand-new sheets and soft blue comforter on the bed,
plumped up the pillows, pushed a footlocker full of music
books under the bed, and hung towels on the bar. It was all I
could do. For the next nine months, my son would share this
spare, fifteen-by-fifteen-foot box of a room with a budding
concert pianist from Arkansas. The life he would live here
would, at long last, be his own.

What I remember most about that day is just how intensely
all my deepest fears for this boy of ours collided with all my
dearest hopes for him. Had we done a good enough job preparing him for what lay ahead? Was he smart enough, good
enough, mature enough, to be here? Would he be happy?

Toward the end of the afternoon, the dean of students stood on a podium before us, all 866 sweaty freshmen and their mothers and fathers, and took on the task of reassuring the parents. "The answer to all your questions," he said, "is yes." There was a ripple of nervous laughter as he continued, "Your son or daughter does belong here. You have done your part. And now it is your job to go home, and allow these young men and women to be college students. I know from experience with my own children that no one ever feels quite ready to be a parent in an empty nest. The only way to learn how, is to do it."

At the end of the program, we all stood as the faculty, the men and women about to take charge of our children's educations, costumed in full academic regalia, proceeded solemnly through the crowd and out the doors. And then, in a well-orchestrated farewell, students were allowed one last moment with their parents before heading off to meet with professors and advisers. The three of us stood together in the crowded lobby, smiling and hugging. For my son's sake, I managed not to shed a single tear.

"Where am I supposed to go now?" Henry asked, looking around as the sea of bodies began to part.

"I have no idea," I answered. "I guess it's up to you to find out."

During his first days of school, Henry auditioned for the freshman men's choir and made the first tenor section. Six weeks later, on an October afternoon, I was on my way home from a run in the woods when my cell phone rang. It was Henry, calling to report that he had just met with the dean of the education department, his piano teacher, and his academic adviser, in order to change his major from Bachelor of Arts to Bachelor of Music and from jazz piano to music education with an emphasis on voice.

"Voice?" I asked, astonished.

Much as he loved piano, he explained, and international re-
lations, and music theory, and all his other classes, it was choir,
and his voice class, that had lit him on fire. He wanted to sing,
to start taking private singing lessons himself, to work with
singers, and to learn everything he could about vocal tech-
nique. He wasn't calling to ask if we thought this was a good
idea. If he auditioned and was accepted to the major, it was
already a done deal.

"Well, good for you," I said. "I can tell that you've really
thought it all out. It sounds great." I slipped my phone back
into my pocket and walked slowly toward home in the golden
light of an autumn afternoon, touched by a relevation. My son
had grown up. He had found his voice.

This afternoon, there is not a spare seat to be had for the year's
final Christmas concert, the nationally known and widely broad-
cast service of hymns and carols that has been a St. Olaf tradition
since 1912. For weeks, rehearsals have taken up several hours of
every day. Choral singing here requires an enormous commitment, and never more so than in the month before Christmas.
My son has loved every minute of it. Never in his life, he told us
over breakfast this morning, has he been a part of something
that's meant more to him than this.

Finally, I am getting the glimpse I've yearned for of this new,
independent life he's leading, the new vocation he's embraced
so passionately. It has been years since my mom and I have
taken a trip alone together, and we are savoring this one. As the
lights dim and the packed auditorium grows quiet, we exchange a look that seems to say it all—how surprising life is,
and how grateful we are, not only for this moment, but for the
millions of moments that preceded it as well, moments that
have somehow added up to this: three generations converging

on a frozen Minnesota hilltop far from home to celebrate a new season in all our lives.

The five choirs file in, one after another, each group wearing a different-colored robe. In the darkness, I strain forward, searching for my son in the crowd. The students, nearly five hundred of them in all, form an enormous circle around the floor. And then, after one suspended breath of perfect silence, the lights come up and they begin to sing.

acknowledgments

*P*ondering my own life required solitude. Yet I can't help but think of this work as a collaborative effort, for many unseen hands contributed to its pages.

Karen Murgolo's out-of-the-blue phone call on a September afternoon was, without question, a door opening. This book would not have been written without her interest and encouragement. Jamie Raab, fairy godmother of the book world, has created at Grand Central Publishing a most welcoming home for authors. I feel blessed to be part of that family. And I am grateful to my longtime friend and agent, Mary Evans, for envisioning such a fine partnership in the first place, and for her astute advice at every turn.

Thank you, Patti Pitcher, for reading drafts of my first attempt to write this book, and for being honest enough to tell me what I already suspected.

Special thanks to eQuanimiti Joy, Nancy Mellon, and Maude Odgers. Each of you contributed more than you know.

I am grateful to the women of Verve for unconditional cheerleading in matters of both literature and life: Carol

Burdick, Stephanie Douglas, Gina Kurban, Debbie Johnston, Susan Leathers, Barbara Lynch, and Carolyn Potter.

My gratitude to Debbie Day continues. Thanks to my dad, John Kenison, for sharing his house and much else. And to my mother, Marilyn Kenison, thank you for, well, everything.

Last but not least, thank you, Steve, Henry, and Jack, for allowing me to turn a chapter of our life together into, if not art, a story.

about the author

Katrina Kenison is the author of *Mitten Strings for God: Reflections for Mothers in a Hurry*. From 1990 until 2006, Kenison was the series editor of *The Best American Short Stories*, published annually by Houghton Mifflin. She coedited, with John Updike, *The Best American Short Stories of the Century*, and, with Kathleen Hirsch, *Mothers: Twenty Stories of Contemporary Motherhood*. She wrote, with Rolf Gates, *Meditations from the Mat: Daily Reflections on the Path of Yoga*. She lives in New Hampshire with her husband and sons.

reading group guide

A word about reading groups . . .

If it hadn't been for mine, this book might never have been completed. Month after month, my book group in my old hometown urged me on. And so it was quite a moment when, at long last, I had copies of the bound galley in hand and a request to think of questions for a Reading Group Guide for the back of my book. Who better to help me come up with provocative discussion topics than the seven passionate readers with whom I've had the pleasure of trading books and opinions for the last nine years?

Since our first, memorable meeting—circled around a crackling fire, while a late-winter blizzard raged outside—we've shared nearly a hundred books and countless hours of conversation. We've revealed our secrets, confessed our fears and failures, celebrated milestones and happy moments, and mourned the inevitable losses and disappointments that are a part of every human journey. Oddly enough, we often feel closer to one another than to some of the friends we see on a daily basis, for together we create a sacred space each month, a place in which who we are and what we say will be neither judged nor betrayed. We trust that what's said in the room stays in the room.

I will not soon forget the cool spring night that my book group gathered to discuss THE GIFT OF AN ORDINARY DAY. My friends' copies of the galley were highlighted and bookmarked and scribbled in, testament to the seriousness with which they'd tackled their task, of coming up with themes and questions. We poured wine, filled our plates with pasta and salad, and settled down to talk. The questions that follow grew out of our conversation that night. I hope they inspire you and your reading friends to pause and reflect on your lives, to attend to ordinary moments as if they mattered, and to come up with some questions of your own. For one thing we've realized is that sometimes the questions themselves are more valuable than the answers, which are always changing anyway.

—Katrina Kenison

DISCUSSION QUESTIONS

1. Trying to describe the restlessness she felt as her sons approached adolescence, Katrina admits:

> I longed for something I could scarcely name but that our orderly, well-defined life seemed no longer to provide. Watching my sons growing and changing so visibly, almost from one day to the next, I sensed something inside me breaking loose and changing as well, something no less powerful for being invisible . . . I was suddenly haunted by all the things I hadn't done, the dreams that might never be realized, the sense that the tidy, civilized life we'd worked so hard to create didn't quite fit the person I really was, or, rather, still thought I might be.

Have you experienced a similar unrest in your own life as your children began to claim their independence? What longings did you experience? What kind of movement resulted from these unsettled feelings?

2. "If you want to grow," wrote Gail Sheehy in her self-help classic *Passages*, "you must be willing to change." Change is a theme that runs throughout this memoir, changes both sought and unsought. As Katrina comes to realize, "our lives are always in the process of becoming something else." What changes have you resisted in your life? What changes have you wished for, and then regretted? What unsought changes have turned out to be blessings in disguise?

3. When Katrina's older son scores poorly on a standardized test, she knows that the numbers do not really reflect his intelligence or his character. And yet, so often our children's potential is judged by how well they perform—on tests, in schoolrooms, and on athletic fields. How do you measure success in your family? Do you believe that attitude is as important as aptitude? Given the competitive culture in which our children are coming of age, how can we help them grow up knowing that who they *are* is even more important than what they *do*?

4. Katrina falls in love with the dilapidated red cottage at first sight; her husband thinks she's lost her mind. In the end, she prevails, but then doubts all of the impulses that drove her to want it in the first place. How do you make big decisions in your life? Do you trust your intuition, or do you listen to an inner voice that is more practical and well reasoned? How do you deal with the negative, as well as positive, results of those decisions?

5. The solstice party is an act of desperation, an attempt to cheer a demoralized family at the end of a long, hard week. And although only three people show up, it works. What do you think makes for a good party? How do you create magic in less-than-ideal circumstances?

6. While stripping the paint off a collection of two-hundred-year-old doors, Katrina allows herself to peel away some of the protective layers of her own persona as well. In solitude and silence, she initiates a long-postponed conversation with herself. In the process, she begins to practice a more mindful cultivation of gratitude. What layers might you be willing to strip away in order to look more deeply at who you are in this moment? What would it mean to become a better friend to your authentic self? How can you make time do this if you feel overcommitted?

7. As we begin to honor our everyday experience, to value the ordinary, we become more open to the extraordinary. What ordinary moments did you notice and appreciate today?

8. Marion Woodman has written: "A mother who is identified with being mother has to have children who will eat what she gives them to eat and do what she wants them to do. They must remain children."

A central theme in THE GIFT OF AN ORDINARY DAY is the challenge all mothers face, of learning to let go, so that our children can grow up to be the adults they are meant to be. Where are you in this process? How difficult is it to step back and trust that your children will find their way? What part of letting go has been the hardest for you?

9. You could say that the author's search for a home is central to the book's story, but perhaps it would be more accurate to say that her real quest is to arrive at a new understanding of what home truly means, once home is no longer a place where children are growing up. How do you define home? How has your vision of home changed as your children have grown up and away? How much of your idea of home is attached to a physical place? How much of it is a state of mind?

10. Katrina comes to see that the years of moving and transition have enabled her to avoid some of the hard questions she needed to ask herself as her children moved through adolescence, questions such as "Who am I now?" and "What am I called to do?" Have you had to answer those questions in your own life? What finally prompted you to ask them?

11. Perhaps it is human nature, but most of us fail to appreciate our ordinary days until something happens that robs us of the very life we so easily took for granted. Have you had such a wake-up call in your life? What was it, and how did it change the way you view an ordinary day?

12. In an early morning conversation, Jack muses about how much he's come to care about people he never would have expected to be his friends. Debbie and eQuanimiti Joy appear as characters in Katrina's new life, but become unexpected friends. How do you make new friends as an adult? Have you welcomed people into your

life whom you might not have embraced when you were younger?
What unlikely soul mates have aided you on your journey?

13. Throughout her book, Katrina draws on the wisdom of many
other writers whose words have inspired and supported her. Which
quotes resonated with you? Whose insights help you to live the life
you aspire to?

14. Hard as it was to leave a home and a life her family loved, Katrina eventually comes to see that for everything they lost, they have
gained something as well. What have you been asked to release in your
life, and what gifts have been placed into your open hand in return?